ABBEVILLE PRESS
ENCYCLOPEDIA OF NATURAL SCIENCE

The World of Birds is one of the first four volumes in Abbeville Press's outstanding new collection of pocket encyclopedias of natural science. Written in scholarly yet easy-to-understand language, the series is packed with information that will fascinate student and nature buff alike. Beautiful full-color illustrations on every page supplement the lively text.

The World of Birds offers a comprehensive overview of the structure, habitat, ecology, behavior, and classification of birds. The volume combines the usefulness of a reference work with the readability of a browsing book, perfect for anyone attuned to the splendor of our natural world. It both explains and illustrates how birds build their nests, why they migrate, how they fly—and more.

Together with *The World of Fish, Insects,* and *Amphibians and Reptiles,* these books form the cornerstone of an indispensable home library—one that is almost guaranteed not to sit idly on the shelf.

The World of
BIRDS

BY GIANFRANCO BOLOGNA

TRANSLATED FROM THE ITALIAN BY Simon Pleasance

ABBEVILLE PRESS • PUBLISHERS • NEW YORK

Designers/Artists
Illustrations drawn by Sergio Rizzato together with the following:
Piero Cozzaglio, Brescia: 14–15, 34, 35, 102, 111. Ugo Fontana, Florence: 9, 20, 21, 42, 48, 50, 51, 68, 71a, 80, 84, 96, 99, 104, 105, 113, 118, 123, 146, 156, 157, 201, 210, 213, 214, 225, 226, 241b, 245. Raffaello Segattini, Verona: 16–17, 36–37, 46, 56, 62, 66, 79a, 86, 166, 167, 169, 172b.

Photographs
A. W. Ambler, National Audubon Society, Inc., New York: 139. Archivio Mondadori, Milan: 13, 172a, 198–199; Walter Bonatti: 106–107; Mario De Biasi: 242–243; Giorgio Lotti: 67. Ardea Photographics, London: Clem Haagner: 193; Peter Steyn: 249; Wardena Weisser: 8. D. Bartlett/Bruce Coleman, Uxbridge, Great Britain: 22–23. F. Carrese, Milan: 79b, 235b. Gastone dalle Vacche, Livorno: 221. André Fatras, Paris: 47, 91, 92, 136, 148, 149, 158. Jacana, Paris: Bel et Vienne: 110, 117; Brosselin: 124b, 176, 197, 237: Brosset: 122; Chevalier: 134; de Klemm: 72, 246; Dubois: 133, 215; Fatras: 227, 238; Metais: 141; Rebouleau: 124a; Renaud: 93, 149c; Robert: 151, 229; Roux: 165; Solaro: 25; Souricate: 144–145; Suinot: 44; Thibout: 10; Tollu: 241a; Varin: 127b, 247; Vielliard: 138; Visage: 82, 103, 148cs, 162–163. Magnum Photos, Paris: 228. Aldo Margiocco, Genoa: 224. Guiseppe Mazza, Milan: 114, 115, 148bd. Mario Pasotti, Garda (Verona): 144. Lino Pellegrini, Milan: 194–195. Pictor, Milan: 184–185, 210, 232–233. G. Pizzey/L. H. Newman's N.H.P.A., Westerham, Great Britain: 74–75. Luisa Ricciarini, Milan: Giuliano Cappelli: 135, 149b, 208–209; Nino Cirani: 182–183; R. Longo: 140, 175a; Sandro Prato: 142–143, 187; Angelo P. Rossi: 83, 94, 220–221. Fulvio Roiter, Venice: 129. Ina Watson, Victoria, Australia: 45.

Library of Congress Cataloging in Publication Data

Bologna, Gianfranco.
  THE WORLD OF BIRDS.

  (Abbeville Press encyclopedia of natural science)
  Translation of Il mondo degli uccelli.
  Bibliography: p. 252–3
  1. Birds. I. Title.
QL676.B6913   1979   598.2   79-1190
ISBN 0-89659-028-3 pbk.

Copyright © 1975 by Arnoldo Mondadori Editore S.p.A., Milan

English Translation Copyright © 1978 by Arnoldo Mondadori Editore S.p.A., Milan

All rights reserved. No part of this book may be reproduced or utilized in any form or by any means, electronic or mechanical, including photocopying, recording, or by any information storage and retrieval system, without permission in writing from the Publisher. Inquiries should be addressed to Abbeville Press, Inc., 505 Park Avenue, New York, N.Y. 10022.

Printed and bound in Italy by Officine Grafiche of Arnoldo Mondadori Editore, Verona.

Contents

Introduction	6
Structure	26
How Birds Live	98
Habitats	180
Birds and Man	218
Classification	244
Bibliography	252
Index	254

Introduction

Airborne animals: the conquest of flight
Birds are feathered creatures. The front limbs have been transformed into wings, so they are able to fly. This extraordinary adaptation to flight has dictated their entire body structure. It has enabled them to colonize the Earth with great success, not only in terms of the variety of habitats in which they are found but also of their geographical distribution, which extends over every area of the globe (apart from the 'heart' of Antarctica). The morphological and anatomical structure of birds is therefore designed in accordance with this essential activity which characterizes the entire group (although there are certain birds which cannot fly and have adapted themselves instead to swimming and running, like penguins and the Ostrich).

In the vast sweep of geological time which embraces the presence of life on Earth, it was some 200 million years ago that birds evolved from reptiles. They still retain some of the latter's features today. In order for them to conquer the air, however, they have had to achieve a whole series of specific adaptations. Because of this, these animals have a structural make-up which has evolved gradually according to the requirements of aerial movement. It is also evident that the present-day evolutionary success of birds is closely bound up with this faculty, which enables them to move in all the three environments: land, air and water. The capacity to fly is the result of the combination of favourable conditions which have been concentrated in the structure of a bird. Lightness, aerodynamic properties, strength and energy are the conditions which, together, enable these creatures to move in and on air. If we look at the structure of a bird, we can see that the necessary conditions are in fact rules. Any feature, be it

▲ Costa's Hummingbird *Calypte costae*

anatomical or physiological, whose presence might compromise the lightness, has been eliminated. The bones are strong but light; reproduction is oviparous (an embryo developed internally would mean an increase in weight); there are no reserve stores. The external morphology of the body tallies with the aerodynamic condition: there are no outer appendages. Beak, head, neck, legs and tail are all structured in such a way that they form a streamlined contour. The bulk of the internal organs is near the animal's centre of gravity. The tough, light skeleton, the musculature and the lightness of the feathers which form the flying surface all have the strength required for aerial movement. The functioning of the circulatory, respiratory and digestive systems requires a consistently very high metabolic level – a level maintained by the physiological make-up which needs a great deal of energy to sustain a bird.

▲ Wandering Albatross *Diomedea exulans*

At the present time the Class Aves (birds) includes more than 8,600 species. Structurally speaking, they show a certain uniformity, but the remarkable variety of forms and adaptations in other respects makes this class one of the most fascinating of all animal groups. The variety within the Class Aves can be briefly summarized by giving, by way of example, certain data about the size and weight of one or two distinctive species. Wilhelm Meise (in Grzimek, 1972) gives the ranges of certain measurements as follows: (a) the total length, calculated from the tip of the beak to the tip of the central tail feathers, varies from the 6 cm of a hummingbird to the 235 cm of a peacock or the 600 cm of the Phoenix (or Yokohama Cock), one of the varieties of Japanese cocks; (b) the height, calculated from the tip of the beak or bill to the lowest point of the legs, reaches 300 cm in the Ostrich (it used to reach 400 cm in the Great Moa, which is now extinct); (c) the wingspan,

▲ Ostrich *Struthio camelus*

calculated from the point where the wing meets the body to the tip, varies from the 2·5 cm of the Bee Hummingbird (*Acestrura bombus*) to the 340 cm of the Wandering Albatross (in the now long extinct giant Nevada Vulture it reached as much as 500 cm): (d) the weight of the chicks when they hatch from the egg ranges from 0·19 g for *Acestrura bombus* to 1,000 g for the Ostrich, or even 6,500 g for the extinct

Madagascan Elephant Bird (*Aepyornis*); (e) the weight of adult individuals ranges from 1·6 g for a hummingbird to 144,000 g for the Ostrich, not to mention the 450,000 g of the extinct Madagascan Elephant Bird.

Evolution
The natural world is the product of millions of years of evolutionary processes, through which each species has undergone modifications, adaptations and diversifications which have brought it to the form, way of life, status and position which it occupies in the present environmental context. Numerous species have vanished in this natural process, and others have given rise to new species. Evolution can be defined as a change in the genetic constitution of a population, this latter term being taken to mean a group of organisms of the same species spread over a given distribution area with features typical to the group and not to single individuals (Odum, 1971). The modern study of population genetics enables us to make the above definition more specific: evolution is a change of the genic frequencies.

The idea of evolution has taken rather a long time to establish itself: before 1859 (the year in which Darwin's *Origin of Species* was published) it was thought that the living world had been as it was from the moment in which the Creator had created it. Many thinkers and scientists tried to challenge this prevailing view, putting forward the idea that the living species were derived from other species through an evolutionary process. It was Charles Robert Darwin and Alfred Russel Wallace who first showed that evolution was a real process. Gradually, the belief in the immutability of the species crumbled. The discovery of fossils and the study of living populations both played a very important part in the growing confirmation and acceptance of the evolutionistic concept and its implications.

The evolutionary mechanisms do not act on the individual, but on groups (populations). The term population means a group of living beings, belonging to the same species, which freely exchange with one another their hereditary assets by means of mating. It is a term which embraces many dimensions: populations may consist of small groups, usually called demes, which occupy very small areas (such as the area beneath a stone, or a puddle of water) or of large groups covering a vast area. The inherited units in a population are the genes, and the overall set of genes in a population constitutes the common genetic legacy. It can be said that every new-born

INTRODUCTION

individual draws at random from the genetic legacy of the population (via its parents) a series of genes which, by interacting with the environment, form the structure of the new individual. In practice, every generation presents the same proportion of genes of the preceding generation, because the genes are drawn at random and the number of individuals produced is usually large. The frequency of the genes remains substantially constant down successive generations. This only happens if certain conditions are respected: new genes must not be produced through mutation or admission; reproduction must be random so that every gene has an equal probability of being transmitted, and the individuals which present different combinations of genes must have the same probability of survival. In natural populations there are often violations of these conditions. The stability of the genetic legacy is modified by mutations, that is by alterations occurring at gene and chromosome level. If subjected to favourable selective pressure, the mutating genes increase their frequency in the population. Other modifications to the genetic legacy occur when non-random reproduction takes place. This happens in various cases. For example, when a population is extremely reduced in numbers, some genes are lost because of the small number of individuals who can receive them (the phenomenon of genetic drift); or, when there is a situation of isolation, the exchange of genetic material occurs within the isolated population and does not give rise to random reproduction. Natural selection is a fundamental agent of evolution because it favours those genes which show themselves best suited and adapted to survival.

The history of birds

To get some idea of the great many changes which have taken place in the different geological periods, before man made his appearance on Earth, we must base our enquiry on the study of fossils, which provide evidence of the past. Fossils are parts of living beings which existed in past times and which are usually found squeezed between rocks, and are often transformed into rocky matter. The process of fossilization begins when the hardest remains of animals and plants become covered with soft sediments, like mud or clay for example, which then solidify and preserve the fossil with its structure complete. While it is not very difficult to find fossil remains of mammals' bones or the remains of shells, fossils of birds are particularly rare because the bone structure of these creatures is very fragile. As a result the work of the palaeontologist concerned

▲ *Archaeopteryx lithographica*

with winged creatures is fairly problematic. The remains of birds' bones, generally covered in mud or sand, have been subjected over millions of years to successive stratifications and superpositions. This lengthy process has modified the original matter, which is invaded or replaced by mineral substances, although the original shape remains much the same.

INTRODUCTION

The history of the Class Aves must have started, as proposed by the ornithologist Harrison, some 225–180 million years ago, in the period known as the Triassic in the classification of the geological periods laid down by palaeontologists. That period saw the slow evolution which gave rise to birds, from reptiles. In support of this derivation we find that birds still retain certain reptilian characteristics. In particular the legs and toes have horny scales like those of reptiles, and similar claws. In the skeletal structure, both birds and reptiles, in the articulation between the cranium and the spinal column, have a single occipital condyle situated beneath the cranium (in mammals, the cranio-spinal articulation is achieved with two occipital condyles which reduce the mobility of the head). Like birds, certain reptiles, the Chelonia (tortoises and turtles) and the Chamaeleontidae, also have air sacs which act as extensions to the pulmonary cavities. Birds and the vast majority of reptiles lay eggs and the young use a special 'tooth' at the tip of the beak or nose to break out of the egg. In addition, the pecten is found in the eye structure of both birds and reptiles. This is a special comb-like structure with a large number of blood vessels which apparently acts as an oxygen

▼ A Triassic reptile *Saltopsuchus*

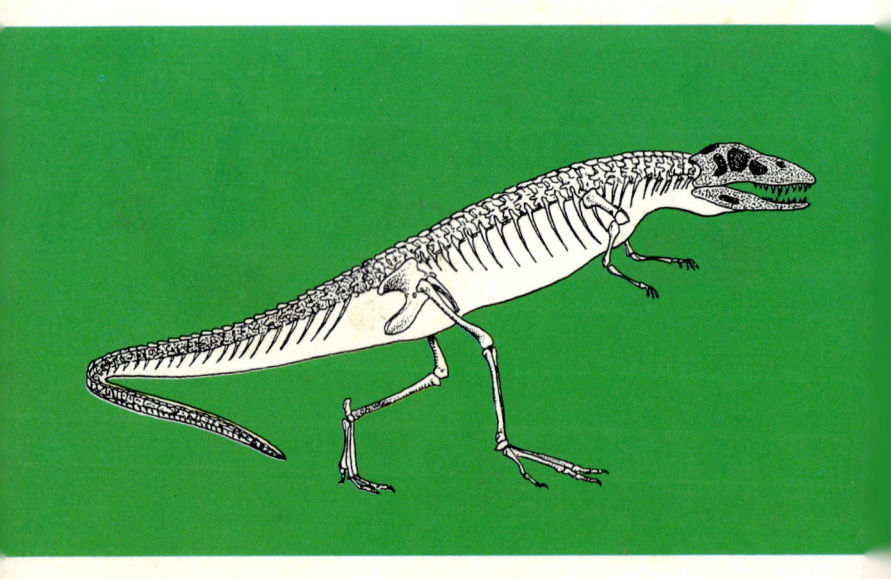

INTRODUCTION

supply reservoir, although this is not certain. There are also various similarities in the blood of the two classes. This is discussed on page 92.

The discovery of a very important fossil added greatly to our knowledge of the transition from reptile to bird. The first discovery of this fossil was made in 1861 at Solnhofen in Bavaria, a site which, some 150 million years ago in the Jurassic Period, must have been a lagoonal area with large plants where mud had gradually accumulated. Over long periods this mud turned into extremely fine limestone which, in the nineteenth century, was cut into slabs and used for lithographic printing. When the slabs were being cut various fossils of organisms preserved by the soft ooze were unearthed. One of these slabs yielded the first fossil skeleton of a bird called *Archaeopteryx lithographica*, now in the British Museum (Natural History) in London. A second skeleton was found in 1877 at Blumenberg, near Eichstatt, about 20 kilometres from Solnhofen. A further fossil was also discovered in the same quarry at Solnhofen, and another hitherto unnoticed specimen was identified in the collection of a Dutch museum. At first, palaeontologists considered these

▼ *Archaeopteryx lithographica* ▼ A modern bird

▲ *Ichthyornis*   ▲ *Hesperornis*

remains to belong to two different species, *Archaeopteryx lithographica* and *Archaeornis siemensi*, but subsequent research has shown that they belong to just one species, that of *Archaeopteryx lithographica*.

  Birds derive from the diapsid reptiles (those having two temporal fossae in the skull). *Archaeopteryx* still has the skull of a diapsid reptile, the upper limbs are almost wing-like, fairly short and with three free toes; there are feathers, the tail is long, and the upper and lower jaws both have teeth. Following one system of classification Padoa (1969) places *Archaeopteryx* as the only member of the subclass Palaeornithes (or ancient birds), as opposed to the subclass Neornithes (or new birds). In this latter subclass are three superorders: the Odontognathae, with two fossil genera from the Cretaceous Period, *Ichthyornis* and *Hesperornis*, with the basic characteristics of present-day birds, although the maxillary arches are equipped with teeth; the Palaeognathae and the Neognathae, subdivided on the basis of the structure of

▲ *Phororhacos* ▲ *Diatryma*

their bony palate. Members of the Palaeognathae include the ostriches, the rheas, the cassowaries, the kiwis, the emus and the tinamous; the Neognathae embrace all the other birds. Various other scholars make a distinction between birds having a sternum or breastbone with a carina or keel (i.e. with a strong ridge for the attachment of the pectoral muscles which are so vital for flying), and birds having a sternum without a carina (keel), known technically as ratites. The former include all the birds except the so-called runners, which form the second group and which are flightless precisely because of the absence of this keel. Following the latest classifications, Fisher and Peterson (1964) divide the Class Aves into three subclasses: Sauriurae (the first birds), to which they ascribe *Archaeopteryx*; Odontoholcae (birds with teeth) to which they ascribe the fossils *Hesperornis, Baptornis, Enaliornis, Coniornis* and *Neogaeornis*; and lastly the Ornithurae (typical birds) to which they ascribe *Ichthyornis, Apatornis*, various other fossil forms and all birds currently living.

INTRODUCTION

The first known fossil, the connecting link between reptiles and birds, is *Archaeopteryx*, dating to the Jurassic Period in the Secondary (Mesozoic) Era (about 181 million years ago). In the Cretaceous Period, still in the Secondary Era (about 135 million years ago) birds with teeth emerge, and certain birds similar to present-day types make their appearance. Among the major fossil finds are grebe- and diver-like forms such as *Enaliornis*, *Hargeria*, *Neogaeornis*, *Lonchodytes*, and *Baptornis*; goose- or flamingo-like forms such as *Gallornis*; gannet-like forms such as *Elopteryx*, tern-like forms such as *Ichthyornis* and other forms like *Hesperornis* and *Apatornis*. In the Tertiary Period birds began to expand numerically: in the Eocene and Palaeocene Epochs of the tertiary Period (63 million years ago), 27 families of modern birds appeared, and other primitive groups became extinct. Among the fossils unearthed we should mention *Odontopteryx*, like a large cormorant; *Prophaethon*, like present-day tropic birds (Phaethontidae) and *Diatryma steini*, 240 cm tall. In the next epoch known as the Oligocene (about 36 million years ago) we find the first Procellariiformes, Colymbiformes, Ciconiiformes, Charadriiformes, Coraciiformes and other modern groups, while in the Miocene Epoch (some 25 million years ago) most of the present-day families and some of the modern genera were in existence. Some primitive families became extinct. By the Pliocene Epoch (about 13 million years ago) most of the modern genera probably made their appearance and birds seem to have been at their most diversified. The moas, ostriches, tinamous and Caprimulgiformes (nightjars) come into existence. We come to the Quaternary Period, and the epoch known as the Pleistocene (some 2 million years ago), in which all modern orders and families are represented and most of today's species are present. About 750 extinct species are known. As a result of glaciation many species became extinct, especially the large birds without a carina. In the four identified glacial periods, known as Günz, Mindel, Riss and Würm, the polar ice-cap spread slowly towards areas previously having a temperate climate. Between one glaciation and the next there were inter-glacial periods during which the climate became milder. There were major movements in the distribution of the various species, especially mammal and bird species, with subsequent modifications in the distribution areas. In the Holocene or Recent Epoch we find the current number of species: the dominant order is the Passeriformes. Because of man's activity certain species, especially those found in islands, have become extinct.

INTRODUCTION

Species and evolution
A species (from the Latin *specere*, to observe or look) was defined in the past as a 'different thing', an entity which 'has a different appearance', 'a different form' (Mayr, 1963). Continual progress in this area of inquiry has gradually led to the formulation of a biological concept of the species, the significance and meaning of which are accepted throughout the world. The current definition of a species can be stated as follows: a species is a group of natural populations effectively and potentially capable of reproducing themselves by interbreeding. A species, therefore, has acquired a state of reproductive isolation in respect of other species, and its members have a common hereditary legacy. As a result of these new considerations, the definitions based exclusively on morphological differences, which had been established as fundamental elements for interspecific distinction, have been largely superseded.

Despite the new definition, the possibility that two species may cross-breed, and produce hybrids, has not been rejected; in fact such occurrences are by no means rare in nature although, unless a hybrid has real biological likenesses, it will rarely be fertile. Between one species and another a whole series of isolating mechanisms exist, designed to avoid the incidence of cross-breeding. These mechanisms are part of the heritage acquired by genetically isolated populations which then become species. Cases of hybridization do occur: for example on 27 May 1970, in the colony of pratincoles nesting in the Camargue National Park (Bouches-du-Rhône, France) the ornithologist Walmsey observed a pair made up of a Collared Pratincole (*Glareola pratincola*) and a Black-winged Pratincole (*Glareola nordmanni*). On June 6 the nest of this pair was found with three eggs; the first two chicks hatched on June 14, and the third on June 15. All three were later killed by predators. This case has nevertheless raised the question whether these two birds should be considered as two different species, two subspecies, or simply two forms with different coloration.

In the vast store of evolutionistic terminology there are the 'twin species' populations which are morphologically similar or identical, but isolated where reproduction is concerned. Within a species (in particular when it appears to be distributed over a very wide area) there can be a heightening of the differences due to hereditary modifications and a difference in local environments. These differences can give rise to populations with distinctive aspects called subspecies or races. The

INTRODUCTION

distinctive features which these present are generally to do with variations in shape, colour, weight and size. A subspecies is particularly interesting because it can illustrate a basic phenomenon of evolution: the formation of new species. Ornithologists have singled out numerous subspecies. The Russian Dementiev, for example, found 22 subspecies of the Peregrine Falcon (*Falco peregrinus*). By studying the variability of features in the different populations of some species, one can see various phases of coloration or morphism. A particular case in point is the sexual dimorphism observed in various species of birds, where the male and female present conspicuous morphological differences. There are two fairly extreme cases. The Huia (*Heteralocha acutirostris*), a passerine

▼ Great White Heron *Egretta alba*

▼ Common Rhea *Rhea americana*

▲ Common Cassowary *Casuarius casuarius*

◀ Emu *Dromaius novaehollandiae*

INTRODUCTION

of the family Callaeidae (New Zealand wattle birds) today extinct but once widespread in New Zealand, had pronounced sexual dimorphism in the form of the beak: in the male it was in the form of a chisel like a woodpecker's, and in the female it was long and curved. This difference in shape enabled them to find food in different ways. Nothing has been seen or heard of this bird since 1907, when two solitary males were spotted. Another interesting case of sexual dimorphism is that of the Eclectus Parrot (*Eclectus roratus*) found in New Guinea, where the two sexes are so differently coloured that they were thought to be two different species.

Other species exhibit polymorphism: in other words in the same population there may be two (dimorphism) or more (polymorphism) distinct forms, especially in the coloration of the plumage. These forms are usually called phases as in

▼ A group of White Pelicans *Pelecanus onocrotalus*

INTRODUCTION

the two phases of light and dark coloration of the Fulmar (*Fulmarus glacialis*) and the various phases shown by different species of birds of prey such as the Common Buzzard (*Buteo buteo*) and the Honey Buzzard (*Pernis apivorus*).

Similar environmental conditions may coincide with similar adaptations. One example is that of two unrelated species of Passeriformes, the North American *Sturnella magna* and the African *Macronyx crocea* – the *Sturnella* being an icterine bird and the *Macronyx* a member of the Motacillidae. As well as being very alike in appearance, they both have similar habitats and behavioural patterns because they live in similar habitats, although in different continents. This is known as convergent evolution. Essentially, penguins in the southern seas and the extinct Great Auk, clumsy in flight and from the Northern Hemisphere, inhabit similar environments, use their wings for

INTRODUCTION

underwater swimming, and as a result look alike. It can happen that from a common original strain different forms emerge, living in the available ecological areas in the territory colonized. This is known as adaptive distribution.

When two similar animal populations living in the same distribution area do not produce hybrids (do not cross-breed) it can be said that there is an efficient isolating mechanism; this makes the two populations two distinct species, which are called sympatric because they live in the same geographical area. Conversely, two animal populations which are similar but isolated from the viewpoint of geographical distribution are called allopatric, although, with no actual proof of reproductive isolation, they might be thought to be two different subspecies. (Note that a river, a mountain range or even a clearing in a forest may be sufficient cause for geographical isolation.) Two allopatric species with surprising morphological similarities, the Canadian Nuthatch (*Sitta canadensis*) and the Corsican Nuthatch (*Sitta whiteheadi*), found in just a few parts of Corsica, were thought to be subspecies of one and the same species. Detailed studies by Hans Lohrl showed that they were two different species: in fact they have behavioural, singing and eating habits which are so different that reproductive isolation exists between them even if they are kept together in captivity.

The Eurasian Golden Plover (*Pluvialis apricaria*) and the American/Asian Lesser Golden Plover (*Pluvialis dominica*) are very alike morphologically, but in Siberia where the distribution areas of the two species overlap there are no hybrid populations. The overlapping areas in Central Europe between the distribution of the Hooded Crow (*Corvus cornix*) and the Carrion Crow (*Corvus corone*), on the other hand, have numerous hybrid examples. Many ornithologists consider these to be two subspecies:*Corvus corone corone*, the Carrion Crow, and *Corvus corone cornix*, the Hooded Crow.

Then there are species which, in their distribution area, have one or more subspecies, and others, on the contrary, which do not have any such sub-divisions. These latter, known as monotypic species, are generally species which have appeared recently in the history of life on Earth, or which have a distribution confined to clearly defined geographical areas without any great possibility of further dispersion. The term polytypic refers to species which have sub-divisions into one or more subspecies. These are species which, on the whole, appeared early in the evolutionary history of birds, with a broad geographical distribution and the possibility of

▲ A pair of Griffon Vultures *Gyps fulvus*

dispersion – both features which facilitate the formation of subspecies. In time, as a rule, every monotypic species tends to turn into a polytypic species unless the group in question concerns very localized forms which have few evolutionary possibilities.

The formation of new species from a parental species is called speciation. A classic example is the speciation of the Chaffinch in the Canary Islands. From the typical subspecies *Fringilla coelebs coelebs*, which had colonized the islands, the subspecies *Fringilla coelebs tintillon* and a new species, *Fringilla teydea* later evolved. It is currently held that speciation takes place basically because of geographical isolation, which would favour the formation of distinct populations within one and the same species. In the course of time, these populations may themselves become species, achieving reproductive isolation from the parental species. This type of speciation, occurring because of geographical isolation, is known as allopatric speciation. Some ornithologists see the possibility of speciation because of other reasons; for example, as a result of mutations which might modify certain populations within one and the same species. This type of speciation is known as sympatric speciation.

Structure

Flight is the most distinctive feature of the Class Aves. The ability to fly has numerous requirements concerning the optimum weight, strength, power and lightness of the various structures. The skeletal and muscular apparatuses are perfectly adapted, and complemented by the feathers.

Plumage
In vertebrates, the cutaneous or integumentary apparatus is formed basically by the skin (also called integument or cutis) which covers the entire body surface and consists of two layers: a superficial layer called the epidermis and a deeper layer called the derma or dermis. The various structures found in these animals – glands, scales, feathers, hairs, nails, claws, horns, luminous organs – are derived from these two layers. The forms and functions of the organs so derived are extremely varied. In birds, the skin is very thin and has no glands, except for the uropygial gland (preen-gland) near the tail, which

secretes an oily substance used by the bird to smear over its feathers with its beak, making them waterproof. In waterfowl this gland is especially well developed but, conversely, it is absent in the Ostrich, cassowaries, bustards, various Columbiformes and parrots. The plumage acts as protective covering which stops the dispersion of body heat because of the large amount of air trapped within the feathers, keeping the body temperature high. In many cases the plumage is brightly coloured, a basic requirement in the social life of birds. More important it provides the essential supporting surface which gives them the capacity to fly and satisfies in every way the requirements of lightness, flexibility and resistance which are all fundamental to flight. Although it derives from the papillae of the dermis, the plumage is biologically a dead structure, and as a result does not need to be supplied with blood because, in effect, it remains detached from the rest of the body. The feathers are horny formations derived from a thickening of the

STRUCTURE

dermis and are fed by a dermal papilla. When the feather has formed into its components, the dermal papilla retracts, leaving it devitalized. If a bird loses a feather, for either natural (moulting) or accidental reasons, the cells of the papilla produce a new one. Feathers are thus regularly produced, inasmuch as birds moult annually. There are three types of feather: the feather proper, or contour feather, the plumule, or down feather, and the filoplume. The feathers known as contour feathers, because they cover the body, are formed by a central structure divided into two parts: the calamus and the rachis. The calamus runs from the point where it is attached to the skin, where there is a groove called the lower or inferior umbilicus, to an upper groove called the superior umbilicus; inside, it has a few horny laminae. The rachis runs from the superior umbilicus to the outermost tip of the feather. Two lateral series of barbs emerge from the rachis, and each barb has two series of barbules, one turned towards the tip of the feather and a lateral series. Usually, the barbules turned towards the tip of the feather are equipped with hamuli which are hooked to the lateral series of barbules on the adjacent barb, thus forming a very fine and close-knit surface. This interlocking system is known as the vexillum or vane. In general, at the superior umbilicus is a small tuft of barbs and in some instances (in the feathers of birds of prey, in certain passerines, in the Anatidae, the Ardeidae, cassowaries and the Emu) there may be a smaller structure with a rachis, barbs and barbules, in miniature, which is called the hyporachis or aftershaft. Some feathers have barbules with no hamuli, and as a result the vexillum is not closely knit as with the feathers of the Ostrich. If a twig or some object passes through a feather, the components of the vexillum simply separate, but a flick of the bird's beak will place everything back in its correct position.

The plumules, on the other hand, have a calamus which is open at the base and at the top, at the level of the inferior and superior umbilici, and usually have no rachis. As a result a series of barbs emerges directly at the upper tip of the calamus. In some cases the plumules do have a rachis, in which there are barbs. The plumules form the downy plumage of chicks – precocious nestlings are born with their feather covering and, although they do not stray far, are able to move about both inside and outside the nest soon after hatching. In species which have helpless young (young which are born with their skin bare and remain for some time in the nest before becoming independent), the first feathers to appear are contour feathers and not plumules. However, the plumules are found together with the contour feathers in the plumage of many adult birds, particularly in the ventral area of the body where they form a fairly thick plumage, for example in waterfowl. It must be remembered that in birds (excluding the penguins and the ratites, where it is present uniformly on the skin) the plumage does not form over the entire skin, but only on certain parts of it, known as pterylae. The bare regions are

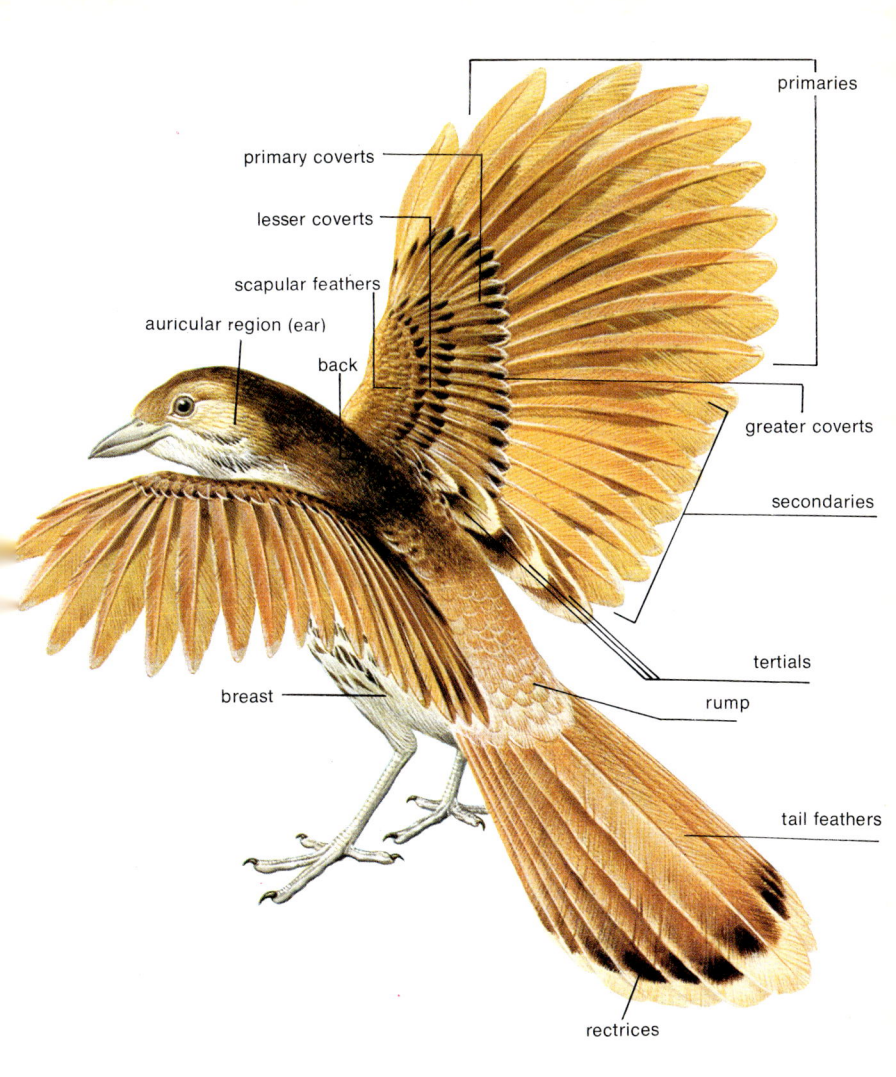

29

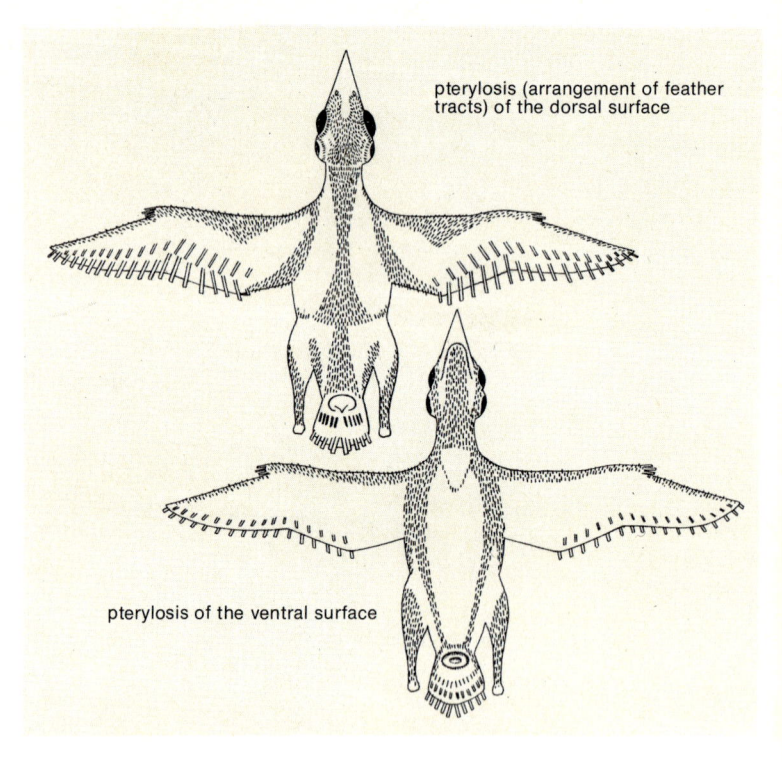

pterylosis (arrangement of feather tracts) of the dorsal surface

pterylosis of the ventral surface

▲ Examples of feather distribution

called apteria. When present, however, the down covers all the skin. The filoplumes, lastly, have no vexillum: here the rachis is usually bare or has just a few barbs at the tip.

A bird's body has various filoplumes. As well as the feathers, plumules and filoplumes there are also the so-called vibrissae, which look like whiskers, have no barbs and are found often at the base of the beak of some birds, such as birds of prey; and also so-called pulverulent (or powdery) down, which is present in herons, bitterns and tinamous, and has the feature of continually breaking up and forming a sort of fatty powder which these birds use for cleaning and preening their plumage.

The average weight of the feathers in relation to the bird's total weight usually works out at about 6 per cent, dropping to 3–4 per cent in penguins and rising to 12 per cent in titmice.

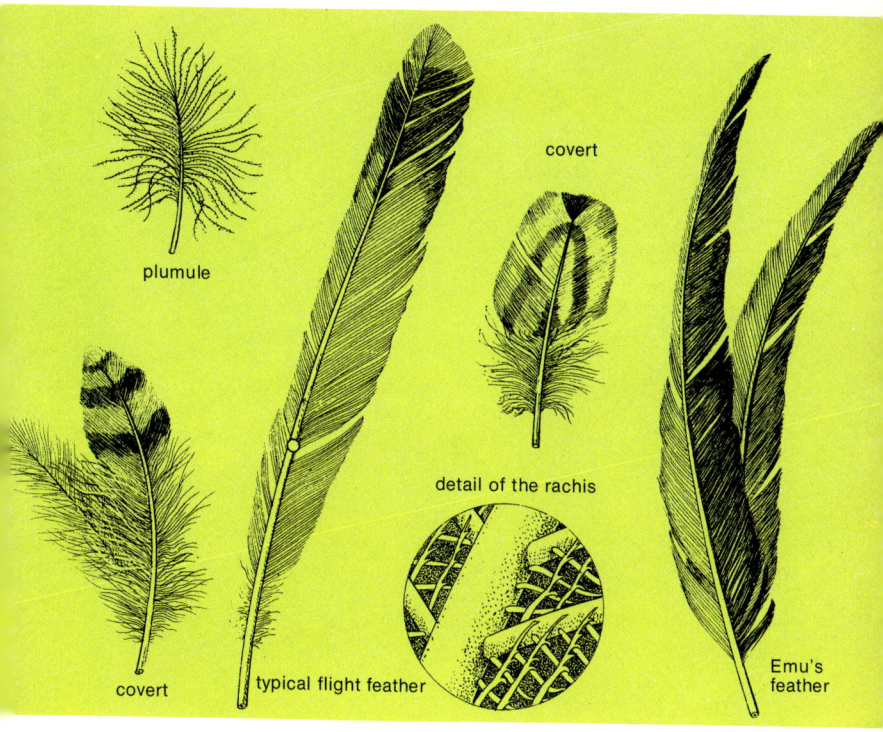

▲ Types of feather

The feathers are arranged over the bird's body in an extremely ordered way. For flying, the feathers on the front limbs are of prime importance. Depending on where they are situated, they can be divided into: (a) the 'thumb' remiges or wing-quills, there being three or four on the thumb, forming the alula or bastard wing, which is important in flying; (b) the primary wing-quills, situated on the manus or hand and the middle 'finger', 9–12 in number, and on average 10; (c) the secondary or cubital wing-quills, situated on the ulna or 'forearm', ranging from six in small Passeriformes, to 40 in the large albatrosses; (d) the tertiary wing-quills, situated on the humerus or upper armbone. Each wing-quill is protected at the point of fixture, both above and below, by other feathers called coverts, which take on different specific names depending on where they are situated. Wing-quills and coverts thus form a

STRUCTURE

perfect, tough structure vital for flight. The tail feathers, called rectrices, are very important for flying.

A bird is subject to periodic moulting of its plumage. First it sheds its fledgling's down, and develops an early plumage. If almost naked at birth, feathers gradually grow, eventually covering its body. Later the feathers are replaced at least once a year, usually at the end of the mating season. During moulting all the feathers are gradually and systematically replaced. In certain species moulting occurs twice a year: one before and one after reproduction. Prenuptial or winter moulting is mostly only partial and does not affect the feathers most vital for flying – wing-quills and tail feathers. These latter are shed progressively and replaced during the postnuptial or autumnal moulting, so that the bird's ability to fly is never completely endangered. In some species, however, the flight feathers are shed all at once, and during this period these species (in particular waterfowl: certain Anatidae, Procellariiformes and waders) are unable to fly, and have to hide themselves from predators. The period of moulting varies in length from species to species: it is usually short in the case of most Passeriformes and Charadriiformes but very long in the case of albatrosses, pelicans, boobies, gannets and birds of prey. Because they moult, birds may have different coloured 'dress', which can make them difficult to identify in the wild. In many species, as well as the different coloration between the plumage of young and adults, there are also major differences between the winter and summer plumages, especially in ducks and waders such as plovers and curlews. Depending on the species, the young achieve their adult 'dress' at different times: the Shore Lark (*Eremophila alpestris*) acquires its adult plumage at the first post-nestling moult, about three months after it is born. Various other species, such as certain birds of prey, assume the adult plumage between four and six years old, while the Twelve-wired Bird of Paradise (*Seleucidis melanoleucos*) waits until it is seven before this occurs.

Moulting occurs in birds as the result of a series of major endocrine activities. Vital roles in causing moulting are played by the thyroid gland and the front area of the hypophysis. If the thyroid gland is removed from a bird, moulting does not take place; conversely, it can be brought on by giving a bird injections of thyroid hormones. The action of the hypophysis is affected by light, which plays a major role in causing moulting by activating the hypophysial-thyroidal hormonal axis. The sex glands and the adreno-cortical gland also help to affect moulting.

The skeleton

There are two main features in the skeleton of birds: the transformation of the front limbs into wings, with the subsequent loss of some bones and the merger of others (made necessary in order to obtain the maximum compactness which is crucial for flight); and the overall lightening of the skeletal apparatus. The bones are strong but for the most part porous and hollow, although some marrow may occur in the bones of young specimens. This allows the penetration of air from the lungs through the air sacs connected to the bronchial tubes.

Birds have two ways of locomotion: namely on land, and in the air, and there are adaptations for moving in or on water. In the air, the most essential bones are those in the front limbs, and in the rib-cage as a whole; on the ground they are the spinal column, the pelvic girdle and the lower limbs.

The skull or cranium of birds includes an element derived from the cutaneous apparatus, the beak, bill or rhamphotheca, which forms a horny sheath around the jaws. Sutures between the various bones of the cranium, though present in other vertebrates are not visible in birds – particularly in adult specimens. The structure of the palate has been used as a determining factor in some classifications of the whole class. The vertebrae range in number from 39 in certain Passeriformes to 63 in swans. The neck has a varying number of vertebrae, from 11 in some parrots to 25 in swans; in mammals, on the contrary, the neck (including the giraffe's) always has seven vertebrae. The cervical vertebrae are very mobile, and in some species enable the bird to turn its head almost through 180°, to face backwards. The dorsal vertebrae are more inter-linked and in some instances form an actual dorsal bone consisting of three to five vertebrae. In the lumbar region the vertebrae are joined together, while the sacral vertebrae, two in number, fuse with some of the lumbar and caudal vertebrae, of which there are between 10 and 23, giving rise to the synsacrum which supports the attached pelvic girdle. This latter is in turn formed by three similarly fused bones: the ilium, ischium and pubis. The final vertebrae are the caudal ones: the first, between four and nine, are free, while the last, which may number up to ten, are fused and form the so-called pygostyle, which carries the tail feathers. The tail of *Archaeopteryx* is very long when compared with those of present-day birds. Today only the ratites and tinamous have divided tail vertebrae. The rib-cage and front limbs are vital elements for flying. The ribs, ranging from three to nine, have a vertebral and sternal segment and in some cases an uncinate system as

STRUCTURE

well, and run from the spinal column to the sternum. This latter is very well developed, especially in the species which fly, where it has a full keel acting as a support for the pectoral muscles. In the group of runners or ratites there is no keel, but just a small plate, which is why these birds are known also as Acarinatae. The scapular girdle is situated on the sternum; at the front the shoulder bones are joined by the clavicles or collarbones which are fused to form the so-called furcula. The wings are formed by the humerus, the radius, the ulna and a series of bones which are mostly fused into an elongated complex which is the equivalent of the hand in mammals. As

▼ Skeleton

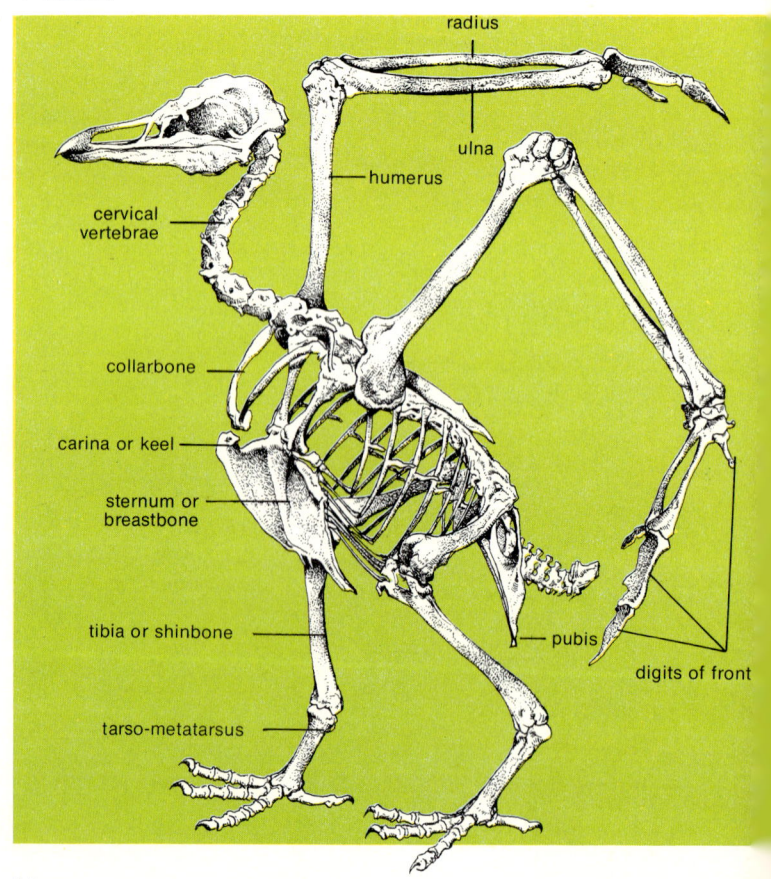

STRUCTURE

far as fingers are concerned, the index finger and, in the most rudimentary form, the thumb and the middle finger occur. The others are missing. In the lower limbs the femur is articulated to the tibia (shinbone), with a thin fibula alongside. There is then a further segment deriving from the fusion of the distal elements of the tarsus and the metatarsus, hence the term tarso-metatarsus: this is the part of the bird which is commonly called the leg. The foot has four toes at most. Usually there are three forward-turned toes and one at the back, but in various species there are two forward and two back, as is the case with birds such as woodpeckers.

▼ Types of feet

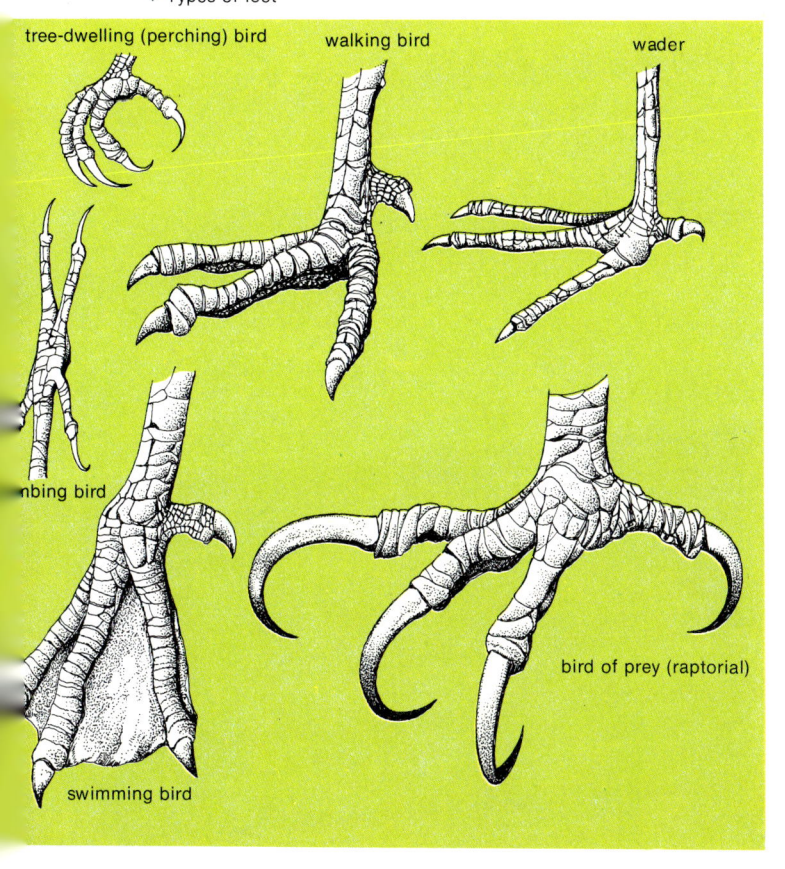

tree-dwelling (perching) bird   walking bird   wader

nbing bird

bird of prey (raptorial)

swimming bird

35

STRUCTURE

The muscular apparatus

The muscles form a tight cover over the skeleton and help to make the body streamlined and aerodynamic. The neck and all the limbs have a powerful musculature. The wings are controlled by muscles extending from the breastbone and the keel. The large pectoral muscle controls the lowering of the wing and is the most highly developed of the wing-muscles; the small pectoral muscle, also known as the rear coraco-brachialis muscle, completes the action of the former. The supra-coracoid or middle pectoral muscle controls the raising of the wing. These three muscles are the most important of the 50 or so involved in the wing movement. In the hind limbs, the simultaneous action of the front and rear muscles of the thigh produces the extension of the limb, their action being important in the jump preceding take-off; muscles working in the other direction bend the tibia over the tarsus. In the femur, tibia and tarsus the extensor muscles dominate the flexor muscles, while in the foot, on the contrary, the flexor muscles

▼ The hummingbird's flight

normal flight

STRUCTURE

are more powerful than the extensors: these produce the closure of the foot and the elongation of the limb. They are important, together with the other muscles in the hind limb, at the moment of take-off and landing. The remarkable suppleness of the foot gives the bird its ability to roost or perch. The flexor muscles of the toes which enable birds to grasp hold of a perch automatically mean that they can sleep in peace in such a position, without any danger that their hold will slacken.

Flying

In the cross-section of a wing the upper surface is convex and the lower concave. Birds fly on the same principles that apply to aircraft. Both have similarly shaped wings — this is because air moves faster over the larger curve of the upper surface of a wing, causing greater pressure beneath the wing and hence the lift necessary to remain airborne. Flapping or beating the wings provides forward propulsion. Upward

hovering flight

backward flight

STRUCTURE

thrust and maintaining altitude are provided by the form of the wing. In addition the alula or bastard wing directs a layer of air across the upper surface of the wing, thus reducing turbulence and allowing a smooth landing. The variety found in the forms of birds' wings permits different types of flight. A distinction is generally made between gliding or soaring, and flapping flight.

Gliding or soaring means that the bird does not beat the air for a certain period of time. It is typical of birds with large, wide

▲ Phases in the flapping flight of a duck

wings and slender bodies. With this type of flight they often manage not only to avoid losing height, but also to gain height. Birds such as vultures, other large birds of prey, storks, pelicans and so on, use warm rising currents. Open areas which are warmed by the sun's rays increase the temperature of the air layers above which, as a result of a reduction in density, move upwards; similar warm rising currents occur in regions which are hilly and mountainous. Soaring birds move from one

STRUCTURE

warm rising current to another, losing height as they make the move and then regaining it once the other current has been reached.

Sea birds are the experts at soaring. Except in very specific conditions, there are no warm rising currents available over the sea (during migration the large land-based species avoid crossing large stretches of sea and stick close to coastlines, making use of straits and narrows like Gibraltar and the

Bosphorus). Thanks to their slender build, sea birds (such as albatrosses and shearwaters) can take advantage of the currents produced at wave level by the wind hitting the waves, and skilfully use any variations in the wind speed. They keep aloft without losing height, moving with the wind when it slackens, and moving into it when it increases. The perfect knowledge possessed by these birds of the rapid variations played by winds at sea is assisted by special tactile organs, as

▲ Mute Swan *Cygnus olor*

evidenced by the morphology of the nasal fossae in species belonging to the order Procellariiformes, which includes the most able marine soaring birds.

Flapping flight, conversely, in its many forms, is the commonest technique of flying used by birds. In this type of flight the wing is regularly raised and thrust downward, beating the air each time: the regular wing-beat enables the bird to stay aloft and move from A to B. Depending on the various morphological structures and the respective aerodynamic features of the various birds, there are variations in the phases of flying. Certain Passeriformes have an undulating wing-beat, whereas other birds have a straight trajectory during which the more developed secondary and tertiary wing-quills give a

Species	Wingbeats per second	Species	Wingbeats per second
Cormorant	3.9	Peregrine Falcon	4.3
Pheasant	9	Herring Gull	2.8
Coot	5.8	Guillemot	8
Grey Heron	2.5	Blackbird	5.6
Mallard	5	Magpie	3
Mute Swan	2.7	Hummingbird	70

Wall Creeper
Tichodroma muraria ▶

◀ Fulmar
Fulmarus glacialis

Manx Shearwater
Puffinus puffinus ▶

broader supporting surface. Other passerines remedy this situation by maintaining a constant forward movement, due to the force of inertia and the aerodynamic form of the body, which enables them to penetrate the air regularly.
Woodpeckers have an alternating flight pattern: dives with the wings almost closed, then energetic wing-beats which enable them to make up the height lost in the dives. Other species (in particular certain birds of prey, kingfishers, terns and shrikes) sometimes use a type of flight in which they remain motionless in a given spot, with their wings beating very fast. This typical position of hovering enables the bird to keep an eye on its potential prey before plunging down on it.

Basing their views on the shape of the wings in various species of birds, some ornithologists have drawn up a specific classification. Four categories are generally acknowledged, based on the ratio between the length and breadth of the wing: (a) birds with rounded or elliptical wings (Galliformes, woodpeckers, certain pigeons and doves, certain passerines, etc.); (b) birds with long, narrow wings (waders, swallows and swifts, bee eaters, falcons etc.); (c) sea birds which soar; (d) land-based birds which soar. The ratio between body-weight and wing-area has also been measured in various species and produced significant results.

Other important factors in any analysis of the flight of birds are take-off and landing, inasmuch as the ways in which both these tricky manoeuvres are handled by the various types of birds differ widely. Before taking-off, some species have to reach an adequate horizontal speed. This applies to vultures, large sea birds, and various species of waterfowl such as coots which run quickly across the water beating both wings and feet before becoming airborne. In other cases take-off is helped by the bird launching itself from a raised place. Other species manage to take-off without much trouble by making a leap and then rising vertically into the air beating their wings. When it comes to landing, the bird has to slow down its horizontal speed by opening its tail, using its wing-beats as brakes and arranging its body vertically. The stress undergone by the legs and pelvis in this manoeuvre is considerable but these parts of the body are tough and can stand the impact. An extraordinary type of flight, known as vibrating flight is peculiar to and typical of hummingbirds. These creatures are capable of flying and staying in the same place all at once, by constantly beating their wings and flying backwards. They can do this because the special formation of the bones in their front limbs where the humerus, ulna and radius form a kind of fixed 'V' which is controlled by extremely strong muscles.

The large amount of energy used by a bird when in flight means that when a group of birds is on the move, particularly during migrations, they abide by special flight formations designed to save energy. In various of the largest species we find single-file flight formations (cormorants for example) in which each bird follows the one in front of it in the line, and upside-down V-formations (geese, ducks, pelicans, cranes and certain waders). In this latter formation the wing-beat produces a rising eddy at the tip, and enables the bird nearest to support itself on this rising current, and thus save energy – the birds change places, taking it in turns to occupy the key positions.

The flying performances of birds are remarkable, and when migrating they manage to cover incredible distances. The famous Arctic Tern covers 17,000 kilometres in its postnuptial flight. Every day the Common Swift will cover 1,000 kilometres, while the delicate little Blue Tit, with its endless to-ing and fro-ing (30 or 40 journeys a day) to the nest to feed

STRUCTURE

its young will easily cover 100 kilometres. As far as speed is concerned, a distinction can be made between a flight in search of food, a flight to and from the nest, or to peg out a territory, and quicker flight when the bird dives on to its prey, or when it swoops to escape from a predator. The speed reached in a migratory flight lies between the two above types. When migrating, a quail can reach 48–91 kilometres per hour and the Turtle Dove 61–72 kilometres per hour; a Peregrine Falcon plunging on to its prey from the sky may reach a speed of 290 kilometres per hour, the highest speed recorded for any bird. Swifts can reach speeds of around 200 kilometres per hour (although their average speed is somewhere around 90–100).

▼ Adelie Penguins *Pygoscelis adeliae*

Rainbow Lorikeet
Trichoglossus haematodus ▶

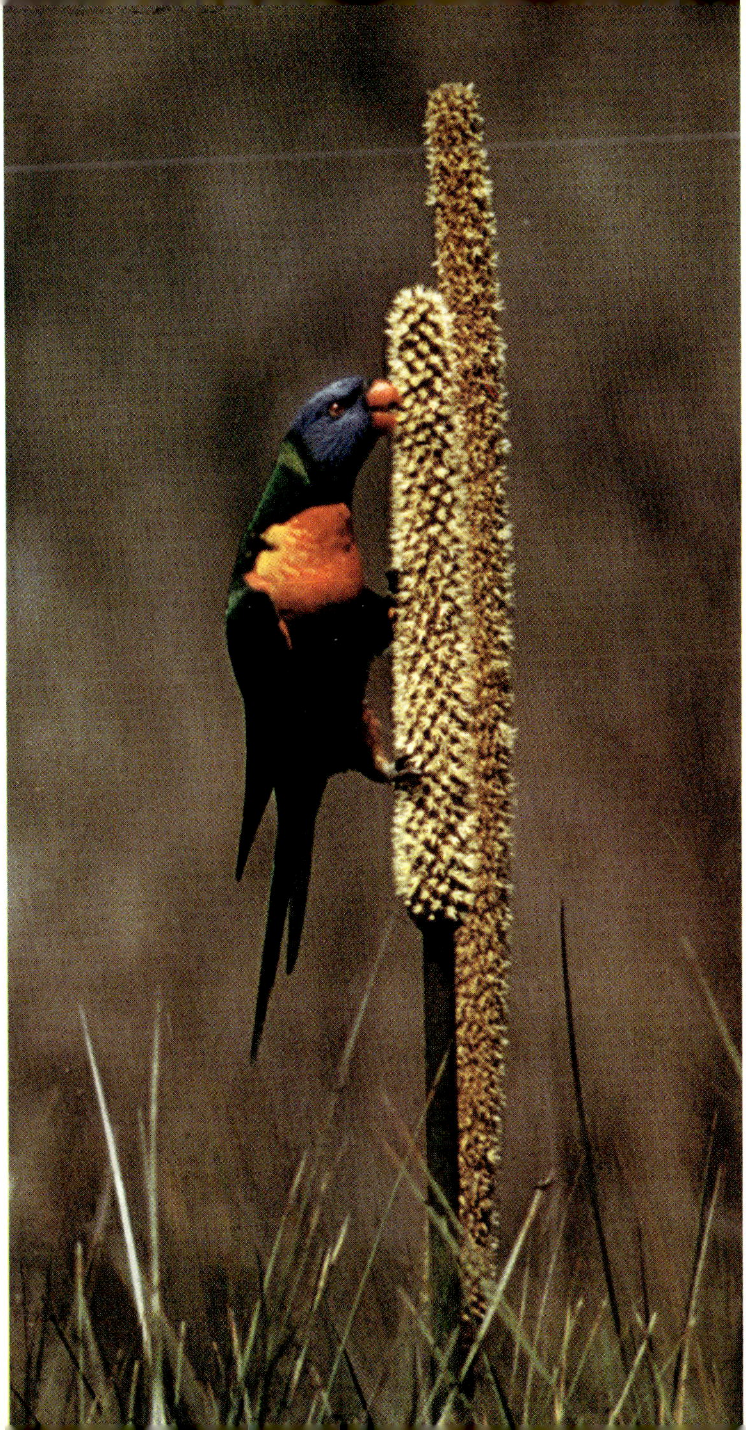

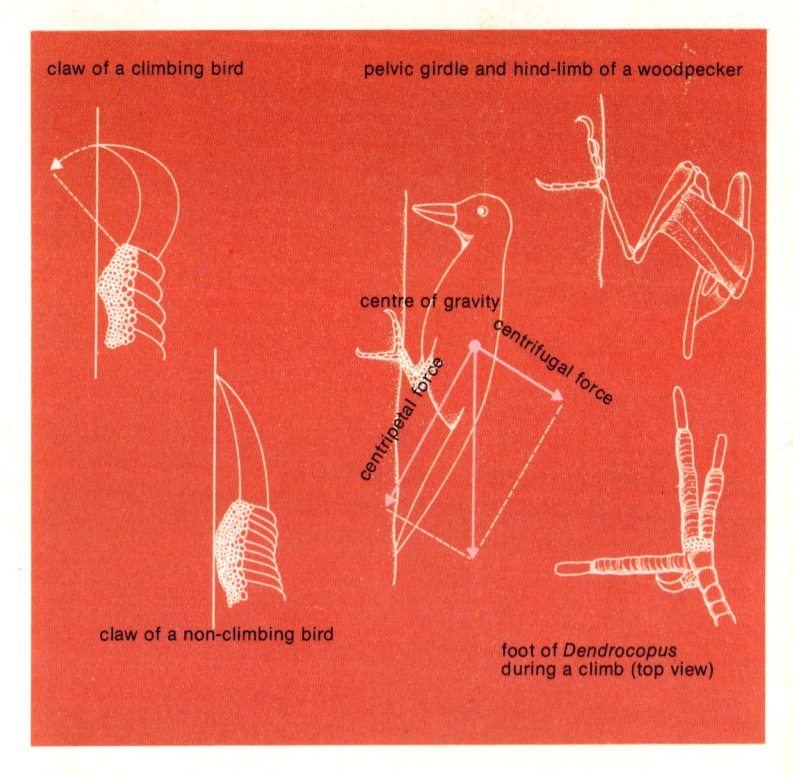

Special features which enable such birds as woodpeckers to climb ▲

Altitude varies a great deal from species to species: the Andean Condor has a remarkable record, reaching 6,000 metres above sea level in the Andes, as does the Bearded Vulture which reaches 8,000 metres in the Himalayas. When migrating, various Anatidae and waders cross the Himalayas. A record was set up by some Indian geese, at Dehra Dun in India, at 9,000 metres. The ornithologist R. C. Laybourne reported that on 29 November 1973 a commercial aircraft collided with a Rüppell's Vulture over the Ivory Coast in Africa at an altitude of 12,000 metres.

Birds move in various ways on the ground. In the large runners, which are flightless, the legs are highly developed and enable them to move safely and speedily on land. Swifts, hummingbirds and certain Artamidae (wood swallows)

Great Spotted Woodpecker *Dendrocopus major* ▶

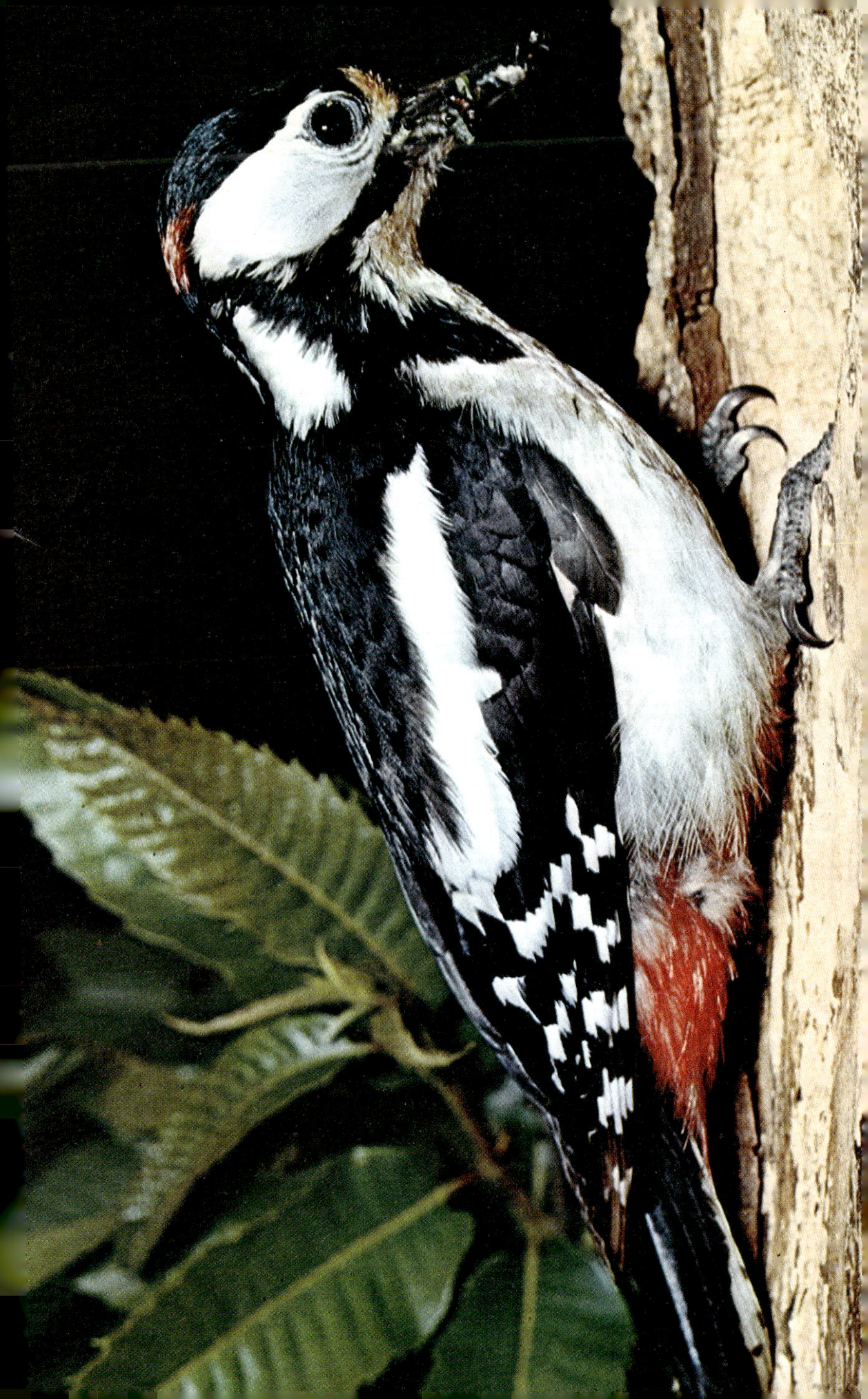

STRUCTURE

practically never come to rest on the ground because the particular structure of their legs means that they can only find a footing on vertical walls or perch on branches. Numerous birds move on the ground by moving their legs forward alternately; these species are the most conspicuously land-based and they will in many cases only take to the air when confronted by some serious danger. Others move on the ground with small hops and jumps; this form of movement applies to smaller birds, and those that are tree-dwelling. There is a remarkable variety in the form of the legs depending on the adaptations and habits of the various species. Some birds have climbing habits and their legs are perfectly adapted to this purpose: strong, with two toes in front and two behind, and curved claws, all features which

▼ Black-throated Diver *Gavia arctica*

help to make climbing easier. In woodpeckers, which are classic examples of climbing birds, the tail feathers also have an extremely strong structure and form an additional support for use when climbing.

Many species of birds move in water: they swim, float and dive, often reaching remarkable depths. Grebes can reach depths of 55 metres and dive on average to between five and 10 metres. The dives last varying lengths of time, but not usually more than a minute or two. Penguins have a special relationship with water. The body structure is perfectly adapted to moving through water, so much so that the front limbs are used like a fish's fins and they can reach speeds of more than 45 kilometres per hour in water. The plumage of waterfowl, which is particularly waterproof, is smoothed or sleeked and further waterproofed with the secretions from the uropygial or preen-gland, the only external gland in a bird's body.

Coloration
Birds have particularly keen eye-sight and a remarkable ability to discern colours. Their means of communication is therefore mainly visual, whereas mammals, with the exception of the primates, are governed predominantly by the sense of smell. As a result the plumage of birds is brightly coloured and plays an important part in their social and sexual behaviour. Dorst (1974) explains how the colours are produced in different ways: some derive from pigments while others are the result of more complicated optical effects, such as reflection and light interference, on subtle structures. Among the various pigments responsible for coloration we find the melanins (coming from foodstuffs containing amino acids, transformed into melanin by specific enzymes) which are the base of black, grey, brown and brownish yellow colorations; the carotinoid pigments, also known as lipochrome pigments because they are soluble in fats (likewise deriving from food) which are the basis for most yellow or red colorations, with their respective variations; the porphin group (porphyrins) which is responsible for certain red colorations, and so on. A particularly interesting pigment is the turacin pigment, which can fade or run directly on the living animal without harming its feathers. This pigment is present in the dark red marking in the wings of species belonging to the turacos (family Musophagidae, order Cuculiformes), found in tropical Africa. If one takes hold of a turaco or plantain eater, the hands may become stained red, without damaging the bird. Turacin fades

▲ Crested Seriema *Cariama cristata*

or runs in weakly alkaline water. The green colour of the rest of the turaco's plumage is produced by another distinctive pigment, turacoverdin.

The blue seen in birds does not originate from any specific pigment, but derives from the reflection and absorption of incident white light over or through heterogeneous media. This is because the blue part of the spectrum is reflected to a greater degree than the red. The blue colour in birds is produced by highly specialized feathers, absorbing most of the red rays. Except for certain cases, as with the turacoverdin pigment of the turacos, both green and violet derive from the same phenomenon. Other colorations derive from interference. They vary according to the incidence of the light, giving the plumage a metallic sheen. These interferences

▲ Carmine Bee Eaters *Merops nubicus*

generally occur in the pigmentary granules of the feathers' barbules. Various physical factors, as well as the chemical structure of pigments, are thus responsible for the brilliant colours we see in birds. Different types of coloration are present in the plumage of a single species and sometimes even in a single feather. Additional colours in the plumage of birds derive from the secretion of the uropygial gland which, in certain species, is coloured by iron oxide (from dirt or pollution) which darkens the plumage particularly in the ventral area. A classic example of this is the rust-coloured area in the lower parts of the magnificent Bearded Vulture. Modifications to the colorations of plumage come about as a result of wear and tear to the plumage itself, and sometimes, in various species, occur after moulting.

Digestion

Flying requirements have been decisive factors in the development of light, functional structures in the anatomy of birds, and the digestive system is no exception to this rule. In birds there is no complete masticatory apparatus, as there is in mammals: the beak and the mouth carry out the task of grasping food, tearing it free, and breaking it up or smashing it (in the case of seeds or fruit) to make it easier to swallow. No chewing takes place inside the mouth and food is swallowed whole. Given their high metabolic level, birds need to eat rather frequently and as a result their digestive apparatus is structured in such a way as to ensure rapid digestion of any food eaten and also an equally swift metabolization of this food which, obviously, supplies the fuel used to move the body. Not all birds have the high metabolism of certain Passeriformes, hummingbirds and swifts, and only the flightless species have permanent fatty deposits.

The digestive apparatus

The beak is a horny sheath formed from a series of plates which are so tightly inter-fused that there is no likelihood of sutures appearing (with the exception of the Procellariiformes, in which the plates are separated; in the Ostrich, in skuas and tinamous the beak has retained a primitive structure). In parrots, diurnal birds of prey, pigeons and certain Cracidae (curassows), there is an area of bare skin at the base of the beak which is often brightly coloured, called the cere, where the nostrils are situated. The articulation between beak and skull is structured in such a way that the mouth has a certain degree of mobility. In just a few groups (for example parrots) the upper part of the beak is also mobile. The beak is obviously used a great deal, and the inevitable wear and tear to which it is subject is compensated for by continuous growth at its tip. It is also equipped with sensory organs which help many birds to seek out and identify their prey. This is the case with waders in particular, which are specialists when it comes to seeking out prey, rummaging through the ooze in swamps with their beaks, at the tip of which there are small fossae with tactile properties. The tongue, which has tactile corpuscles, is extremely mobile and, like the beak, comes in many forms. With the exception of the rearmost section, the mouth is fairly hard and keratinized. In swallowing, a jerk of the head carries the food into the rear part of the pharynx. Next, with a reflex movement, the choanae or internal nostrils close (these are the apertures which link the nasal cavities with the palate), and at the same time the larynx

Flamingo *Phoenicopterus roseus* ▶

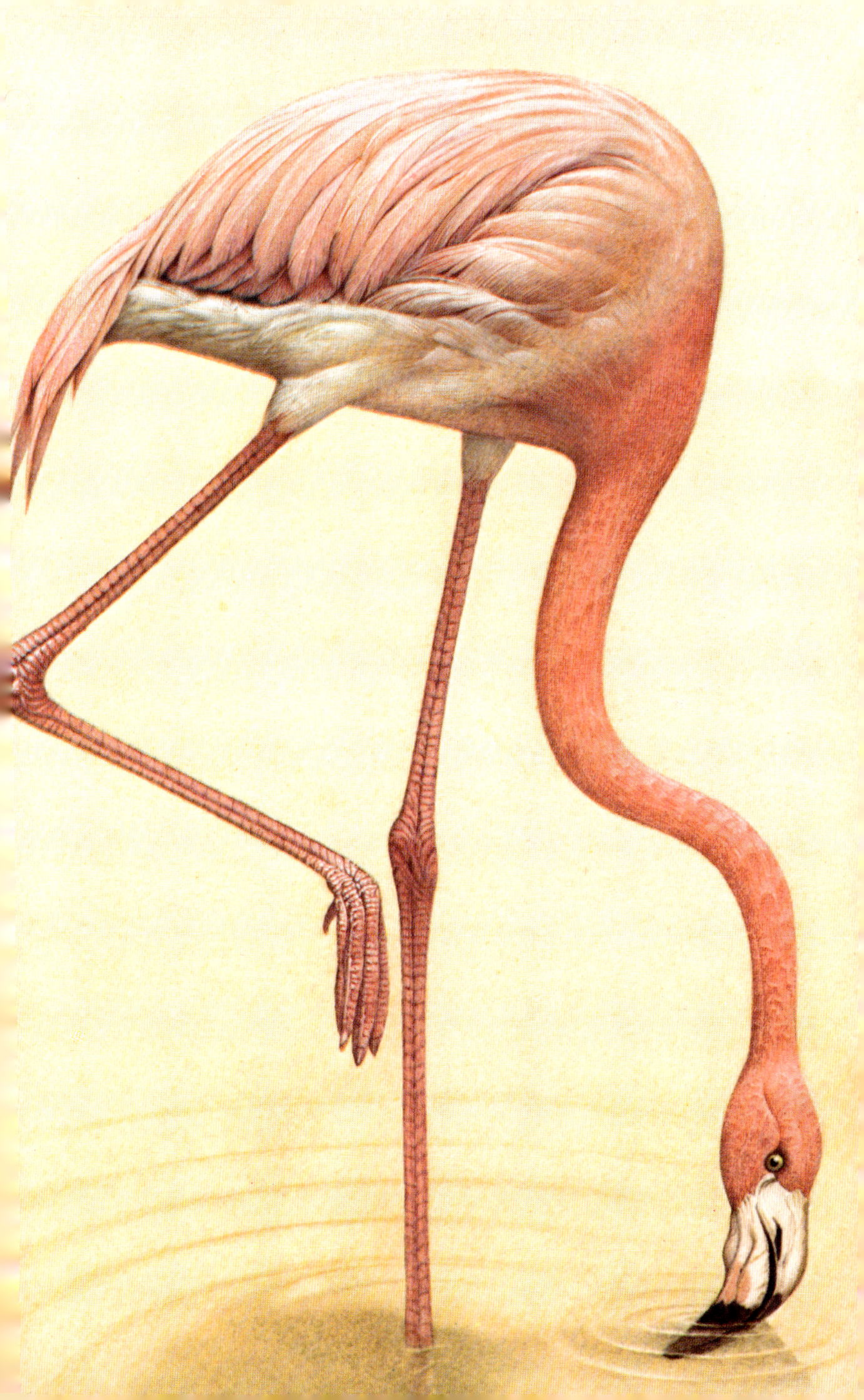

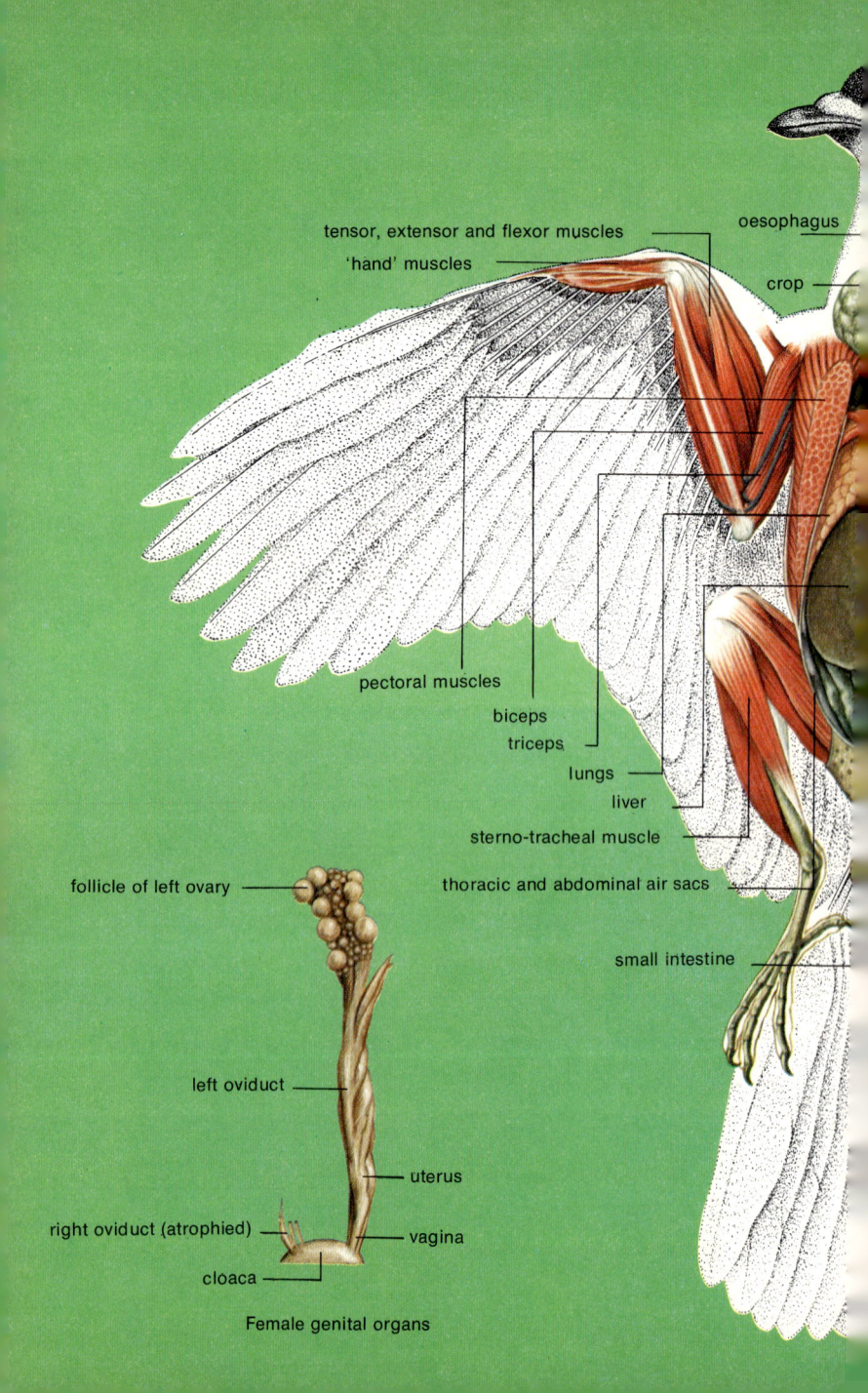

tensor, extensor and flexor muscles
'hand' muscles
oesophagus
crop

pectoral muscles
biceps
triceps
lungs
liver
sterno-tracheal muscle
thoracic and abdominal air sacs
small intestine

follicle of left ovary
left oviduct
uterus
right oviduct (atrophied)
vagina
cloaca

Female genital organs

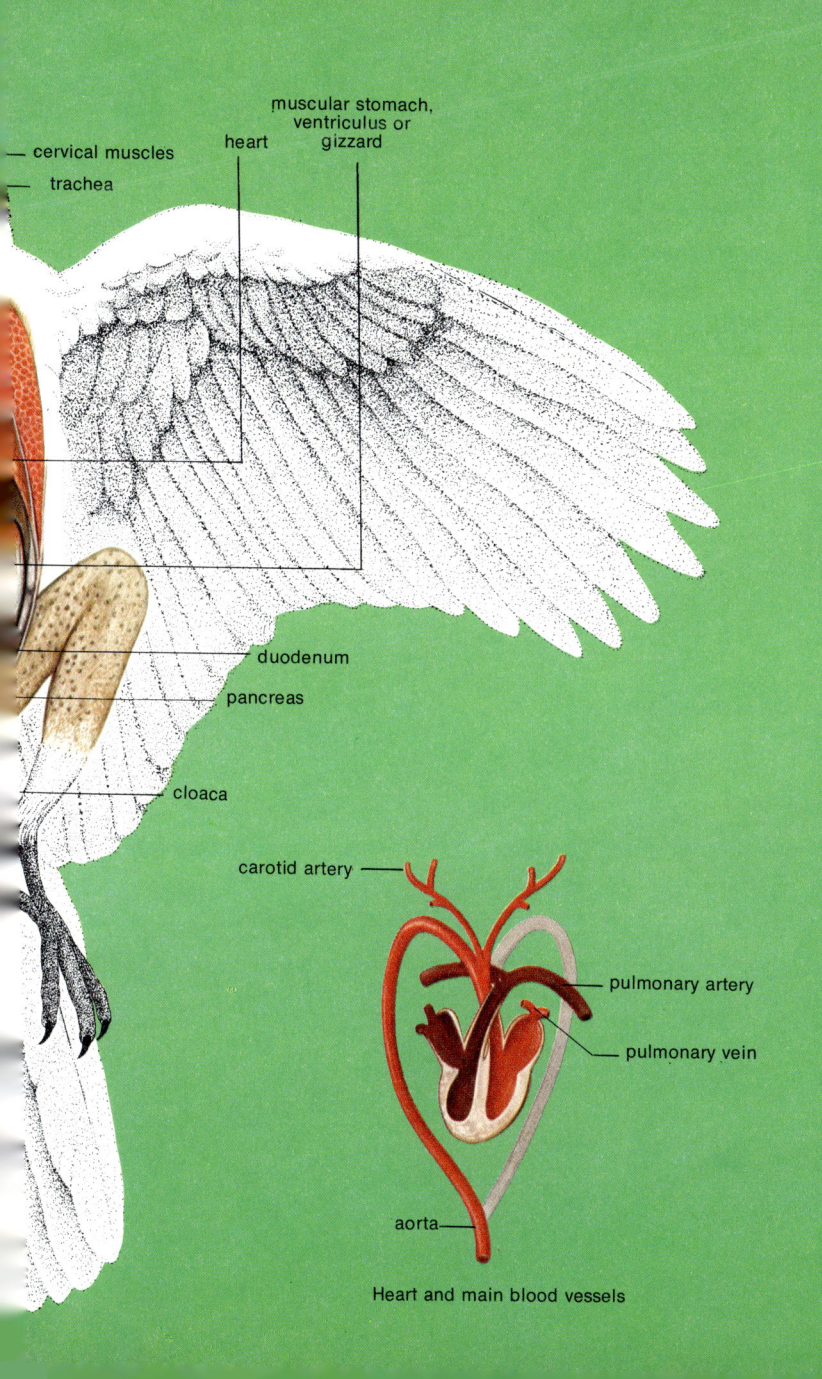

- cervical muscles
- trachea
- heart
- muscular stomach, ventriculus or gizzard
- duodenum
- pancreas
- cloaca

- carotid artery
- pulmonary artery
- pulmonary vein
- aorta

Heart and main blood vessels

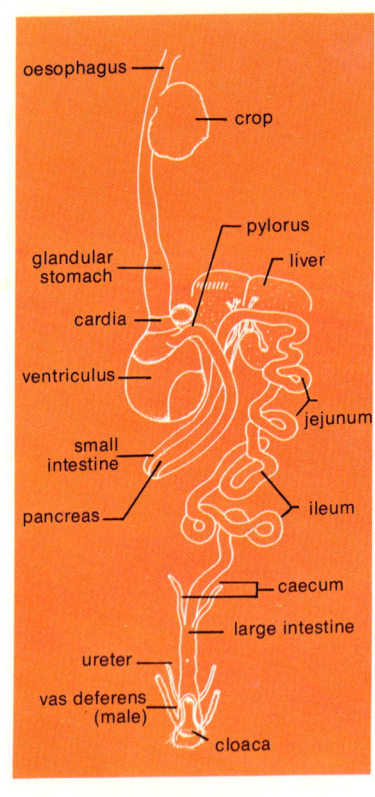

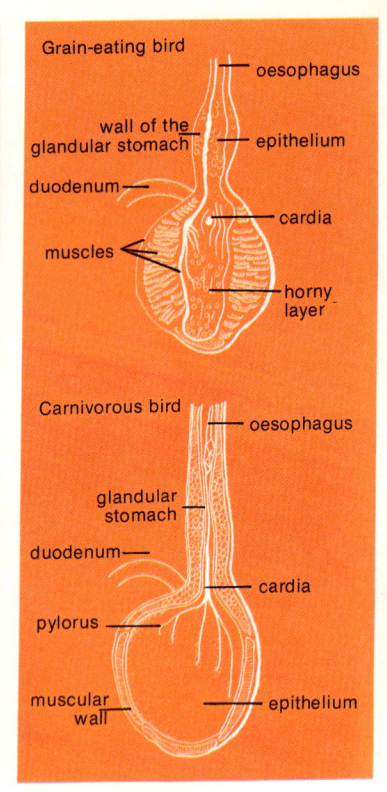

▲ Digestive apparatus of a bird   ▲ Ventriculi of birds

blocks off the respiratory tract. The food thus passes into the oesophagus. The salivary glands are fairly well developed in the granivorous and insectivorous species, but much less so in waterfowl. They are most developed of all in woodpeckers: at the base of the buccal cavity woodpeckers have two glands which make their long tongue sticky; the tongue is then inserted into holes in tree trunks to catch insects. It is also well developed in jays, and in swallows and swifts in particular. In the latter two species the salivary glands increase in size during the mating season because the saliva is used to construct the nest with mud and bits of plants. In swiftlets belonging to the

◀ Preceding pages: anatomy of a bird

genus *Collocalia*, one can even find nests built exclusively with hardened saliva, which are used in eastern cooking.

The oesophagus is situated between the pharynx and the stomach. In certain species it has a widened section which acts as a temporary food-store and in various species (pigeons, parrots and game birds) it takes on the form of a large, extendable pouch called the crop. Food is quickly warehoused in the crop and then pushed down into the stomach to be digested. In the breeding season a strange phenomenon takes place in the crop of pigeons: from the eighth day of incubation, in both sexes there is a secretion from the lining (caused by the action of the hormone prolactin) which continues until the sixteenth day after the eggs have hatched – the purpose of this, unique in the world of birds, is to feed the nestlings in the first days of their life. This whitish secretion contains fats and proteins. A similar secretion also occurs in the flamingoes, the Emperor Penguin and certain petrels. The crop in birds also has a certain digestive function which only assumes any importance in the distinctive Hoatzin (*Opisthocomus hoazin*). This species, living in the forests of South America, has a huge crop, with strong muscular walls, of a type found in no other bird. The size of the crop has reduced the dimensions of the sternum thus restricting this bizarre bird's ability to fly, and in practice has taken on the function of the stomach.

The stomach consists of two distinct parts: the glandular stomach, also known as the proventriculus, and the muscular stomach, ventriculus, or gizzard. These two parts combine to carry out two basic digestive functions: the glandular stomach, with its gland-filled walls, is in charge of the chemical action designed to attack the alimentary proteins with gastric or peptic juices; the muscular stomach is in charge of the mechanical process of grinding-up the food. Unlike in mammals, then, in birds the chemical action precedes the mechanical process. The muscular stomach comes in different forms, depending on the bird's diet. In the carnivorous species (birds of prey, fish-eating species and so on) the ventriculus is an extendable sac with reduced musculature; in the grain-eating species it is a tough muscular sac, covered internally by a thick membrane which carries out the task of shredding and breaking up food, sometimes made easier by the habit of swallowing small stones. The indigestible parts are regurgitated by various birds (in particular by birds of prey but also by herons, gulls and bee eaters) and then expelled from the mouth in what are known as pellets. By analysing these rejected parts and identifying the remains (the skulls and

STRUCTURE

bones of rodents, small birds, the wing covers of beetles, and so on) it is possible to study the diet of the bird.

A bird's intestine does not have the clearly distinctive features that it does in mammals. After the ventriculus there is a duodenal loop to which the pancreas and then, via the bile ducts, the liver are connected. The pancreas secretes the pancreatic juice, which is used in the digestive process, and various hormones, the best-known of which is insulin. In birds, as in other animals, the liver is the largest gland in the body; it consists of two lobes. Its extremely important functions can be summed up as follows: production of bile, storage of iron, regulation of the amount of glucose in the blood, production of red corpuscles (in young birds) and elimination of waste-matter from the blood. In the intestine, after the junction with the bile ducts, is an ileum, two coeca (which are absent in Procellariiformes, birds of prey, parrots and kingfishers, very reduced in swifts and hummingbirds, and highly developed in herbivorous species), and a rectum, which opens into the cloaca, which is where the excretory and sexual ducts also open. On the wall of the cloaca, in young birds, there is the bursa Fabricii. Its function is unknown.

As well as carrying out the digestive function with the help of various juices coming from the walls and connected glands, the intestine is important as a place where food is absorbed and waste-matter collected. The digestive activity in birds generally enables them to assimilate food quickly. As well as the digestive activity carried out by the various juices and secretions, a bacterial digestive function which helps degrade cellulose, also takes place within the intestines.

Excretion

Given their high metabolic level, birds must also be able to dispose of waste-matter quickly. The excretory apparatus satisfies this requirement very well. The kidneys are broadly similar in structure to those of all the vertebrates. They are composed of glomeruli, more plentifully than in other vertebrates, which filter the blood and eliminate all waste-matter. The urine consists mostly of uric acid (as in reptiles) and not of urea, as it does in other vertebrates. Birds have no urinary bladder, except for the Ostrich, where the bursa Fabricii carries out the functions of the bladder. The urine is a clear liquid which merges with the faeces in the cloaca and is expelled with it. Sea birds which can drink salt water also take in salt through their food; these amounts of salt are eliminated by special glands which open into the nasal cavities.

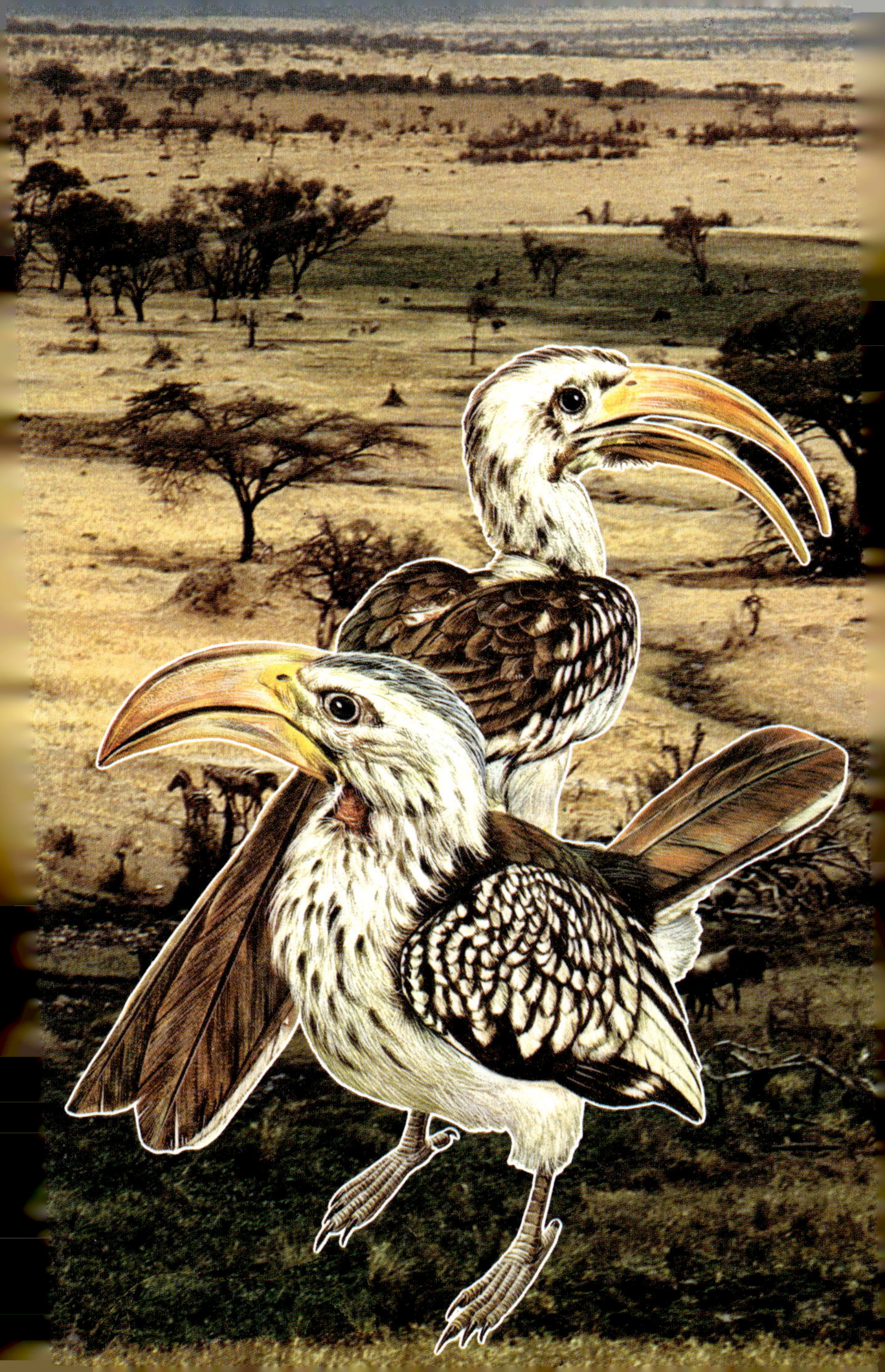

Reproduction
Birds are oviparous creatures and have thus retained the reproductive patterns of their ancestors, the reptiles. This reproductive process allows another economy on body-weight (mammals on the contrary, are viviparous and carry the embryo in their body for long periods of time in the prenatal stage). It also means, however, they have to lay and hatch eggs, which are particularly exposed to adverse environmental conditions and predators.

The sex organs
Again for maximum efficiency in the air, the two testes in the male are situated in the abdominal cavity, above the kidneys, and not in an external scrotum as in mammals. During the breeding season the testes not only increase considerably in size, but move downwards around the abdominal air sacs, where their temperature lowers, helping the formation of the spermatozoa (spermatogenesis). These latter are evacuated via the epididymis and the vas deferens which then runs into the cloaca. There is no penis in birds: only in the ratites, ducks and Cracidae (curassows) can a primitive structure which is erectile and can be evaginated, acting as a penis, be found. Copulation takes place by positioning the two cloacal regions together, and the act is swift and often repeated.

In the female genital apparatus only the left ovary functions, developing in the breeding season. Except in the case of certain Falconiformes, where it is non-functional, the other ovary remains atrophied. Once released from the ovary and fertilized, the eggs pass into the oviduct, consisting of a glandular part, the magnum, in which the albumen envelops the egg; the isthmus, in which the membranes of the calcareous shell are secreted; and a uterus, where the formation of the fertilized egg is completed. From the oviduct it passes to the vagina and finally into the cloaca.

Sexual characteristics
In birds the number of chromosomes is generally large and varies between 60 and 84. Sex is determined genetically. On hatching, the ratio between the sexes is usually 1:1. However, males seem to be favoured in certain passerines and ducks whereas in certain birds of prey and game birds the opposite seems to be the case. In many birds we find sexual dimorphism, with fairly marked differences between the sexes. There are also instances where the females are more vividly coloured and take on roles usually reserved for males: the female will take

the initiative when it comes to copulation often mating with several males, or will not build the nest or look after the eggs and young, these duties being assumed by the males. These deviations from normal reproductive behavioural patterns occur with painted snipes, phalaropes and certain other groups. The seasonal variations in plumage result from the combined action of genetic factors and associated hormonal ones, for example, from the influence of the sex glands and the hypophysis. The hormonal action caused by these glands has been studied by experimentation: while the removal of a cockerel's testes does not cause any change to the plumage, the removal of a chicken's ovary brings about a masculinization of the plumage.

Other experiments have studied the various actions of the hormones. Influences brought about by the sex hormones, for example, affect the plumage, the fleshy appendages (such as the cockerel's comb) and the beak, which sometimes takes on a different coloration during the mating season. Cases of hermaphroditism occur among birds, too. The sex hormones are important in determining the behaviour of both sexes. Manifestations associated with reproduction (singing, presence of the territorial instinct, nuptial displays) and aggression are caused by the hormones. Proof of this is provided by the fact that with castration this type of behaviour does not occur. All the phases associated with the reproductive cycle are thus directly controlled by the hormones (particularly by the sex glands and the hypophysis), while the actual hormonal action is determined by external stimuli. Among the external factors important in determining the conditions favourable for reproduction, the photoperiod or length of daylight assumes an undoubtedly crucial role. The photoperiod stimulates the internal physiological rhythm of birds, a rhythm which is mainly regulated by the hypophysis, on whose activities the action of the endocrine glands depends, as do the occurrence of moulting and the emergence of the internal state which leads to migration. The internal hyphophysial action is so important that in some cases certain species of birds in the Southern Hemisphere, which have been moved to the Northern Hemisphere, have retained their original seasonal reproductive rhythm. Dorst (1974) explains that birds react to the approach of spring with the sense of time adapted to their place of origin. Migratory birds have evolved a sense of rhythm so that sexual maturity coincides with the seasonal rhythm of the place where they reproduce, which may be far away from the place where they winter. The photoperiod plays a part in these rhythms.

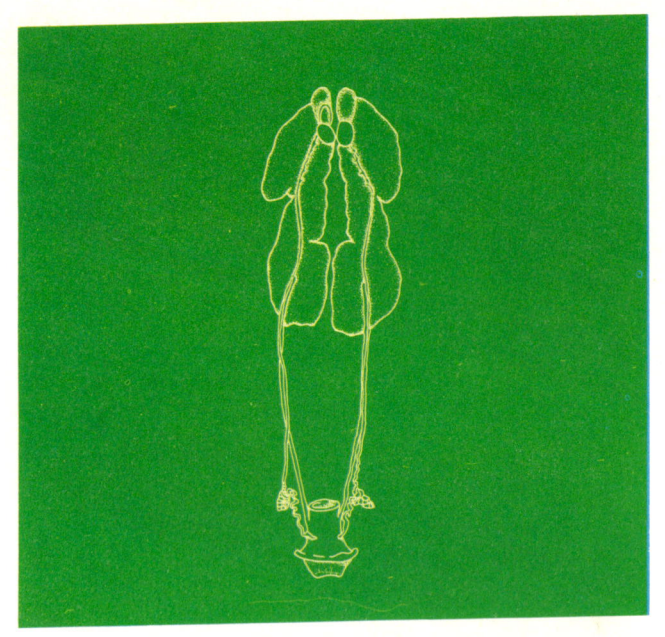

▲ Urogenital organs of a male sparrow

▼ Structure of a chicken's egg

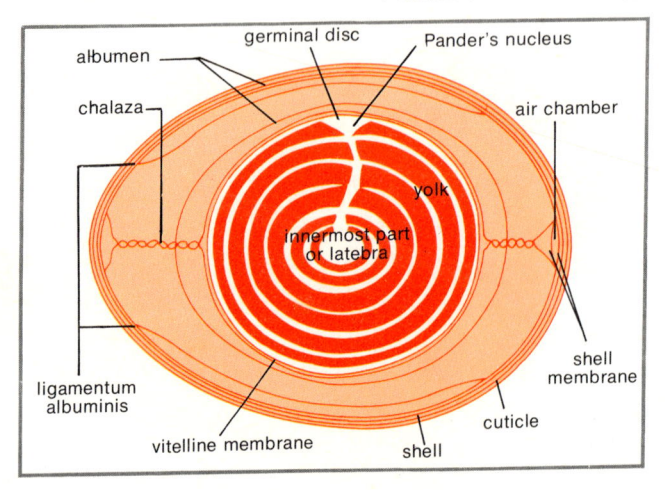

STRUCTURE

Appropriate experiments carried out on various species have shown that by artificially increasing the length of daylight, it is possible to bring about an 'extra-seasonal' development of the sex glands. Light and the length of daylight must be determining factors in the production of sex cells in the pair, whereas the temperature and the amount of food available in the habitat would seem to be responsible for the occurrence of ovulation and nest building. There is, however, a further period after reproduction in which, even if subjected to longer daylight, birds do not nest again. This is why the migratory birds in temperate zones, which fly to the tropics shortly after nesting, when the cold season sets in, do not nest on arrival. The occurrence of the reproductive cycle therefore depends on various external factors such as the availability of food and the climatic conditions, which is why nesting takes place when the most favourable conditions are found: the internal rhythm, photoperiod and environmental conditions, which together bring about nesting depending on the requirements of individual species.

The egg

The egg forms in the female's genital tract. After copulation, the female oocyte, or egg-cell, is fertilized by the spermatozoon and then passes into the parts of the oviduct where the shell is secreted and its formation is completed. Between fertilization and being laid the egg spends several dozen hours in the genital tract. When laid it is almost completely self-sufficient in the way it protects and nourishes the embryo. All it needs is oxygen to which the shell is permeable. An egg consists of the shell (almost exclusively calcareous containing up to 97 per cent of calcium carbonate) which is divided into three layers; the albumen (white of egg) the chemical composition of which is usually specific to the various species; the vitelline membrane; the yolk; and the germinal disc (or blastodisc). The development of the embryo, after the union of oocyte and spermatozoon, starts before the egg is laid, ceases on laying, and starts again when incubation begins. The shell may be quite thin, as in the case of the pigeon's egg and the eggs of the waders, or very thick (in the Black Francolin's it weighs up to 28 per cent of the egg).

An indication of the chemical composition of an egg can be gained by knowing that the egg of a chicken contains 65·6 per cent water, 12·1 per cent protein, 10·5 per cent fats, 0·9 per cent sugars and 10·9 per cent mineral salts. The structure of a chicken's egg is shown on the opposite page.

STRUCTURE

The senses
Birds live in a world governed by visual and aural perception. Activities involved in day-to-day survival, the reproductive cycle with its nuptial displays and songs, social relationships, defence and attack mean that the social life of birds is extremely active. Accordingly, their senses of sight and hearing are highly developed to enable them to tackle these needs. The other senses are less well developed, although to differing degrees. The sense of smell, for example, is usually quite poorly developed. Recent studies by the School of Ethology in Pisa have shown the considerable importance of the sense of smell in the homing instinct of pigeons, and studies of certain vultures have shown that their sense of smell is used to detect corpses.

The nervous system
In the nervous apparatus there is a central nervous system, a peripheral nervous system, an autonomic nervous system and the sensory organs. The central system consists of a cerebro-spinal axis or neurite embracing the encephalon, which is enclosed within the cranium and the spinal cord, contained in the vertebral duct. The encephalon and spinal cord do not come into direct contact with the bony surfaces in which they are contained as they are surrounded by the meninges, in which the cerebro-spinal fluid is contained. The peripheral system consists of those structures of the nervous apparatus which are not present in the neurite, the nerves and ganglions (or nerve centres). The nerves may be spinal or encephalic, depending on whether they derive from the spinal cord or the encephalon. The autonomic nervous system governs those body functions not under conscious control, and is concerned with the ganglions and nerves which fan out into the intestines, glands and blood vessels; it is further broken down into the sympathetic and parasympathetic systems.

The brain
The encephalon is divided into the anterior or fore-brain, the middle or mid-brain and the hind-brain (the prosencephalon, the mesencephalon and the rhombencephalon, in that order). The fore-brain is divided into two cerebral hemispheres beneath which is the diencephalon. These hemispheres consist of an outer layer of grey matter (the cerebral cortex) and an inner layer of white matter. The higher psychic acts are associated with the cerebral cortex. In a bird this cortex is considerably reduced in comparison with a mammal's. It is not

associated, as it is in mammals, with the spinal cord. Conversely, the two hemispheres responsible for instinctive behaviour are well developed in birds. Likewise the mid-brain, which is associated with sight among other things, is well developed and plays a vital role in the perception of surroundings. In the hind-brain, the most important of its various parts is the cerebellum, the co-ordinating centre of movements and muscular contractions. This is also well developed. The size of the brain varies from species to species. Dorst (1974) records the weight of the brain in birds whose weight ranges between 80 and 90 g: Common Quail (*Coturnix coturnix*) 0·73 g; Spotted Crake (*Porzana porzana*) 1·1 g; Common Starling (*Sturnus vulgaris*) 1·8 g Scops Owl (*Otus*

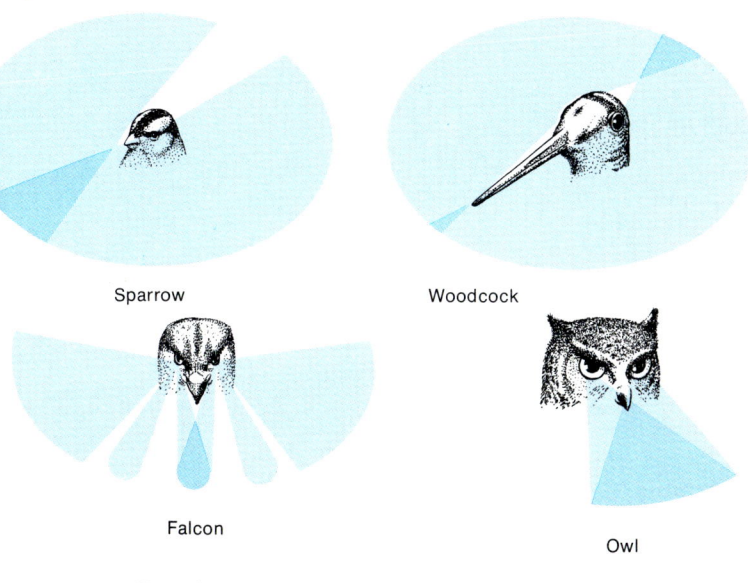

Sparrow

Woodcock

Falcon

Owl

▲ Examples of field of vision

scops) 2·2 g; Great Spotted woodpecker (*Dendrocopus major*) 2·7 g.

It has been found that the birds with the highest degree of psychic activity are crows, woodpeckers, owls and parrots, and those with the lowest are game birds.

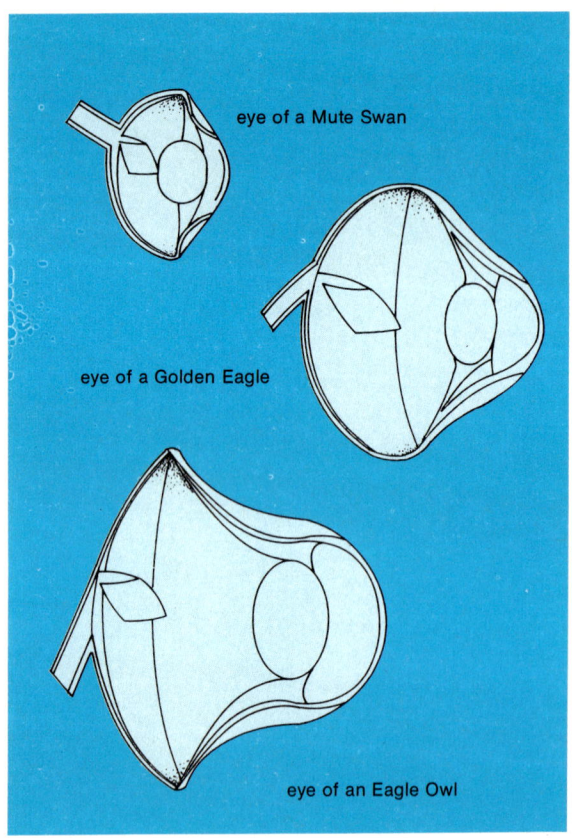

▲ Various forms of eye

Sight

All birds have well developed eyes since the sense of sight is so vital to them. The development of the eyes is clearly visible in some birds, such as owls and diurnal birds of prey, where the eyes are extremely large when compared with the human eye. Most birds have their eyes positioned on the side of the head. The angle formed by the optical axes reaches 120° in some passerines and 145° in pigeons; in diurnal and nocturnal birds of prey the angle is around 90°, because the eyes are positioned particularly far forward. This feature is a specific adaptation of

▲ Golden Eagle *Aquila chrysaetos*

various species: birds of prey, for example, need sharp binocular vision to single out their prey. On the contrary, other birds need wide monocular vision to keep a close eye on their surroundings and spot possible enemies as quickly as possible. The Woodcock (*Scolopax rusticola*), found in enclosed environments like woods, has its eyes placed well back, enabling it to extend its monocular vision backwards as well as forwards. It can, therefore, keep an even better watch for enemies, find food more easily and, in the event of danger, fly off instantly into the thick undergrowth without dashing itself

STRUCTURE

against branches. The ocular arrangement in predators means that these species have to turn their head if they wish to look behind them or to the side. The predominantly monocular vision of birds does increase their field of vision but makes it hard for them to judge distances and obstacles. The pigeon has a field vision of 300°, so only a 60° blind spot remains behind the head when the bird is facing the front; but, to the front, the fields of vision of the two eyes only coincide for 30°, which makes their binocular vision very meagre. Conversely, in a species which hunts like the Barn Owl, the overall field covered by both eyes is 160° (much less than the pigeon's), but the angle of binocular vision accounts for 60°. In the Strigiformes (owls) the ability to turn the head round to face the back makes up for the small field of monocular vision. When discussing the mobility of the neck, Josselyn Van Tyne

▼ Brown Kiwi *Apteryx australis*

observed that the reflex movements of the eyes tend to be replaced, in birds, by reflex movements of the neck. In fact the eyes of birds do not move in their sockets, only in a few exceptions like the Bittern (*Botaurus stellaris*). But this immobility is made up for by the swift and frequent movements of the head.

The anatomical structure of a bird's eye is roughly like that of the other higher vertebrates. There are certain distinctive features. The retina, the light-sensitive area at the back of the inner eye, has a large number of cells (cones and rods) the ratio of which varies within the bird groups. The cones, cells which make it possible to see colours, are present in very large quantities per surface unit (in the Yellow Wagtail there are up to 120,000 cones per square millimetre, whereas in the human retina the density of cones for the same surface unit is about 10,000). The rods, cells which are sensitive to minimal amounts of light, are very numerous in nocturnal birds which have virtually no cones at all. There is no point in these species being able to detect detailed colours, whereas it is of prime importance for them to have high visual sensitivity (which is ensured by the rods). In some parts of the retina the density of the cells adds up to impressive numbers: up to a million rods per square millimetre in birds of prey, as opposed to man's 200,000. In the middle of these areas are the foveae, which are the zones of maximum visual acuteness. In man there is only one fovea. In many species of birds, especially predators, there are two foveae: the *fovea centralis* and the *fovea temporalis*. They correspond to the double vision present in these birds, the *fovea centralis* being used for monocular vision, and the *temporalis* for binocular vision. A bird's eye also has a special structure called the pecten (present in reptiles as well, but no longer in mammals) which forms a vascular membrane, the function of which is not altogether clear. It would seem to be some kind of supply reserve. The eye is protected externally by three membranes: an upper, a lower and an intermediate membrane (called the nictitating membrane). It has many important tasks; in waterfowl, for example, it protects the eye under water.

As well as the features listed, the eye of a bird has the classic structures which exist in higher vertebrates: sclera or sclerotic coat, cornea, iris, retina (see above) and the crystalline lens. This latter, due to its elasticity, enables swift visual accommodation, particularly in birds of prey. This is an important asset for creatures such as birds which rely so greatly on their sight.

STRUCTURE

Hearing

Birds have no external ear with a pinna, but just a tubular cavity protected by feathers. The ear duct leads to the middle ear, bounded by the tympanum or ear-drum, which acts as a resonating chamber and communicates, via the Eustachian tube, with the mouth. Beyond the tympanum there is no series of tiny bones as in mammals, but simply a bony and cartilaginous structure called the columella. In the liquid-filled inner ear, three semicircular canals connect to the utricle which, with certain adjoining elements, forms the cochlear region, essential to the bird's hearing. The hearing of birds is excellent; their maximum acuteness of hearing reaches sounds between 2,000 and 4,000 cycles per second (hertz) and generally (except in cases like parrots and small owls) sounds in excess of 10,000 cycles are not all that well received (Dorst 1974). The localization of sounds is very good, particularly in nocturnal birds of prey, where it is considerably helped by the asymmetrical arrangement of the ears, an arrangement which is important when picking out prey in the dark. Various experiments have shown that in many instances these birds catch their prey due to their extraordinary ability to hear and then isolate sounds. They have mobile, feather-covered folds of skin which function virtually as a pinna (outer-ear).

The organ of balance

In the inner ear there are three semicircular canals opening into the utricle. This structure, which exists in all vertebrates, forms the organ responsible for balance, and is only important as such in birds. The anatomy and physiology of this structure are fairly complex. Suffice it to say that the three semicircular canals, arranged in the three spatial planes, contain two liquids: endolymph and perilymph. As the body moves it causes these liquids to shift and touch highly sensitive nerve-ends which are stimulated and inform the bird about its movements and the position of its head. Other structures do this when the bird does not move its head.

The sense of smell

The nasal cavities, which is where the sense of smell is based, are separated by a partition-like structure and divided into three parts: a fore part or atrium, a central part linked to the mouth, and a lower part positioned behind and above the central part. The nasal septum which divides the two cavities has a surface covered with filaments which filter, heat and humidify the air. The sense of smell is still something of an

◀ Storm Petrel
Hydrobates pelagicus

▼ Californian Condor
Gymnogyps californianus

STRUCTURE

unknown quantity in birds. It is partly atrophied in the vast majority of birds, even if in some species it seems to work fairly well. Kiwis for example have their nostrils right at the tip of a long bill. The nocturnal habits of these birds and their weak eyesight lead one to suppose that they locate and detect food by their sense of smell. Likewise, in species belonging to the order of Procellariiformes (shearwaters, albatrosses) there is

▲ Martial Eagle *Polemaetus bellicosus*

a fairly functional olfactory organ, proof of this being provided by experiments carried out by tipping strong-smelling fish oil into the sea which attracted these birds through their sense of smell. Vultures have been the subject of a long controversy over the idea that these birds home in on the smell of carrion. Numerous experiments have been carried out: fans are used to blow the smell of carrion into up-currents of air, and dead

STRUCTURE

animals, which have been embalmed and do not emit the typical smell of dead bodies, are laid out on the ground. These experiments have shown that some species of American vultures and Old World vultures only use their eyesight, and fly at high altitudes to detect possible dead animals below. One American vulture on the other hand, the Turkey Vulture (*Cathartes aura*) seems capable of locating dead bodies by its

▲ Oilbird *Steatornis caripensis*

sense of smell. The olfactory organ in this species is quite well developed and this vulture is found in regions of the Amazon forest (in habitats, in other words, where there are few open spaces which can be surveyed in flight) where it can only find food by using its sense of smell. Another American vulture with a fairly well developed olfactory structure is the King Vulture (*Sarcorhamphus papa*) which is brightly coloured.

▲ Budgerigars drinking

There are also accessory functions carried out by the nasal structure of birds. Dorst (1974) explains the function of the triangular valve which opens towards the front on each side of the septum in Procellariiformes: it acts as a kind of pressure gauge and anemometer by filling with air, when the bird flies, and creating pressure which appears to be proportional to the air inhaled and to the movement of the bird. Shearwaters and albatrosses glide in the air currents which blow across waves without beating their wings, so they need to know with precision any changes in speed or direction of an air current.

Other senses
The sense of touch is situated in various corpuscles: Grandry's corpuscles situated on the tongue and palate, and Herbst's corpuscles which are situated in the beak of the snipe and woodcock and in the tongue of woodpeckers, as well as in the mouth of the Anatidae, on the edges of the beaks of nestlings, in the legs and in other places around the body. Herbst's corpuscles are capable of perceiving vibrations of a given frequency and of a low intensity. The ability to detect these vibrations was in the past attributed to the sense of hearing.

STRUCTURE

Birds on the ground or perched in trees can detect things that man cannot. For example they can anticipate earthquakes.

The sense of taste is based in taste-buds like those of other vertebrates, although they are not gathered in papillae as in mammals, but spread over the rearmost part of the tongue and in the mouth. Experiments carried out on the use of the sense of taste have shown that various species can distinguish between sweet, sour, acid and salty substances.

The vocal organ

The vocal organ is extremely important in the vast majority of birds, where it is generally used as a means of communication. In the world of birds, wide use is made of visual and audible signals. It is no coincidence that the most functional sensory organs are sight and hearing. Birds' faculties for making sounds vary considerably depending on the various groups: they are extremely rudimentary in waterfowl and sea birds in general, extremely diversified and elaborate in numerous passerines, especially those of the song birds which form a subgroup in the order of Passeriformes called the Oscines.

In the other vertebrates it is the larynx which has the job of emitting sounds; in birds, the organ of phonation, called the syrinx, is positioned at the junction of the trachea and the two bronchi. The special structure of this organ varies according to the species: in some it is formed by the modification of certain tracheal or bronchial rings, in others (some Passeriformes) it is a complex structure. Some species of Passeriformes belonging to the families Conopophagidae (gnat eaters), Formicariidae (antbirds), Dendrocolapridae (wood creepers) and Furnariidae (ovenbirds) are called tracheophonic because in their case the syrinx is formed by the lower section of the trachea and by one to three pairs of muscles. Similarly, in the Passeriformes known as sub-Oscines to which the tyrant flycatchers (Tyrannidae), manakins (Pipridae) and Cotingidae belong, there are between one and three muscles, whereas in the Oscines there are between five and nine pairs of muscles attached only to the bronchial rings. The function of these muscles is to regulate and control the bird's vocalizations. Three membranes form the vibratory organ: one is situated at the base of the trachea, and the other two are each positioned inside the base of the two bronchi. These membranes vibrate as the bird breathes out, worked by the nerves which stimulate the syrinx. The sounds emitted are modified both by the trachea and by the mouth. In certain cases the trachea has numerous circumvolutions which are folded and rest on the

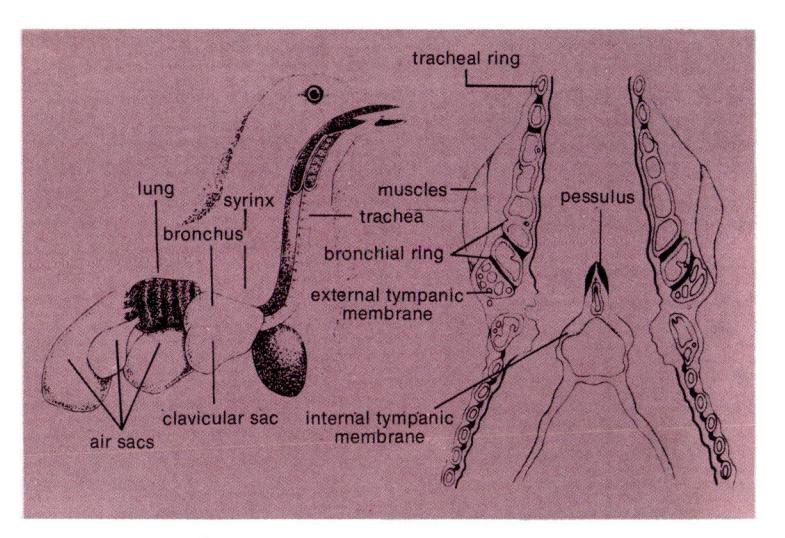

▲ Vocal organs of a song bird and section of a Blackbird's syrinx

breastbone; in cranes and swans the trachea may be up to 1·5 metres long. The power of the sounds made by these birds is considerable; the Common or Grey Crane (*Grus grus*) for example, has a cry which can carry for two kilometres. The inter-clavicular air sac is vital for the production of sounds since the bird loses its vocal capacities if this is opened.

The study of birds' songs is particularly important in field ornithology as recognition of the songs of the different species leads to quick identification. For a long time a scientific analysis of these sounds posed a problem since onomatopoeics – the translation into letters of birds' songs – is not very successful. Acoustic devices have made it possible to study the physical characteristics of birds' songs. By recording them on tape, with ever more sensitive microphones, accurate analyses of the frequencies, intensity, volume and timbre, for example, have been made as well as studies of the acoustic signals used by birds. The songs can be transposed to sonograms, where the lines of the abscissae mark the times and the lines of the ordinates the frequencies. Birds emit sounds with higher frequencies, which vary from species to species, than those occurring in the human voice – they have correspondingly sharper hearing. The sounds do not remain on the same frequency for long but are modulated.

STRUCTURE

Homoiothermy (warm-bloodedness) in birds

The term homoiothermy (from the Greek *homois*, identical, and *thermos*, heat) applies to the state existing in some animals of having an internal temperature which does not change with the external temperature variations. In the animal kingdom, only mammals and birds are homoiothermic – the others are poikilothermic (from the Greek *poikilos*, varied, and *thermos*, heat). They have a body temperature which varies according to the temperature outside. Even among mammals and birds there are cases of poikilothermy or, more accurately, of temporary hypothermia (in nightjars, some hummingbirds, and the Common Swift one finds states of winter or temporary hibernation). The food assimilated by a bird is used to fuel the physiological activities necessary for its life and survival, to produce heat to maintain the state of homoiothermy by counterbalancing the loss of heat transmitted to the environment (thermogenesis, or production of heat, which offsets thermolysis, or loss of heat). The standard functioning of the living structure, apart from in specific physiological activities or states such as digestion of food, ovulation, moulting and the reproductive cycle, is analysed by measuring the basic metabolism – the consumption of energy required by an organism to stay alive. In birds, the examination of data taken from such studies reveals a high metabolic level.

Metabolism

In birds, as in all vertebrates, the larger the species the lower the metabolism. The intensity of the metabolism is inversely proportional to body-weight. In the small species there is a greater loss of heat because the surface area per unit of weight is larger. In young animals the basic metabolism is more intense, because the body is smaller and because young, growing animals have greater energy requirements. In adults, the intensity of the metabolism varies according to the physiological conditions of the subject and according to the activities associated with day and night: obviously a bird flying has a higher metabolic level than a bird resting.

Temperature

Given the high metabolic level, birds have high internal temperatures, which range on average between 39–42°C and reach 44°C in some Passeriformes. They are higher than the temperature of mammals which ranges, on average from 36–38°C. The internal temperature of birds is constant, although it is subject to fluctuations during the day, due to

A crane's sternum and trachea ▶

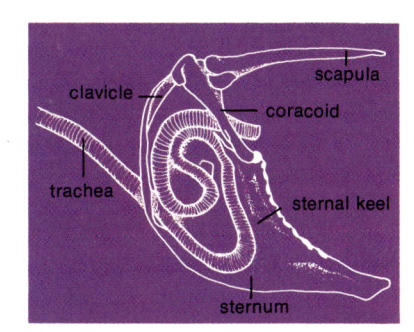

▼ Robin *Erithacus rubecula*

STRUCTURE

specific physiological situations. It covers a range which includes, at the limit, critical temperatures. Once exceeded, these critical temperatures endanger the metabolism, even the life of a bird when they touch either the lower lethal limit (hypothermia) or the upper one (hyperthermia).

Thermoregulation
Although the range of temperatures fluctuates, homoiothermy makes birds fairly independent of their immediate environmental conditions by keeping them internally stable. The balance existing between thermogenesis and thermolysis allows the state of homoiothermy. The internal constitution of the body is protected by the cutaneous apparatus and the

▼ Bald Eagle *Haliaeetus leucocephalus*

Greater Sulphur-crested Cockatoo *Kakatoe galerita* ▶

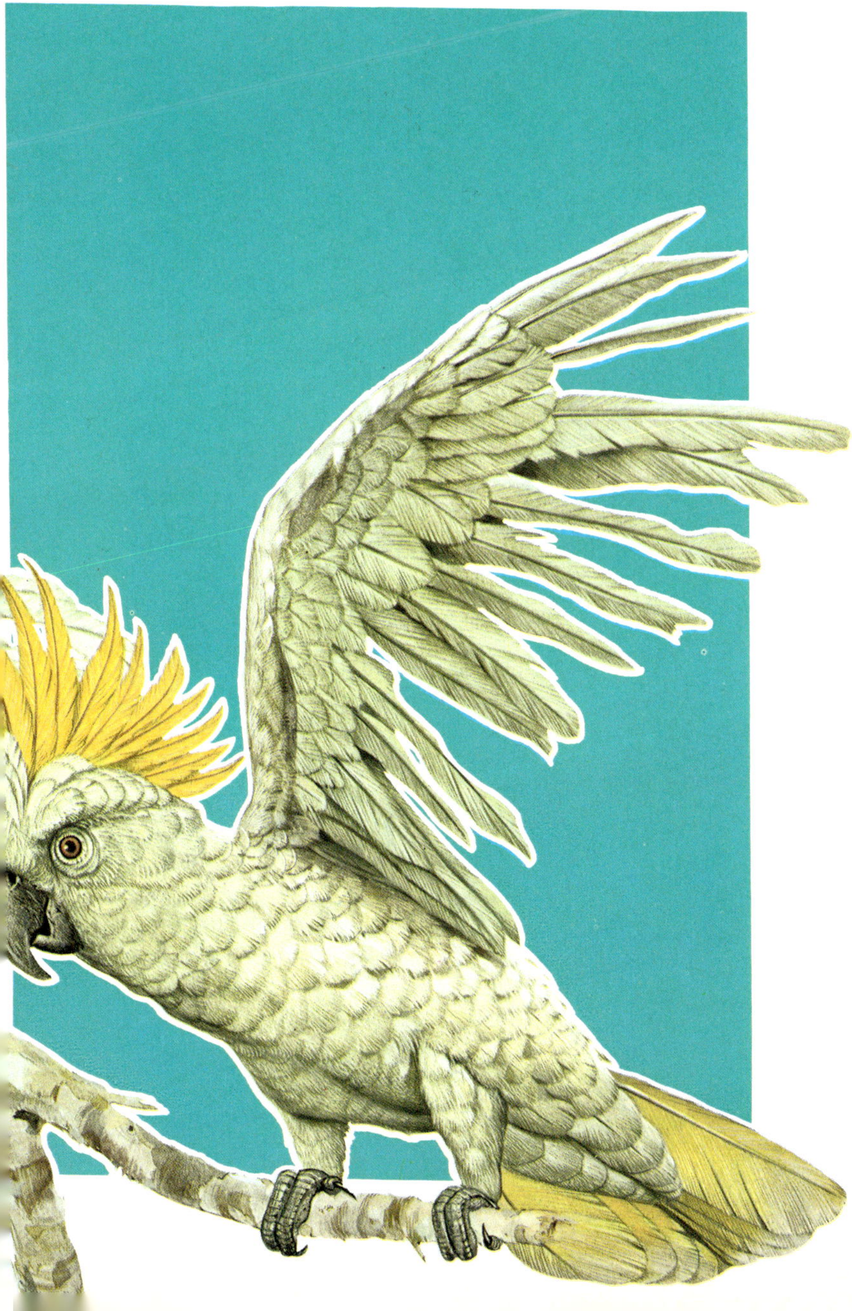

▲ Hummingbird

plumage, which act as thermal insulators. Thermogenesis occurs with the intake of food which varies in accordance with the energy requirement, and then increases with the muscular effort made by the body. Thermolysis occurs because of phenomena such as evaporation (because of the absence of sweat glands in birds this occurs by means of the respiratory apparatus). The process of thermoregulation does not occur immediately after birth. In nidicolous or altricial nestlings (young which remain in the nest for some time before becoming independent), as Yapp reports (1970), thermoregulation does not occur for three or four days. In nidifugous or precocial birds (those which leave the nest almost as soon as they have hatched) on the other hand, it

▲ Swift *Apus apus*

occurs, when the fledgling leaves its shell, or just a few hours later. The regulation here is, however, still imperfect and the young are protected by their parents during the coldest hours. Several days have to pass before thermoregulation reaches the efficiency with which it functions in adults. This state of poikilothermy in young birds is very important in certain cases. Young Common Swifts (*Apus apus*) manage to withstand long periods of fasting (up to 12 hours at times) by greatly reducing the body's energy consumption: the temperature drops as low as 21°C and the breathing rate from 40 (normal average per minute) to as low as eight. Detailed studies of the Common Swift have been carried out by Jukka Koskimies who observed, in adults of this species, the capacity to lower the internal

▼ White Storks *Ciconia ciconia*

STRUCTURE

temperature to as low as 20°C with the arrival of semi-lethargic periods. Swifts thus manage to fast for as long as five days; this capacity appears to be an adaptation to the possible shortage of insects on days when the weather is bad.

As a defence from excessive cold, the plumage makes an excellent thermal insulator. Birds in general, in winter, have more feathers than in summer. In the postnuptial moulting of the non-migratory species the contour feathers grow slowly, and reach the peak of their growth when the temperature is lower. Also because of the tensor muscles in the skin (the platysmae) the plumage can, depending on the circumstances, be arranged in the best possible way to defend the bird from the outside temperature. The skin temperature is perfectly regulated, so that in Arctic birds the legs have a sliding scale of temperatures ranging from 24°C where they meet the body, to 5°C at the extremity, thus avoiding any loss of heat through conduction or convection. This occurs because of circulatory structures where hot arterial blood from the body and cold

▼ Roadrunner *Geococcyx californianus*

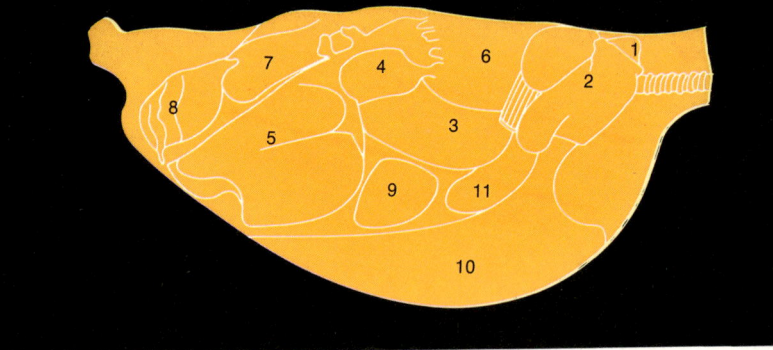

▲ Anatomy of a Pigeon: 1 cervical sac; 2 inter-clavicular sac; 3 front thoracic sac; 4 hind thoracic sac; 5 abdominal sac; 6 lung; 7 synsacrum; 8 intestine; 9 liver; 10 sternum; 11 heart

venous blood from the extremity of the limb mix. In other cases, like that of the American Wood Stork (*Mycteria americana*), the White Stork (*Ciconia ciconia*) and the Marabou (*Leptoptilos crumeniferus*), the legs have the same temperature as the body and disperse any excess heat.

Certain species are forced to seek shelter from the cold (in abandoned nests), while other species behave collectively, sheltering from the cold by huddling together in communal 'dormitories'. Among such species are the Short-toed Tree Creepers (*Certhia brachydactyla*) which sleep in hollows huddled together in groups of up to 15. In intense cold, penguins gather into tight groups, back to back. During periods of high environmental temperatures, the breathing rate increases, involving the 'panting centre', which brings about a series of reactions in the bird by accelerating the respiratory movements, opening the beak and avoiding any increase in their temperature. When exposed to the sun, sea birds in the incubation period eliminate any excess heat by buccal respiration. Other species seek the shade.

Poikilothermia (cold-bloodedness) in birds

The homoiothermous state in birds is fairly flexible and numerous species have a capacity to cope with any temporary drop in their temperature. There are certain specific cases where it is accurate to talk of a real state of poikilothermia, of a variability in the inside temperature based on the outside conditions. There are some hummingbirds (e.g. *Calypte annae* and *Selasphorus sasin*) whose inside temperature during the cold nights in the deserts in the American North West drops from a standard norm of 40°C to a low 19°C, the bird becoming inert with no reflexes. The French ornithologist Jean Dorst in

▼ Snowy Owl *Nyctea scandiaca* ▲ Elf Owl *Micrathene whitneyi*

▲ Grey-lag Geese *Anser anser*

his research in the Andes, observed the hummingbird *Oreotrochilus estella*, which took refuge by night in caves or natural recesses to shelter from the cold. During the night these birds cannot feed to supply their metabolism with fuel; as a result their body functions slow down.

The most classic case of poikilothermia is that of the Common Poorwill (*Phalaenoptilus nuttallii*), a species of nightjar, which nests between southern British Columbia and Mexico, right across the western and central United States. In the winter of 1946–47 Culbertson and Jaeger, working in the Sierra Nevada and the Colorado Desert in California, found several Poorwills in a state of semi-lethargy in hollows in rocks. These birds, whose normal temperature varies between

▲ Black-naped Oriole *Oriolus chinensis*

35–43·5°C had, in this state, a temperature of 18–20°C in an ambient temperature of 17–24°C. These birds did not even react to a bright light shone directly in their eyes and showed no visible signs of cardiac or respiratory movement. It has been shown that the European Nightjar (*Caprimulgus europaeus*) also has a winter period in which the temperature of its body drops dramatically, and the metabolism is reduced. In neither the European Nightjar nor the Poorwill is there a prolonged state of winter lethargy, but short sharp periods (in the European Nightjar not exceeding 24 hours) occurring only in extremely adverse environmental conditions. An internal temperature as low as 7°C in an ambient temperature of 4·5°C has been recorded for the European Nightjar.

STRUCTURE

The circulatory system
In the circulatory system of birds, which still bears certain similarities to that of reptiles, the heart is divided into four cavities (two auricles and two ventricles) and the venous and arterial circulations are completely separate. This division between arterial and venous blood, occurring only in birds and mammals, makes them the only two classes which are homoiothermous. The arterial (left) part of the heart is more fully developed and muscular than the venous (right) part. The two parts are asymmetrically positioned as the arterial part pumps blood throughout the body whereas the venous part only pumps it into the lungs. The weight of the heart varies from species to species and generally follows a constant

Tawny Frogmouth
Podargus strigoides ▶

▲ The young of a White Wagtail *Motacilla alba*

pattern: because smaller birds have a higher metabolism, the weight of the heart is inversely proportionate to the size of the animal. However, an increase in the number of heartbeats per minute can make up for the possibly smaller size of the organ. Directed by nerve centres, the heartbeat is usually quite rapid. Dorst (1974) offers an impressive list of the number of heartbeats per minute in certain species: birds of prey, 301; domestic duck, 212; turkey, 93; domestic chicken, 243–341; pigeon, 192–244; sparrow, 460–800; canary, 1,000; crow, 342. Obviously, the heartbeat increases or drops depending on the bird's physiological activities.

STRUCTURE

The blood of birds has features similar to that of reptiles: the red corpuscles or erythrocytes have the form of an oval disc and have a nucleus. They vary in number in larger and smaller species (the erythrocytes are more numerous in smaller species), in the two sexes (they are more numerous in males than in females), and sometimes at different times of year. Their size also varies from species to species. The differences in the numbers and dimensions of the red corpuscles show a precise relation with the metabolic level. As Dorst observes, the red corpuscles offer a relatively larger surface the smaller they are and as a result there are more intense gaseous

▼ Purple Heron *Ardea purpurea*

Grey Heron
Ardea cinerea ▶

▲ Swifts, *Apus apus,* in flight

exchanges which enable birds to achieve a swifter movement of gas through the body, a factor of great importance for smaller and more active species. The white corpuscles, or leucocytes, are like those of mammals and fairly numerous, reaching in some cases a ratio of 1:70 red corpuscles. In the arterial system the blood circulates centrifugally, through the arteries from the heart to the extremities of the body, conveying nutritive substances absorbed by the intestine and oxygen from the lungs. In the venous system, on the other hand, it flows centripetally, circulating through the veins from the extremities back to the heart, conveying and eliminating the waste-matter from the tissues.

The respiratory apparatus

The respiratory apparatus of birds has features which are unique in the animal kingdom: in addition to the lungs it has large air sacs spread throughout much of the body. The apparatus is linked to the outside by nasal cavities which open in the beak at the base of the upper jaw (except in kiwis where the nasal apertures are at the beak tip). The nostrils are often protected by special feathers called vibrissae; they are covered by opercula or flaps which let air in through a narrow opening, and in some species (gannets and cormorants) they are closed

▲ White-browed Wood Swallow *Artamus superciliosus*

altogether, which is why one cannot see any external nostrils. These species have secondary nostrils which are like fissures in the beak and are protected by an operculum which probably shuts during deep dives up to 20 metres. The nasal cavities communicate with the mouth. Behind the mouth is the trachea which in some species forms large coils, and in swans and cranes makes various loops which have the effect of modifying the shape of the sternum. The trachea then splits into two bronchi, at which point the syrinx, the organ of phonation, is found. The two bronchi then enter the lungs. The lungs are situated in the rib-cage; they are not large, and not unlike those of mammals in structure. In the lungs the bronchi ramify into dorsal and ventral bronchi with a whole series of inter-communicating links formed by the parabronchi, the structure of which consists of hundreds of bronchioles surrounded by a close network of capillaries. Birds' lungs are not divided into lobes, as those of mammals are and the fine structure of their numerous inner ramifications varies from species to species. The lungs then connect with the air sacs, especially in the abdominal cavity. There are usually nine: two cervical sacs situated in the neck beside the spinal column, an inter-clavicular sac in front of the trachea, two sacs at the front of the thorax, two sacs at the rear of the thorax, and two

▲ King Penguin *Aptenodytes patagonica*

abdominal sacs which are the best developed of all. They are all double sacs, with the exception of the inter-clavicular one, although this too is double at the outset and becomes single as the bird grows and develops. They all communicate with the lungs, although in different places; in some species some of the sacs may be fused. The shape and symmetry of the sacs varies in different species. They have diverticula and ramifications between the organs, the muscles, in the bones where to all intents and purposes they replace the marrow, and in the sub-cutaneous layers. There is no diaphragm in birds and the admission of air into the lungs takes place by the contraction of the inspiratory muscles. The air sacs have important functions: helping to cool the tissues, acting as reserves of oxygen-rich air during flight, and as structures which reduce the weight of the

▲ Female Ruby-throated Hummingbird ▲ Streamer-tailed Hummingbird
Archilochus colubris   *Trochilus polytmus*

bird. Nerve centres regulate the breathing rate. As observed by the ornithologist Wilhelm Meise (in Grzimek, 1972), the frequency with which in- and exhalation occurs in birds is remarkable. In a domestic pigeon there are 29 respiratory actions per minute when resting, 180 when moving quickly, and 450 in flight; in a hummingbird the frequency is 250 when the bird is resting and up to 3,000 when in flight. The respiratory rhythm depends also on the internal temperature conditions. An increase in the internal temperature causes a considerable increase in the number of inhalations per minute, thus obviously increasing the volume of air inhaled in that time. Waterfowl do not breathe when they are under water and have to cope with a rise in the level of carbon dioxide in the blood as a result.

How Birds Live

In recent years the study of ethology – the science of animal behaviour – has increased in popularity. This discipline concerns itself with the function of behavioural patterns, the external and internal factors associated with them. It also includes the study of an animal species of evolutionary importance, and the selective pressures to which behavioural patterns are subject.

There was a time, recently, when the study of animal behaviour took place only in laboratories, thus placing the animals under examination in abnormal situations compared with the environmental conditions in which they displayed their normal behavioural patterns. The naturalist Konrad Lorenz and his school raised the study of animal behaviour to a more realistic level: those involved patiently observe the behaviour of the animal in question in its habitat, analyse it as scientifically as possible, and try to avoid anthropomorphic interpretations.

A superficial knowledge of ethology is usually sufficient to understand the distinction between innate behaviour, derived from the hereditary legacy, and learnt behaviour, gained from a gradual learning process through experience and depending on the level of intelligence of the various species. The zoologist

▲ European White Pelican *Pelecanus onocrotalus*

▲ Puffins *Fratercula arctica*

G. Gottlieb observes that for every behavioural pattern there is a kind of genetic remote control, and proposes two important models which demonstrate the derivation of innate and acquired behavioural patterns: genes – structures – maturity – innate behaviour; genes – structure – learning – experience – acquired behaviour.

The ethologist Danilo Mainardi remarks that birds and mammals have a 'social system' in that a new habit invented by an individual is transmitted to other members of the population and absorbed into the 'culture'. He cites primates

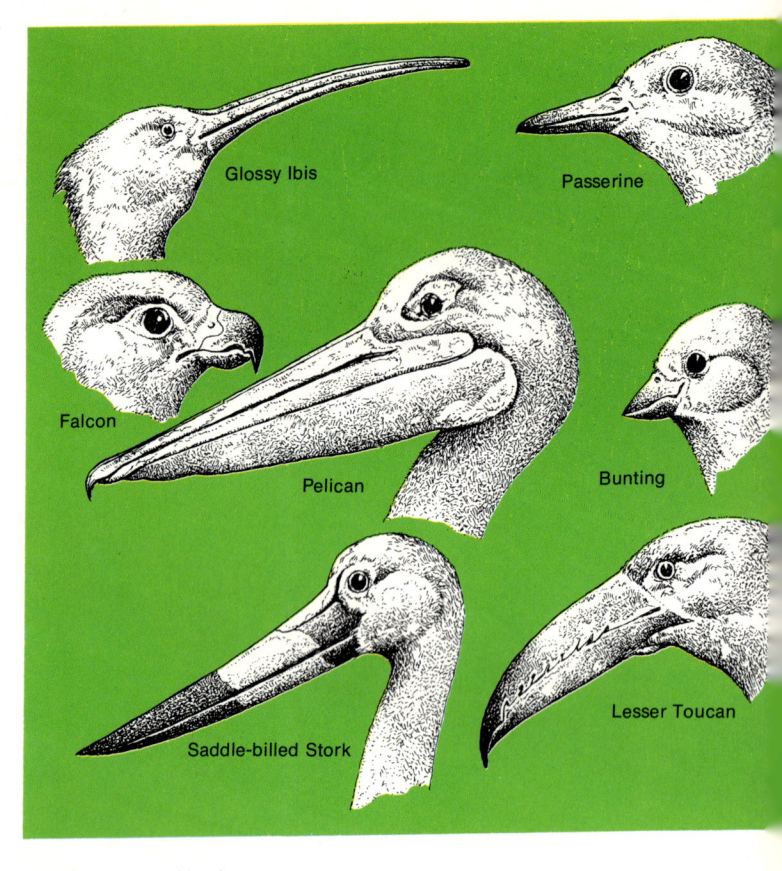

▲ Various types of beak

(macaques, chimpanzees) and birds as examples in which rapid natural behavioural evolution can be seen; and rodents, felines and dolphins where it has been seen in laboratory tests and experiments.

Feeding
By analysing the wide variety of beak shapes and sizes of the various species of birds, it is possible to get some idea of the correspondingly wide variety of food upon which they live. The type of beak is in keeping with the feeding requirements of a

▲ African buffalo with Cattle Egret

HOW BIRDS LIVE

species. There are large, bulky beaks like those of hornbills and toucans; very elongated beaks like that of the hummingbird *Ensifera ensifera*, where it exceeds the overall length of the body; long, curved beaks like those of sunbirds and honeyeaters; beaks where the jaws are crossed, as in crossbills; beaks with the upper part shorter than the lower, as in the Black Skimmer; beaks with a cutting edge; beaks angled to the right (there is just one case of this, that of the Wrybill *Anarhynchus frontalis*, a New Zealand shore bird); long, straight beaks; the hooked beaks of birds of prey, and so on. The common names of some birds derive from the shape of their beak: the Shoebill (*Balaeniceps rex*), the Boatbill

▼ Anhinga, also known as a Darter or a Snakebird

HOW BIRDS LIVE

(*Cochlearius cochlearius*) and the spoonbills (genus *Platalea*).

In the bird world there is an amazing variety of feeding habits and patterns. Shrikes impale their prey (small rodents, lizards and large insects) on thorns, or on the tips of branches, and build up larders. In autumn, nutcrackers prepare stores of nuts and conifer seeds which they stack underground in moss and lichen; these reserves come in very useful when the birds have to raise their young in early spring, when the ground is still snow-covered. Nutcrackers are very clever when it comes to relocating their own secret foodstores. The ornithologist John Sparks (1969) observes how some nutcrackers relocated 86 per cent of their food reserves which were covered by

▼ Common Bee Eater *Merops apiaster*

HOW BIRDS LIVE

50 cm of snow. Indian Black Eagles (*Ictinaetus malayensis*) have very curved talons with which they pick up the nests of other birds, complete with eggs or young. The nests are then carried to a safe place where the eagle devours the contents.

There are two very interesting feeding phenomena which have resulted from the spread of a behaviour pattern, originally acquired by only one individual, throughout the population. The first example concerns the Egyptian Vulture (*Neophron percnopterus*): the ethologists Hugo and Jane Van Lawick-Goodall observed some of these vultures dropping stones on to ostrich eggs in order to get at the contents which are then eaten. The second example concerns the Sharp-beaked Ground Finch (*Geospiza difficilis*) from the Galapagos Islands. Some members of the population of this

▼ Vultures round a carcass

HOW BIRDS LIVE

species living on Wenman island, while cleaning parasites from the plumage of boobies (*Sula sula* and *Sula dactylatra*), must have broken a superficial blood vessel in the wing, and from then fed on the blood. This act was then copied by the other members and now this species of Galapagos finch is a unique case among birds.

Depending on the species, birds need proteins, vitamins, mineral salts and so on, in differing proportions. A brief survey of the different diets is given on page 108.

Each species of bird and its eating habits has, of course, evolved during many millions of years, and its diet at any one time much depends on the food available. Nevertheless, it is amazing how varied diets are, from flies and worms to honey and nectar, and even fungi.

The vegetarian diet

There are some exclusively vegetarian species, and others which complement their diet with plants. Certain species of geese can be considered as herbivores as they usually graze in damp, grassy fields. Geese belonging to the genus *Branta* feed in coastal regions on the strip of shore exposed at low tide, eating plants (especially *Zostera* and the seaweeds *Enteromorpha* and *Ulva*). The beaks of these geese have a cutting edge which is used to cut the stems. Herbaceous plants and their shoots are the basic food for various Passeriformes, such as the Alaudidae (larks), and for birds such as bustards and cranes. The strange South American Hoatzin eats leaves. The digestive system of certain Tetraonidae (such as the Black Grouse and Capercaillie) is equipped with large caecal appendages in the intestine and a marked bacterial fauna; these features enable them to digest cellulose. In winter particularly, these birds feed on juniper and heather shoots, and pine-needles. Some species have a fruit-based diet (frugivorous). They are found mainly in tropical and subtropical areas. Parrots, toucans, turacos, certain pigeons, various Passeriformes like tanagers and cotingas in the tropics and certain Turdidae (blackbirds, thrushes) in temperate zones feed on fruit. Every dietary preference coincides with adequately adapted physical structures: some fruit-eating imperial pigeons found in Oceania, for example, have a beak which can swallow large fruit, 5 cm in diameter.

Another type of vegetarian diet is the granivorous one, typical of many passerines. This type of feeding has effected greater morphological and anatomical modifications than the fruit-based diet because grain and seeds are especially hard and have a low water content (Dorst 1974). In order to break and husk seeds the grain-eating birds have particularly tough beaks, palates and skulls. Using the sharp edges of their beaks, some species husk grain by rubbing it between the upper and lower mandible; others wedge the grain against the palate, which has special ridges, and shatter it. The Hawfinch (*Coccothraustes coccothraustes*) has a particularly large and strong beak, capable of breaking olive-nuts and cherry-stones. Crossbills, with their distinctively shaped beak, feed on conifer seeds hidden among the scales of the cones. Other species, such as woodpeckers, wedge seeds into cracks in trees and then break them open with blows of their chisel-like beak. Grain-eating species, in addition to beak adaptations, also have modified digestive systems: in the oesophagus there is a dilated section called the crop, and the ventriculus or muscular

HOW BIRDS LIVE

stomach is especially well-developed. The work done by vegetarian birds as agents of dissemination is extremely important. The seeds of the fruit on which fruit-eating birds feed are evacuated with the faeces and retain their germinative potential. Many grain-eating species drop seeds in transit or while they are eating them.

Birds which feed on nectar are peculiar to the tropics, and have specific adaptations for this type of feeding: long, slender, curved beaks, and a similarly long, slender tongue, which is divided into two or four parts at the tip, and can be evaginated. The tongue, which is tubular, can be thrust outward to suck up nectar.

▼ Barn Owl *Tyto alba*

HOW BIRDS LIVE

The Trochilidae (hummingbirds) and bananaquits in the Americas, the Drepanididae (Hawaiian honeycreepers), and from the Old World, the Meliphagidae (honeyeaters), Nectariniidae (sunbirds) and lorikeets (a species of parrot) all feed on nectar. The morphological features described above apply to all these birds, except the lorikeets. The nectar-eating birds also eat the insects found near flowers. Some birds use other vegetable resources, such as the sap of trees (much liked by various woodpeckers) and fungi.

The Rainbow Lorikeet (*Trichoglossus haematodus*), a native of Australia and the East Indies, is a typical member of its group. With its slender bill and fringed tongue it is well able

▼ A pair of Short-toed Eagles *Circaetus gallicus*

to suck pollen and nectar from flowers. The Rainbow Lorikeet measures about 37.5 cm and weighs 150 g. As its name suggests, this species is very brightly coloured. The colours of related species vary greatly.

The carnivorous diet
Insects, worms, spiders, crustaceans and other invertebrates, amphibians, fishes, reptiles, mammals, other birds and carrion are all sources of food for many species of birds. Birds help to limit the populations of various invertebrates and vertebrates. There are several species, for example, which feed solely on insects.

▼ Keel-billed Toucan *Ramphastos sulfuratus*

▲ Swallow *Hirundo rustica*

There are interesting adaptations and behavioural patterns connected with the carnivorous diet. One species of Galapagos finch, the Woodpecker Finch (*Camarhynchus pallidus*), wields a spine with its beak to extract insects hidden in the bark of trees. Woodpeckers have a tough skull and beak and a slender, sticky tongue to catch insects in tree trunks. The Black Skimmer (*Rhynchops nigra*) has an upper mandible which is shorter than the lower mandible. This adaptation enables it to cleave the surface of water as it flies and scoop up insects. There are various adaptations for catching molluscs: the Oystercatcher (*Haematopus ostralegus*), for example, has a long, laterally flattened, scalpel-shaped bill which is used for opening bivalve molluscs and eating them. Waterfowl have

▲ Secretary Bird *Sagittarius serpentarius*

HOW BIRDS LIVE

various feeding adaptations. The flamingo, with its long legs and neck, has a bill angled in such a way that it can constantly rummage through mud and ooze; the tongue pumps water into the mouth through horny filters which form the edge of the beak and in this way invertebrates are sifted out of the mud.

Penguins, guillemots, the Razorbill, puffins, boobies, the Gannet and cormorants all eat fishes. Certain herons, with their long, pointed bills, seek out prey by walking through shallows with their wings spread to cast a shadow which cuts out the sun's reflections on the water. Birds of prey are perhaps the most impressive predators of all: some of them have particularly specialized diets, like the Osprey (*Pandion haliaetus*) which feeds solely on fish, and the snake eagles (genus *Circaetus*) which feed mainly on reptiles – especially snakes – amphibians and certain small mammals. Birds which relentlessly devour rodents thus helping to keep down their numbers, include buzzards, kestrels, small owls, barn owls and tawny owls.

▼ Chicken with young

HOW BIRDS LIVE

Nesting

The breeding cycle in birds is usually annual, and in the nesting period there are often two or three occasions when eggs are laid. In the case of species living in habitats which have been marked by very unfavourable conditions for several years, there may be a complete absence of reproduction. In Arctic regions, for example, certain types of birds of prey are dependent for food on the presence of the various species of lemmings – rodents belonging to the Microtidae (voles) living in Arctic zones. There are a dozen or so species, but the numbers of individuals tend to fluctuate radically from one year to the next. These marked fluctuations have repercussions on those creatures which prey directly on lemmings. The Snowy Owl (*Nyctea scandiaca*) manages to lay up to seven or more eggs in the years when there are plenty of lemmings but in years of dearth does not even nest and the adults move out of the Arctic region in search of food. Other Arctic species of birds of prey such as the Rough-legged Buzzard (*Buteo*

▼ Domestic cock (genus *Gallus*)

lagopus) and the Hawk Owl (*Surnia ulula*) also depend on the numbers of the lemmings. Similar situations occur in desert zones, where various birds do not manage to reproduce in periods of extreme drought.

Some species of birds do have a shorter than annual breeding cycle. The population of the Sooty Tern (*Sterna fuscata*) on Ascension Island in the South Atlantic nests regularly about every nine months. However, the populations of the same species found in other parts of the Southern Hemisphere nest regularly once a year. This distinctive bird has been studied in detail by ornithologists N. P. Ashmole, J. P Chapin and L. W. Wing who have observed that the gap between the two nesting periods is associated with the cycles of rearing the newborn, moulting, the courtship period and the next breeding period. In other species of birds, especially in those found on equatorial islands, there are non-annual reproductive cycles. Conversely, some larger birds nest every two years, as is the case with the Wandering Albatross (*Diomedea exulans*) in Antarctica. The breeding cycle of albatrosses is a very slow one. The male sits on the eggs first, then the female. The two partners then take turns, ranging from one to seventeen days. The length of the incubation period varies from species to species: the Royal Albatross (*Diomedea epomophora*) has an incubation period of about 79 days. The offspring is looked after and helped by both parents for a period ranging from three weeks for the smallest species to five weeks for the largest; as a rule it remains in the nest until it can fly. In the case of the Wandering Albatross the first flight takes place at the age of 278 days, in the Royal Albatross at 236 days and in the Light-mantled Sooty Albatross at 139 days. Because of the length of time devoted to rearing the young, in some species the eggs are laid at intervals of two years, while in some smaller species, like the Laysan Albatross and the Black-footed Albatross, breeding takes place every year.

The period and duration of breeding vary considerably depending on the latitude and, obviously, the species. Generally, breeding coincides with the period of optimum environmental conditions for the species and, in particular, the hatching of the eggs and rearing of the young coincide with the greatest availability of food. Adverse climatic conditions are unforeseen developments which can destroy the brood. Moving towards the polar regions, there is a gradual delay in the start of the breeding season, caused by the later arrival of spring in both hemispheres. The equatorial regions do not have

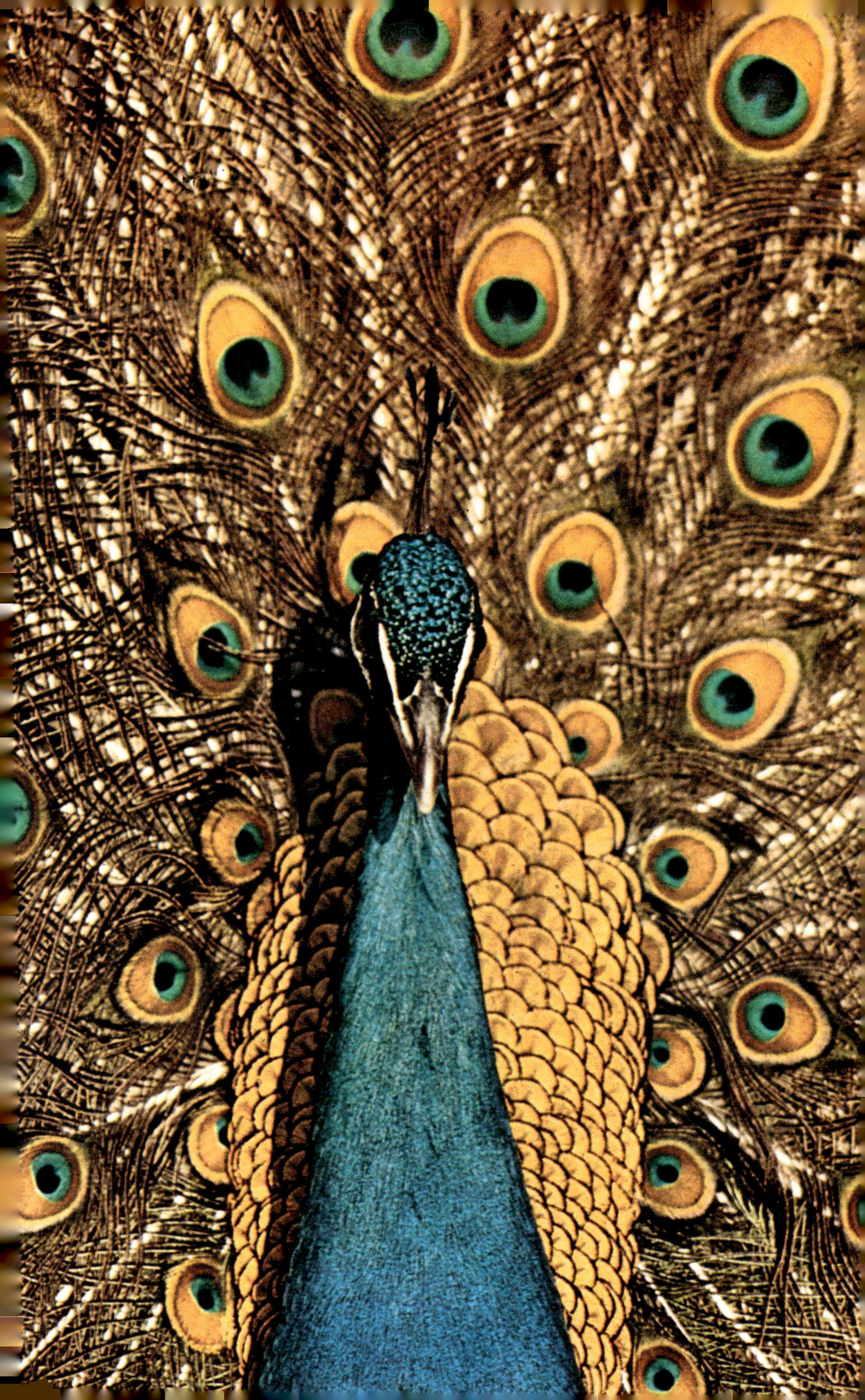

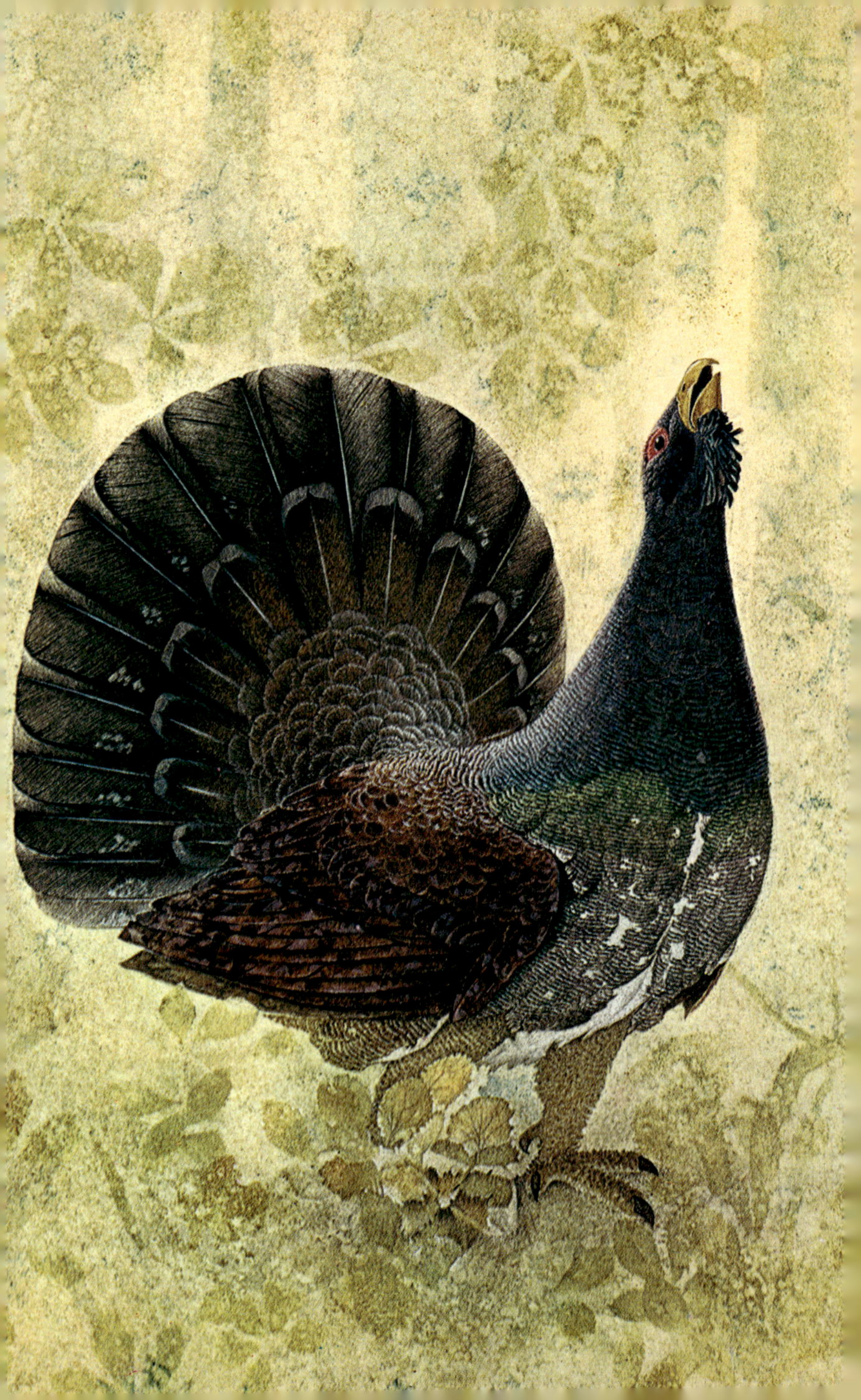

clearly defined breeding periods. In tropical forest habitats some species of birds keep to a rhythm of one, two or even three broods a year with respective periods of sexual inactivity, these cycles being spread over the year. In the intertropical regions, insect- and fruit-eating birds nest in the rainy season, when there is the greatest abundance of plant life and invertebrates; grain-eating birds nest later when seeds have ripened, and birds of prey nest at the end of the wet season when the vegetation thins out, making it easier for them to catch their prey. In dry and arid regions spring is the best time to breed, before the full heat of summer arrives. In temperate and cold parts the breeding cycle lasts slightly longer than in hot regions, but grows shorter and shorter nearer the polar regions where the best environmental conditions last less time than in temperate and hot regions. With the restriction of the breeding season pairs rear fewer broods, on the whole, in high latitudes compared with pairs in low latitudes, although the number of eggs is higher in the former to make up for the lower number of broods. Dorst (1974) has recorded broods in certain species belonging to the genus *Oenanthe* (order Passeriformes): the Wheatear (*Oenanthe oenanthe*), found in cold or temperate regions, has a normal brood of six eggs; the Black-eared Wheatear (*O. hispanica*), found in the Mediterranean region, has a normal brood of five eggs, the Black Wheatear (*O. leucura*) and the Desert Wheatear (*O. deserti*), found in desert areas, have a brood of four eggs.

Territory

At the beginning of the breeding cycle in particular, each male occupies a defined territory which he defends, and which forms the area in which the bird carries out its activities. Since 1868, when J. B. T. Altum scientifically defined the concept, zoologists have spent much time discussing the idea of territory. According to ornithologists G. K. Noble and M. M. Nice, territory is an area which is defended by a bird at some time in its life. Defence is a decisive factor in defining territory. An area used by a bird, but not defended by it, cannot be defined as territory.

There are various types of territory (illustrated on p. 125) which can be identified according to species. A detailed and well documented classification has been drawn up by Margaret Morse Nice which distinguishes the following types of territory. (1) An area whose extent varies depending on the species occupying it where the breeding activities (courtship displays, mating), nesting and rearing young take place and

◀ Capercaillie *Tetrao urogallus*

where the 'owners' find what they need to eat (this type of territory is especially common among the Passeriformes and Piciformes). (2) An area in which all the breeding activities, nesting and rearing the young take place, but where there is no defence where food is concerned, this being sought outside the territory in hunting or gathering areas common to several pairs. There is, therefore, a breeding territory and neutral areas where food is sought which are sometimes defended collectively against possible intruders. This type of territory applies, for example, to certain Passeriformes, grebes, swans, oystercatchers and harriers. (3) An area for courtship displays (*lek*) which has a restricted breeding significance because it applies only to the display put on by males to secure females (the nest is then built elsewhere) and has no feeding connections. This type of territory applies to grouse, cotingas, bowerbirds, birds of paradise, ruffs, and so on. (4) This type resembles the second but differs spatially in that the territory defended only concerns the nest and its immediate vicinity. It is

▼ Oystercatcher *Haematopus ostralegus*

extremely small: beyond the nest the birds use common feeding areas. This type of territory applies particularly to sea birds which nest in large colonies (penguins, boobies, pelicans, cormorants, gulls, terns) as well as to certain herons, various Passeriformes and so on. (5) Some birds divide the territory into two parts: one for nesting and the other for feeding. This type of territory applies to few species. (6) This territory applies to species which maintain their territory not only in the breeding period but also in winter. Various birds defend a territory against any kith and kin who come within a certain range of the area chosen for nesting or hunting: there is a sort of movable territory relating to the area which surrounds the bird and its activities. This is the perimeter defended by shrikes, kestrels, flycatchers and various shorebirds. In the southern winter-visiting areas reached by migratory birds, some species establish a winter territory. This type of territory obviously concerns feeding only. We can also define a seventh type of territory used as a resting-place outside the breeding period. This territory is extremely small in area, coinciding with the space taken up by a bird overnight.

Territory is very important in a bird's life. It governs the distribution of the various individuals, permitting best use of areas suitable for nesting and available food; it keeps conflict down to a minimum, and any aggressive behaviour usually entails displays and threats, or vocal duels; and it gives protection from predators, because the occupant gets to know his territory very well. The first of these territorial functions – as a factor in limiting populations by the distribution and dispersal of individuals throughout the available habitat – is debatable. Danilo Mainardi (in Frugis *et al.*, 1971–2) says given that individuals who do not win a territory do not reproduce, the number of individuals in a population will be proportionate to the available resources in the environment. However, some authors such as the Scottish naturalist V. C. Wynne-Edwards, consider this mechanism valid for species which have different territorial habits. Certain sea birds, for example, confine their breeding areas, in which they form colonies, to rocky areas which restricts the development of the population according to the available seaboard.

The establishment of a territory differs from case to case. As a rule, when their particular nesting period is about to commence, the males of non-migratory and migratory species establish themselves in an area, without definite boundaries as yet, of their chosen habitat. They affirm their mastery over this area visually and audibly. As new arrivals settle among the

▲ Great Frigate Birds *Fregata minor*

birds already established, precise boundaries are set up between territories which begin to take on a definite pattern.

There are areas where the territories are adjacent, making full use of the available habitat. In areas where there are neutral zones between one territory and the next, the boundaries of a territory usually follow physical boundaries: ditches, watercourses, hedges, walls and fences. The males often display themselves on such boundaries, using vocal signals to indicate ownership of the territory. The persistent aggression between males can also affect the size of the territory. In many species the young males may have a smaller territory than adults which have nested before. In most cases the male selects and defends the territory, entices a mate into it and, subsequently, the female defends the territory from intruders as well. In some instances the pair selects the territory, as with ducks, where pairs are formed in winter. Once they have returned to the breeding ground, they choose their territory together. In other species, for example hummingbirds, where the female plays the leading part in building the nest and rearing the young, it is she who displays the territorial behaviour. In species with marked sexual dimorphism, the two partners defend the territory from members of their respective sexes. These are ornithologist Carl Welty's assessments of the territorial areas of various species measured in square metres: Black-headed Gull (*Larus ridibundus*) 0.3; Common Coot (*Fulica atra*) 4,000; Bald Eagle (*Haliaeetus leucocephalus*) 2.5 million; Golden Eagle (*Aquila chrysaetos*) 93 million; American House Wren (*Troglodytes aedon*) 4,000; Blackbird (*Turdus merula*) 1,200; Song Thrush (*Turdus philomelos*) 40,000; Robin (*Erithacus rubecula*) 6,000; Chaffinch (*Fringilla coelebs*) 4,000. These measurements are only indicative, because the size of a territory can vary according to the prevalent environmental conditions. For example, in a study of the ecological relations between skuas and owls, both birds preying on lemmings, at Barrow in Alaska, it was observed that the area of the territories of the Pomarine Skua (*Stercorarius pomarinus*) in the years when there were plenty of lemmings was six to nine hectares but in the years when there were few lemmings it might extend, over an average of 45 hectares.

Singing is widely used by the male in asserting his occupancy of a territory. It is especially important in species living in

▼ Mound Bird (Megapode)

▼ Avocets
Recurvirostra avosetta

HOW BIRDS LIVE

enclosed habitats where visual contact is fairly rare. Specific displays are used by different species. One such is used by the Robin, whose behaviour was closely studied by the late ornithologist David Lack. This passerine adopts threatening postures when confronted by intruders, displaying its red breast which is made even more conspicuous by puffing out the feathers. Likewise, certain types of flight signify territorial defence. Visual and audible behaviour, therefore, signal the presence of the occupant of the territory and serve to avoid conflict with a possible intruder. In view of the density of birds and the proximity of territories, however, conflict and fighting do break out fairly regularly. When this happens, the owner of the territory generally scares off the intruder with threatening behaviour. If a Robin is caged in its own territory, an intruder will flee once the caged owner has put on a display of song and threatening postures. If, on the other hand, this caged bird is placed in the territory of another bird, it will show submission

▼ Different types of territory (● denotes relative area of nest in each territory see pp. 119–20)

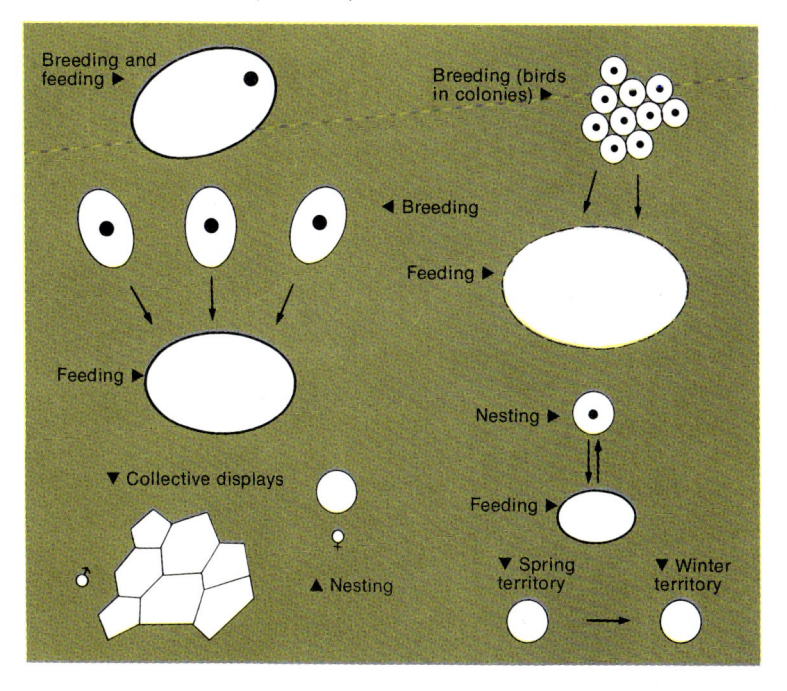

125

HOW BIRDS LIVE

to the legitimate owner, in its cage. Another experiment carried out with Robins involved placing a stuffed Robin in the territory of another subject. The owner of the territory approached the intruder and went through a series of threatening postures. These were to no avail, of course, and the aggressive instincts of the owner were triggered off; it attacked the stuffed body, eventually destroying it. Aggression in animals is extremely important. It is inherited, since by means of specific selective processes it is possible to create races with differing degrees of aggression, the level of aggression being

▼ Red-breasted Goose *Branta ruficollis*

regulated by hormonal factors. Aggression appears to be cyclical: it is more intense in the breeding season and less intense in winter. The concentration in the blood of the male hormone testosterone is, it seems, a major factor in triggering aggression. Aggressive behaviour in animals, especially in

Rooks, *Corvus frugilegus*, nesting ▶

▼ Alpine Choughs *Pyrrhocorax graculus*

animals of the same species, tends to show itself in ritualized patterns which make it possible to establish the dominating from the dominated party without any bloodshed. This ensures the preservation of the species.

Migration studies, by means of ringing, having shown that some birds returned to the territory, or at least to the same area, used for nesting the year before.

Courtship displays

Once a male has established itself in a selected territory, it usually looks for a female with which to mate. In some species the ceremonies used become extremely complex and are called courtship displays. These displays can involve kinds of dances, exhibitions, specific postures, the showing-off of particularly long or colourful feathers, the use of special sounds and so on. Attracted by these displays, the female may, at the outset, be subject to a form of aggressive behaviour from the male, but this gradually turns into wooing, and the pair-bond is formed before very long. The unfolding of the courtship displays follows a precise ritual according to species. Hence, courtships become important elements in analysing possible phylogenetic links between the different groups. Visual and audible stimuli are widely used in courtship displays: the former in species with brilliantly coloured plumage and accentuated sexual dimorphism, the latter in species with more unassuming plumage. The purpose of all courtship displays, is to exhibit to the female the salient features of the male's plumage and song to entice the potential partner. The Peacock spreads out its dazzling tail feathers (in fact they are not tail feathers – in this species these are fairly small – but extremely long upper tail coverts), and the turkey has a similar display. In various Passeriformes the male makes specific movements to show off its distinctive coloration: the male sparrow displays its black throat; the Wheatear fans out its black and white tail, and struts round the female, tail erect; and the Blackcap erects its head and back feathers, and opens and closes its tail. The birds of paradise put on dazzling displays. In the case of Archduke Rudolph's Blue Bird of Paradise (*Paradisea rudolphi*), which has splendid long tufts of blue feathers down its sides, the male flops back over a branch and lets the long blue feathers hang down.

Detailed studies of the behaviour and courtship displays of the Anatidae have been made by ornithologist and ethologist Konrad Lorenz. In the displays performed by ducks, feathers are puffed out, whistling and grunting sounds emitted, the neck

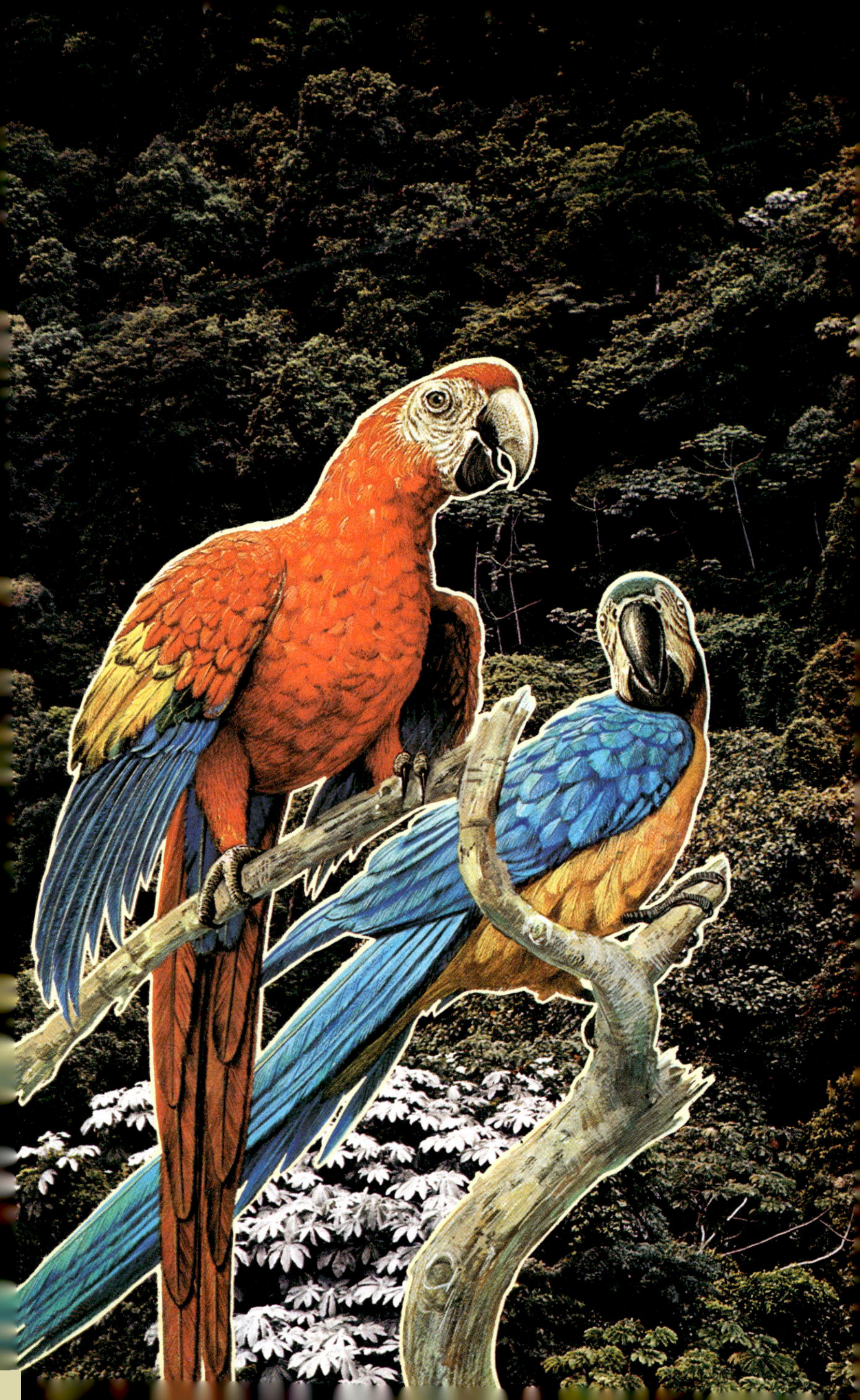

and tail shaken, the head and neck given upward movements, the beak plunged into the water, and so on. The breeding behaviour of certain Ardeidae (herons and bitterns) has been the object of particularly interesting studies. When Grey Herons (*Ardea cinerea*) install themselves in their nesting colony, the males begin their displays.

The Grey Heron's display consists of three main activities, accompanied in some instances by shaking branches with the bill and preening feathers. These activities usually take place by an old abandoned nest or near a branch which looks particularly suitable for nest-building, and consist of a very loud warning cry, a special posture in which the neck is thrown backwards (known as the bittern posture) and a bowing movement. In the view of ethologist Niko Tinbergen, the display, which may last for a matter of minutes or carry on for much longer, has four major functions: the synchronization of the behaviour of the two sexes, orientation (towards the spot where the nest is to be built, for example), the suppression of manifestations other than sexual ones (such as aggressive instincts), and the maintenance of reproductive isolation. Similarly, the Night Heron (*Nycticorax nycticorax*) has an interesting courtship display (studied in particular by K. Lorenz, G. K. Noble and S. Frugis) in which there is a series of dances consisting in raising one leg after the other, until it is close to the head; bowing, with an up-and-down movement of the head; and preening the feathers. In some cases the beak also plays an important part in courtship displays, as do the legs and the inside of the beak and throat when brightly coloured. In the display of the Blue-footed Booby (*Sula nebouxi*), the bright blue feet dilate considerably to reveal the web between the toes.

This species is the largest of the boobies, being up to 86 cm in length. It nests from Mexico south to Peru and Ecuador. It lays only two or three eggs, which hatch in about 41 days. By the 14th week the chicks are fledged, although the parents care for them for a further seven weeks.

Reciprocal displays also exist in which both sexes play more or less equivalent roles as the ceremony unfolds. There are various displays of this type. For example, it occurs in the Great Crested Grebe (*Podiceps cristatus*), studied at length by Julian Huxley in 1914 and subsequently by K. E. L. Simmons. The two partners carry out a series of strange movements such as each snatching a clump of waterweed with the beak and then 'clashing' breast-to-breast and rising up on the water with the clump of weed still in the beak. Another example is that of the

Gannet (*Sula bassana*), studied by E. A. Armstrong. Breast-to-breast, the pair clashes with beaks pointed upwards: this movement serves to heighten the close contact between the two partners and reduce the fear or aggression of the two birds involved. Likewise, albatrosses, in their ceremony, rub each other's beaks.

Depending on the species, courtship displays take place on land, in water, or in the air. The most impressive courtship displays in flight are those of the birds of prey, which carry out strange acrobatics and in some cases (like certain species of eagle) even join together by their feet in the air. The displays in flight of certain passerines are also well known, such as those of the Skylark (*Alauda arvensis*) and the Meadow Pipit (*Anthus pratensis*). In courtship displays there are sometimes symbolic movements during which the female asks the male for food, thus assuming the behaviour of a nestling. Appropriate offerings are made by the male. Her request, however, is not really to do with food, because it is sometimes made in places where food is abundant. This ritual occurs in various Passeriformes, gulls and terns. In other cases the symbolic offering is nest-building material. These acts precede or symbolize the essential nesting activities: the broody female's beakful of food, and the construction of the nest. Very special displays are found in the species of Passeriformes belonging to the family Ptilonorhynchidae (bowerbirds). The biologist G. E. Hutchinson; discussing their behaviour, said that: 'in terms of variety and affectation there is nothing like them in the whole animal kingdom'. Found in Australia and New Guinea, these birds actually build 'bowers' decorated with coloured objects. Using twigs, stalks, grass, leaves and other parts of plants, the males of some species build small huts which are then embellished with glittering objects (in two species these 'bowers' are even painted). Once the 'bower' is complete, the male struts about, performing love dances in front of the female, and then mates with her. Some species simply build a kind of platform in a forest glade, but others build complicated structures like tents, towers and so on. The male of the species *Ptilonorhynchus violaceus* (Satin Bowerbird) takes a piece of bark in its beak and colours his 'bower' blue, as if with a brush, using charcoal and pieces of fruit mixed with saliva as 'paints'. In certain other species the males prepare a clearing in the forest in which to put on their displays. Examples are the Great Argus Pheasant (*Argusianus argus*) and the lyrebirds (genus *Menura*).

In other cases we find collective courtship displays which involve not just one male, or the two partners of the reciprocal

▲ Male Ruffs *Philomachus pugnax*

display, but several individuals which gather in common territories where the displays take place. These territories are called arenas or *leks*. Here there is a hierarchy amongst the males present, and the females choose their partners. A well-known case is that of the Ruff (*Philomachus pugnax*). In the breeding season the males have on their breast a bib-like array of feathers which stretch to the top of the head and their bright coloration varies from individual to individual. These birds gather in spring in some grassy place where they perform their individual displays, and try to avoid fights, in order to attract a female. These collective displays occur among other species, in various forms, particularly in most species of grouse such as the Black Grouse (*Lyrurus tetrix*), the Prairie Chicken (*Tympanachus cupido*) and the Sage Grouse (*Centrocercus urophasianus*). In some of these species the hierarchic order is clearly defined and is important because, for example, in *Centrocercus urophasianus*, up to 74 per cent of mating is carried out by the dominant male. The individuals beneath the dominant male in the hierarchy manage to mate when he is not looking, or tired, while the opportunity of mating for those at the bottom of the hierarchic ladder is literally by chance, or may occur at the end of the mating season. It should, however, be born in mind that in a *lek* 800 metres long in the case of *Centrocercus urophasianus*, there may be groups of up to 400 males. The intermediate stages between the solitary display and the collective display apply to

HOW BIRDS LIVE

certain manakins – Passeriformes belonging to the family Pipridae – where the display arena is common to several individuals (up to 70), but each male retains his own personal territory within the arena. The function of the *lek* seems to be to encourage encounters between the two sexes, which is less easy in solitary conditions, and to ensure the fertilization of the females by the most energetic males who occupy the higher levels of the hierarchy.

Courtship displays demand a considerable amount of energy for birds, given the high level of excitation implicit in them. In species where the courtship displays are very complex, the males use so much energy that once they have mated they will pay no attention to their offspring. Despite this great use of energy, courtship displays fulfil vital functions, mainly concerned with the co-ordination and synchronization of the sexual cycle in both partners, without which reproduction and the survival of the species would not be ensured. The initiative

▼ A Wood Pigeon, *Columba palumbus*, feeding its young.

▲ A Purple Heron *Ardea purpurea* on its nest

in the sexual dialogue is, in the vast majority of cases, taken by the male but there are some exceptions to this rule. In the painted snipes and the button quails, it is the females who make the first move; they take many mates, and do not look after the young. Sexual promiscuity occurs only in a few cases. In some grouse, in certain birds of paradise, in cuckoos and the Ruff, the union of the sexes lasts only as long as it takes to mate; in various other species we find polygamy. In some ratites (the Ostrich, rheas), pheasants and various Passeriformes there are cases of polygyny (a male with several females), but these may be restricted only to certain areas in which the species concerned is found. In the case of the button quails, jacanas, painted snipes and phalaropes we find cases of polyandry (a female with several males). However, most birds

▲ A young Purple Heron

are monogamous: the relationship may last for a season, or the bond may persists for longer than a year, and in some cases it appears to last a lifetime.

The nest

The nest is a structure which in various ways protects the eggs and the newborn young. It is an indispensable necessity, in as much as both egg and nestling (particularly in birds which are nidicolous or hatched naked) are potentially exposed to adverse environmental conditions and to predators. The evolution of the nesting habit in birds has been affected both by environmental factors and by the influence of physiological factors in the animal itself. To some extent, the nesting process in most birds is independent of the more obvious environmental

HOW BIRDS LIVE

factors because of the bird's capacity for thermoregulation; the heat required to incubate the eggs is not derived from the sun nor from fermenting vegetable matter but from the bird's body as it sits in the nest. However, the species belonging to a family of Galliformes, the Megapodiidae, use odd methods of incubation. Found in Australia, New Guinea, Malaysia and on some Micronesian islands, these birds use three major systems of incubation: they build mounds made of dead leaves, twigs, soil and other vegetable matter, and utilize the heat produced

▼ A pair of Little Bitterns, *Ixobrychus minutus,* with young.

as this material decomposes; the heat of the sun's rays; and subterranean sources of heat. The eggs are laid when the appropriately constructed mound reaches a heat of 35–36°C. The incubation period lasts for about 63 days and is one of the longest found in birds. In *Megapodius freycinet*, the pair remains near the nest, keeping an eye on the mound, and ventilating it, thus controlling the temperature. These nesting mounds reach a height of 4.5 metres although as a rule they do not exceed 1.5–2.1 metres, and have a diameter of up to 6 metres. One such mound found in Australia measured almost 15 metres in diameter.

Jean Dorst (1974) writes that nesting patterns must have come about through natural selection. That part of a population of a certain species which used the best system of nesting was at an advantage, and other groups or populations of the same species gradually died out. Among present-day birds, the type of nest is strictly defined, and to such an extent that the outward appearance of the construction enables one, in more cases than not, to identify the occupant. There is still a certain flexibility in those birds which have relatively loose ecological requirements.

The nests built by the various species of birds vary greatly. Some, and especially those with nidifugous young, build fairly rudimentary nests or even lay their eggs on the bare ground. This happens in the case of the ratites, penguins, various sea birds, certain waders (plovers, curlews) and others. Guillemots lay their eggs on rocky ledges above the sea without any nest structure at all (the eggs do not fall off because of their special pear-like shape). Other species use pieces of seashells, a few pebbles, or bits of vegetable matter, and dig a very shallow hollow in the ground. Emperor Penguins sit on their egg by laying it on their feet and then covering it with a fold of skin from the abdomen called the *incubatorium* (they are the only birds to have this feature). Other species lay their eggs in natural hollows in the ground or in rocks, and still others use hollows in trees (either natural hollows, or, in some instances, hollows especially made, as in the case of woodpeckers, and, to a lesser extent, nuthatches and some other species). Various species build a nest structure in tree hollows, using vegetable and other matter (this applies in particular to various Passeriformes). Nests built in hollows are certainly less liable to attack from predators than are open nests, and often ensure higher rates of reproduction for the species using them. There are nests which are more like burrows, either dug in the ground, or adapted by arranging already existing hollows or

HOW BIRDS LIVE

holes. The species which build their nests on the ground include harriers, Rallidae (rails, coots), cranes, grebes, gulls, geese, ducks, terns, divers, various Passeriformes (larks) and others. Then there are nests built in trees, bushes, on branches and so on: in many cases these are very elaborate structures, and some of them are magnificent. Such nests are those of the tailorbirds (genus *Orthotomus*) which consist of large, rolled leaves, the edges of which are almost literally stitched with a strong thread or fibre, and the interiors 'upholstered' with various materials; or the nest of the Penduline Titmouse (*Remiz pendulinus*), with its distinctive bag-like shape; or those used for several years running by birds of prey, which become really huge as the materials accumulate. (Some other species will also re-use nests.) Herrick tells of a Bald Eagle's nest (*Haliaeetus leucocephalus*) which was 4 metres high, 3 metres in diameter, and weighed over 2 tonnes.

Collective nests are used by several pairs. A classic example

▼ The nest of a Desert Lark *Ammomanes deserti*

A Swallow, *Hirundo rustica*, feeding its young in the nest ▶

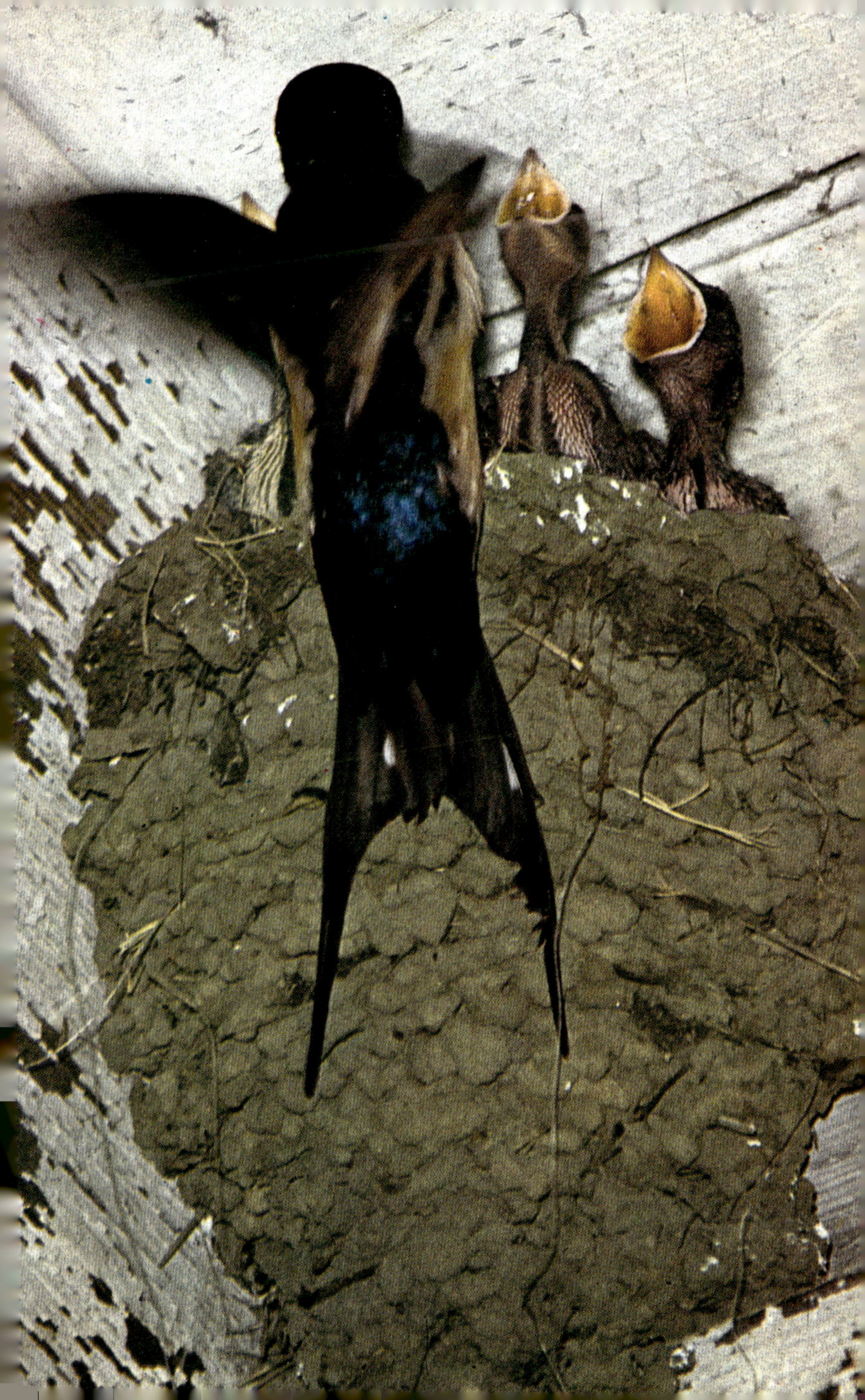

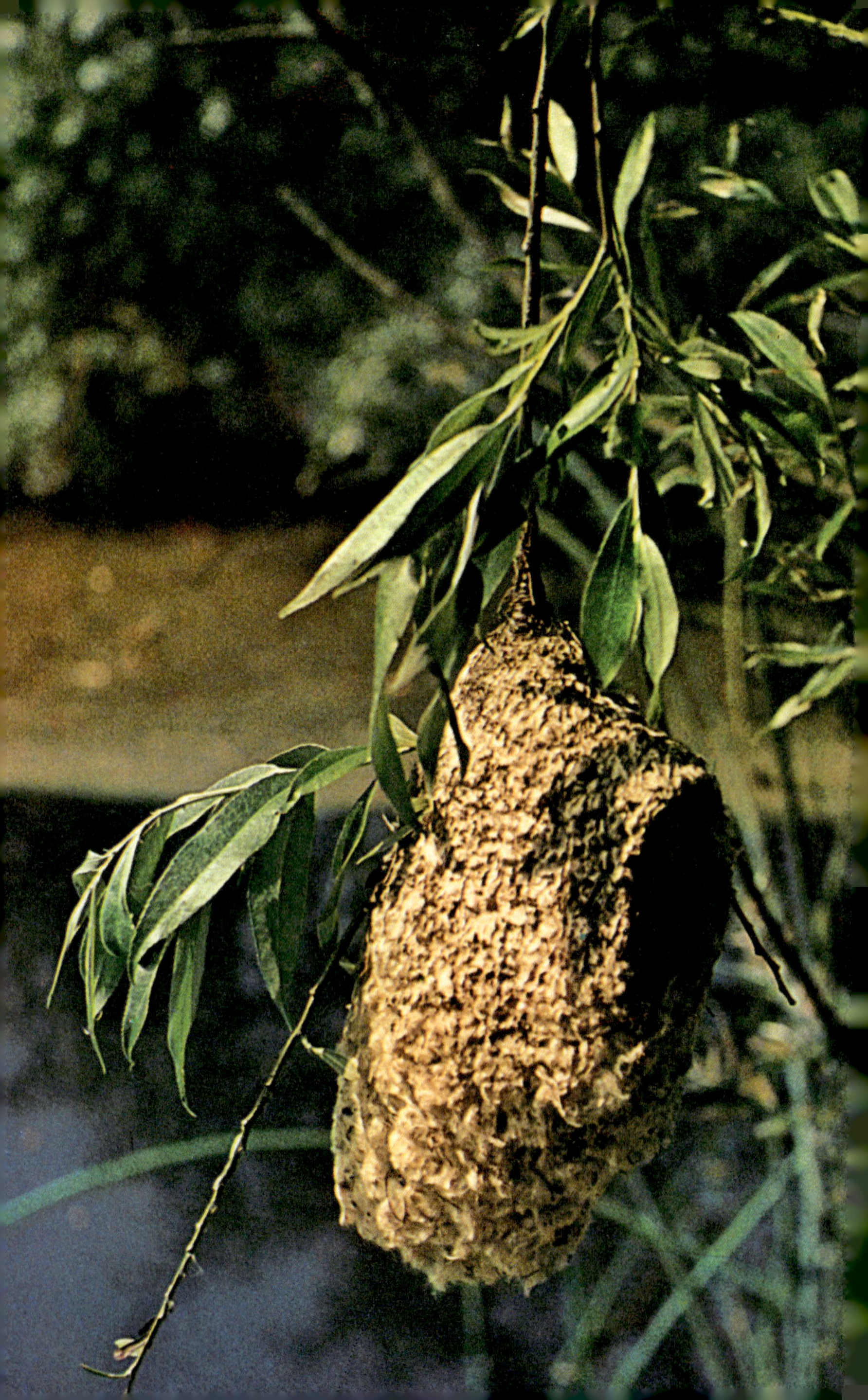

HOW BIRDS LIVE

of this is the Social Weaverbird (*Philetairus socius*): ornithologists N. E. and E. C. Collias saw a colony consisting of four communal nests, the largest of which was 4.8 metres long, 3.6 metres wide and had some 125 apertures. Sometimes a small bird will use the large nest structure of another species, making a small area of it into its own nest (large nests of birds of prey may house the nests of a few small Passeriformes in their structure).

The nest is protected from predators by being built in suitable places, often well concealed, and by the birds avoiding movements which might attract the attention of predators to the nest. When an intruder comes too close to the nest of certain waders – the nest being usually well camouflaged in the ground – they move away, 'moaning', pretending to have an injured wing or leg, thus focussing the attention of the intruder on themselves rather than the nest: this behaviour is known as a distraction display. The nest is a structure used almost exclusively for breeding. Rarely, and in only very few cases, is it used as a resting place, or the stage for displays. The construction of the nest is determined by a series of hormonal influences, associated with the physiological changes which occur in the bird's body in the mating season. The choice of its

▼ The nest of a Sociable Weaverbird *Philetarius socius*

◀ Nest of a Penduline Titmouse *Remiz pendulinus*

Overleaf. Embryo — 12 hrs after the start of incubation; at 90hrs; on the 9th, 12th, 13th and 15th days ▶

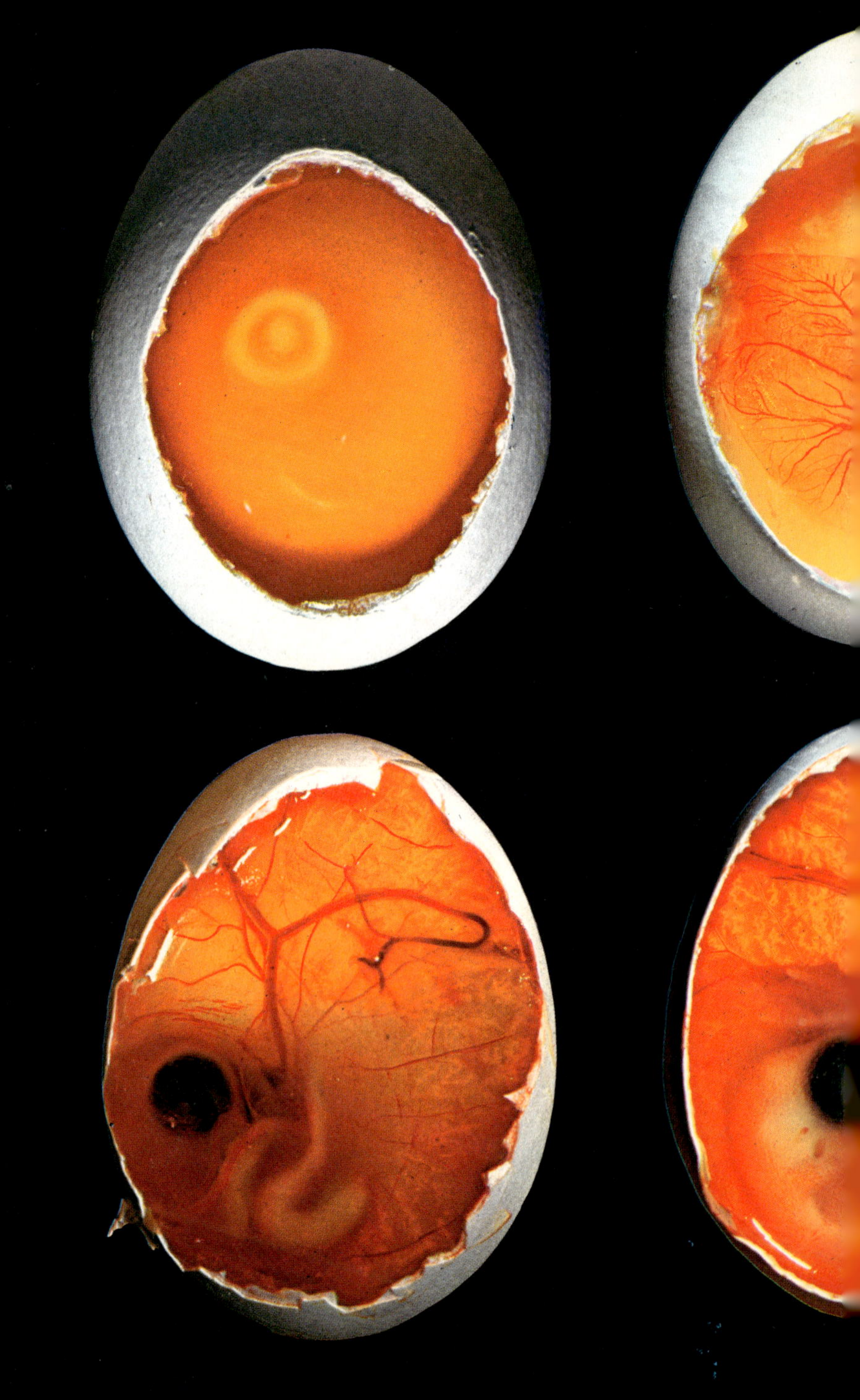

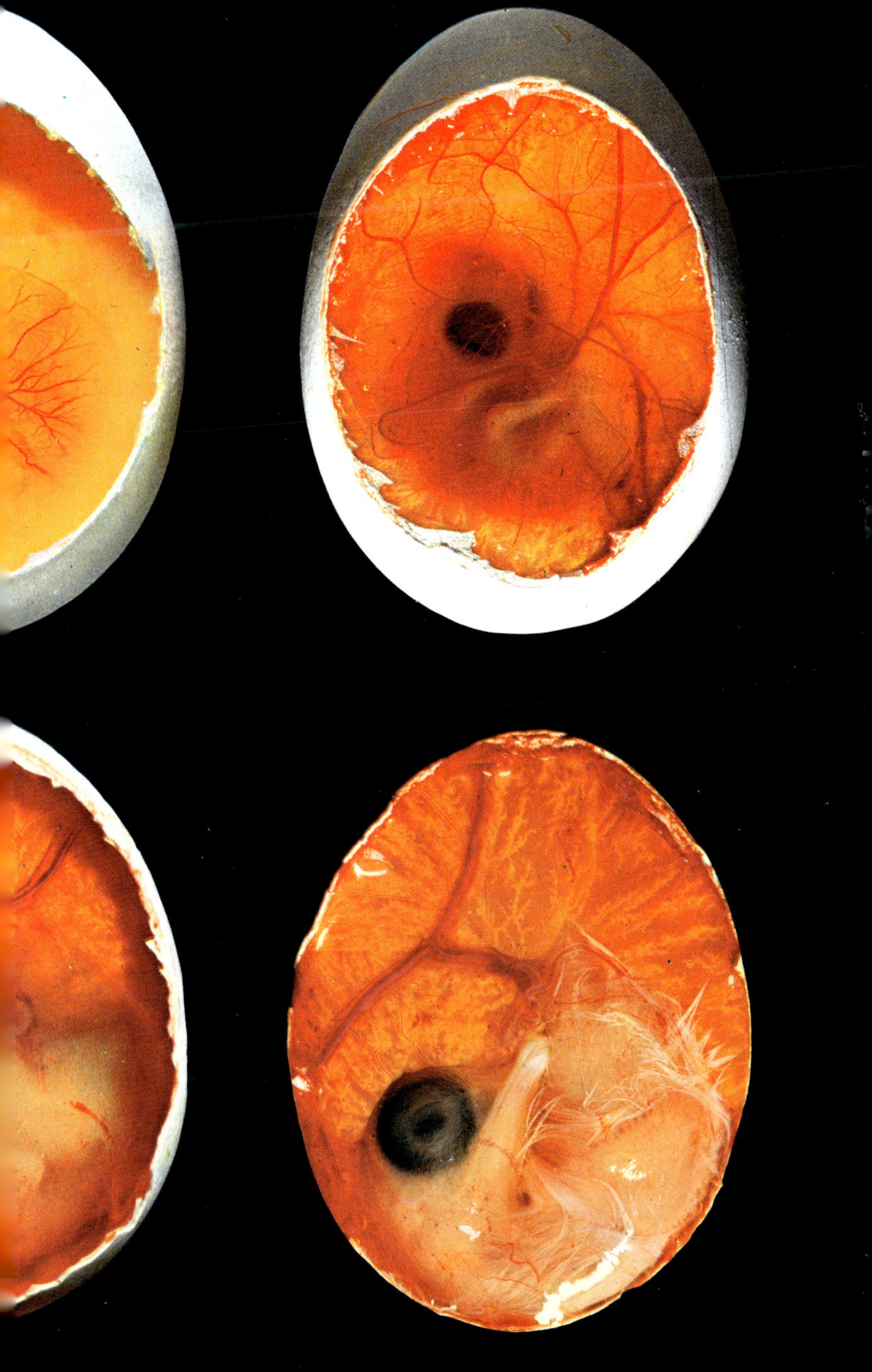

◀ The birth of a chick

HOW BIRDS LIVE

situation, the materials and the actual building are, depending on the species, the responsibility of the male, or the female, or both. The time it takes to build a nest varies from two to six days for some Passeriformes, up to four months for the African Hammerhead (*Scopus umbretta*), which builds an extremely strong nest equipped with three inner 'chambers'.

▼ Three-week-old chicks

HOW BIRDS LIVE

Egg-laying and care of the young
Once the nest is complete, the female lays her eggs in it. The shape, size and colour of the eggs vary from species to species, as do the incubation periods. The young are reared by the parents for a period of time which differs according to the species.

The shape of the egg is usually adapted to the structure of the nest and may be pear-shaped, oval or elliptical, with possible variations. Birds which have a deep pelvis lay spherical eggs (this applies to birds of prey) while those with a narrow pelvis lay elongated eggs (this applies to the Podicipedidae – grebes).

▼ Mexican Stilt *Himantopus himantopus mexicanus*

HOW BIRDS LIVE

Species which hatch several eggs usually lay smaller eggs than species which lay one or few eggs. The size varies and the coloration depends on various factors: species which nest in the open lay camouflaged eggs; those which nest in hollows usually lay whitish eggs. This is a generalization, and there are some exceptions. The eggs of ratites, pelicans, and albatrosses are whitish although they are laid in the open.

The laying period varies from species to species and region to region, but it nevertheless coincides with the period in which the environment presents the most favourable conditions required by individual species. The size of the clutch ranges

▼ The nest of a Coot with eggs and a chick

from the single egg laid by albatrosses, various birds of prey or penguins to the 16 laid by titmice and the 22 laid by some game birds. In some species the number of eggs per clutch is fixed (hummingbirds always lay two eggs), in others there are slight variations or there may be considerable variations. As a rule one can say that every pair produces the number of young which it is potentially capable of rearing. An accurate synthesis of the various studies made on ecological adaptations in bird reproduction, with numerous original annotations, was made by David Lack (1968). Environmental conditions and consequently the geographical position of the regions are very

Little
Ringed Plover ▶

◀ Black Tern

▲ Eider

▼ Hedge Sparrow

▼ Nightingale

◀ Common Tern

Stonechat ▶

Mallard ▶

▼ Linnet

▲ Savi's Warbler

▼ A Coot's nest

◀ Goldfinch

Duck ▶

important in determining the size of the clutch of eggs. Adverse environmental situations, predation and other causes bring about losses. The eggs in a single clutch are laid at intervals ranging from 24 hours in most Passeriformes to five to six days in the Gannet. With some species, if the eggs are gradually removed as they are laid, it is possible to get the female to continue laying until a fairly large number have been accumulated. Some birds lay a single clutch a year, others more than one (up to five in the Mourning Dove *Zenaida macroura*). In some species the destruction of the nest or eggs causes a replacement nesting process.

Sometimes incubation commences when the first egg is laid, or it may not begin until all the eggs have been laid. In the first case the young will hatch at different times and will develop at a different rate. In birds of prey it can happen that the last born are victimized by the first born. which seize all the food brought to the nest by the parents. A brooding bird covers the eggs with those parts of its body (apteria) known as incubation plates or brood spots; blood vessels enlarge in these regions during the breeding season to convey heat to the eggs being incubated. The broody bird moves and turns the eggs to give them all the necessary amounts of heat for successful incubation. If the heat from the sun is excessive the parent bird protects the eggs by opening its wings. In some cases the eggs cope satisfactorily with a drop in temperature, slightly less well with a rise and will even survive not being sat on for a few days. Incubation is constant in some instances and carried out by both parents alternately, in others it is more spasmodic, particularly in species where just one parent is concerned with the activity. In such cases the eggs may be abandoned for varying lengths of time, up to seven days in the case of the Manx Shearwater (*Puffinus puffinus*). Anis belonging to the genus *Crotophaga* build a communal nest, of several pairs, in which the females lay their eggs (as many as 24) which are sat on simultaneously or alternately by various members of the group and the rearing of the young is carried out communally. The duration of the incubation period varies between 11–12 days for certain cowbirds to 78–81 days for certain albatrosses. When the incubation is complete the shell of the egg is thinner, and is broken by the chick with a sort of growth on the upper mandible called the egg-tooth, which tends to disappear as the chick grows. As soon as the chicks are born the parents start to look after them.

Margaret N. Nice (see also Harrison 1975) has classified the new born young of birds by considering their degree of

A young Cuckoo being fed by a Reed Warbler ▶

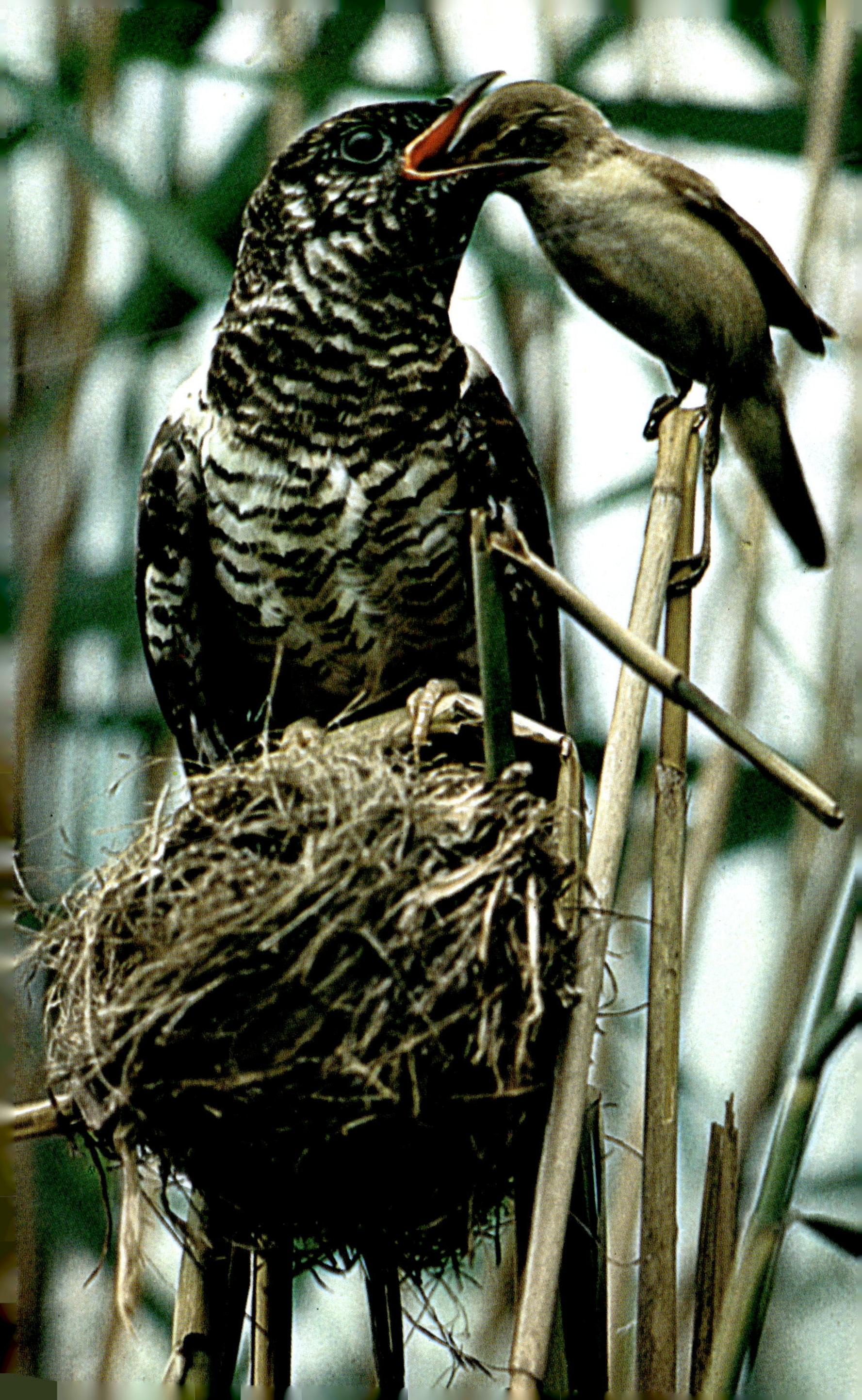

maturity on hatching. She divides them into following groups:
1. Nidifugous chicks hatch with eyes open, are covered with down, and leave the nest on the first or second day. There are the following sub-groups: (a) those independent of the parents (Megapodes); (b) those which follow the parents, but find food for themselves (ducks, geese, swans, sandpipers, avocets, phalaropes, stone-curlews); (c) those which follow the parents, who help them find food (pheasants, partridges, plovers); (d) those who follow the parents and are fed by them (divers, cranes, grebes, rails).
2. Semi-nidifugous chicks hatch with eyes open, are covered in down, but remain in the nest until they learn to walk, being fed by the parents (flamingoes, gulls, terns, skuas, auks, nightjars).
3. Semi-nidicolous chicks are covered with down, but are unable to leave the nest and are fed by the parents. They can be divided into: (a) those with the eyes open (stormy petrels, storks, ibises, herons, falcons); (b) those with the eyes shut (nocturnal birds of prey).
4. Nidicolous chicks have closed eyes, are bare or with little down, are unable to fly, and are fed by the parents (pelicans, gannets, cormorants, parrots, pigeons, cuckoos, swifts, kingfishers, hoopoes, woodpeckers, rollers and various passerines).

Nidifugous nestlings, who do not immediately have a fully functional system of thermoregulation, are kept warm by the parents at night, and in bad weather, for several days after their birth. It is up to the parents to keep watch on them, take them to feeding places, and teach them to react to the various environmental conditions which may occur. Before very long the young learn to feed themselves unattended. Nidicolous young, which have no down, are bare, and sometimes blind at birth, depend entirely on their parents, and their only activity is to open wide the beak to have it filled with food. They do not have an adequate thermoregulation system (a feature which emerges gradually as they develop) and remain in the nest for a period of time, which varies from species to species.

The diet of young birds consists mainly of animal matter, even in those species where the adult diet is predominantly vegetarian. The feeding of the young, be they nidicolous or nidifugous, entails a series of stimuli designed to stimulate this act. The coloration of the buccal cavity is very important in the case of nidicolous young, because it stimulates the adults to place food in it. In birds of prey, for example, the adult pulls the prey to pieces at the nest and then distributes rations to its

HOW BIRDS LIVE

young. In other species the adult simply places the food at the edge of the nest when the young are larger, and in still others the adult inserts its own beak into the chicks' throats and regurgitates the food. Lastly, there are those species where the chicks insert their beaks into the adult's. The frequency of feeding varies from case to case and is obviously proportionate to the amount of food brought to the nest each time. Whereas some large birds of prey bring to the nest on average one prey twice a day, a Great Tit will feed its nestlings 60 times in a single hour. In addition, although this does not apply to all species, the parents also make sure that the nest is kept clean.

Rearing the young takes from 13–20 days in some Passeriformes, to eight and a half months in the case of albatrosses. As a rule, when it takes to the air, the young bird has reached the size and weight of the adult, or may even be heavier. Its plumage is not the same as that of adults, and is called the juvenile plumage. As a result of moulting and the attainment of sexual maturity the young bird gradually assumes its adult plumage. In some cases the young abandon the nest although they are still not altogether independent, even where their flying is concerned, and remain near the nest for a few days. Once they have learnt to fly, the young stay with their parents for a time. In some species they remain with them until the next mating season, in others they accompany the parents on the postnuptial migration, and the parents here become invaluable mentors. The young may scatter, moving far from their parents and from their place of birth.

The phenomenon of parasitism must be considered. In one species of duck, the Black-headed Duck (*Heteronetta atricapilla*), in numerous species of cuckoo, in certain species of the family Indicatoridae (honeyguides), in the family Icteridae (American orioles) and in the family Ploceidae (weaverbirds), the eggs are laid in nests of other species, which then rear the young intruders as if they were their own. With the Common Cuckoo (*Cuculus canorus*) for example, once mating has taken place the female goes in search of the nests of Passeriformes where she lays just one egg in each nest, laying in all between 12 and 26 eggs. These develop in just under a fortnight, often in a shorter time than the eggs belonging to the host species. The newborn cuckoo wastes no time removing any eggs and other nestlings from the nest, and is reared on its own by its adopted parents. Species belonging to the Indicatoridae (order Piciformes) are parasitic mainly on Picidae (woodpeckers) and Capitonidae (barbets), but also on bee eaters, the Hoopoe, swallows, starling and various other Passeriformes. The

HOW BIRDS LIVE

honeyguides' young, at birth, are equipped on both jaws with a strong hook which disappears when they are a fortnight old: these two hooks are used to kill any other young in the nest. Among the Icteridae is an extremely interesting case of parasitism. A species, the Giant Cowbird (*Scaphidura oryzivora*), is parasitic on the clutches of other species of Icteridae belonging to the group of oropendolas (in particular the *Zarhynchus wagleri*). The nests of these oropendolas are plagued by flies belonging to the genus *Philornis* which lay their eggs on the nestlings. The larvae of these flies, once born, dig

▼ Great-tailed Grackle *Cassidix mexicanus* (family Icteridae)

tunnels into the bodies of the young birds and if one has more than seven larvae in its body, it may well die. When the nest of the oropendola is used by the parasitic *Scaphidura*, the latter removes with its beak the eggs and larvae of the *Philornis* from the bodies of the small oropendolas, thus obviously rendering them a great service. In the group of widowbirds (family Ploceidae) we find a strong similarity in the hosts selected for nesting: the song, basic pattern of the opened mouth of the nestlings and the plumage of the young are extremely similar in both parasite and host. This marked resemblance is partly explained by the fact that the young widowbirds do not evict the host nestlings from the nest. Widowbirds are parasitic on species belonging to the family Estrildidae (waxbills), showing a considerable degree of specialization because each species of widowbird is, from preference, parasitic on a single species of Estrildidae although it may be parasitic on other species to a lesser extent. The problems posed by parasitism are many and varied, depending on the species. The parasites must adapt to the reproductive cycle of the hosts; the eggs, nestlings and voice must be fairly alike, and the parasitic nestlings must also make do with the food provided by the host.

Voice
Among the various vocal expressions used by birds a rough distinction can be made between cries and calls designed to attract, actual song, and the sub-song or juvenile song. The first group may have different meanings. In some species (such as penguins and albatrosses) the sounds may have a sexual significance as well, because they are made during the breeding season. In numerous cases they indicate the position of the bird and this serves to maintain contact between the members of a group or colony, to maintain the bonds uniting a pair and to ward off any intruder in the territory of the bird. In other cases cries are emitted to provide information. Alarm calls are given when there is some danger imminent or when a bird is caught by a predator or is otherwise in danger. In still other cases, calls are connected with food or feeding.

The song proper differs from calls and cries in the length of utterance and wealth and variety of notes of which it consists. Songs are sung principally in relations between the two sexes and in territorial behaviour. It is a particular attribute of certain Passeriformes (the Oscines) although other species do make sounds which can more or less be defined as real song. Bird song may well have evolved from the simple cry aimed at attracting attention; in some species it has a range which is

▲ Great Reed Warblers *Acrocephalus arundinaceus*

truly remarkable and audible 5 kilometres away. On the whole the male is the singer, with a rhythm that varies with the species and depends on the stage of the breeding cycle, because singing is controlled by the male hormones.

The sub-song is an elementary form of song. It is sung by young birds which have yet to perfect their voices. Many ornithologists have carried out very interesting research to find out how young birds learn to sing. In particular, W. H. Thorpe has made studies of the Chaffinch. In the voice of the young bird, it is possible to distinguish between an innate part, genetically determined by heredity, and an acquired part, determined by experience. The learning ability of species varies. In some we find a marked ability to imitate, and there is a tendency to assimilate the song of different species. This applies in particular to certain parrots and the mynah birds, which can even mimic the human voice. The ability to imitate is

▲ Wren *Troglodytes troglodytes*

remarkable in various other species too: in species belonging to the American genus *Mimus*, in particular the Northern Mockingbird *Mimus polyglottus*, members manage to copy the

▼ Rufus Scrub Bird *Atrichornis rufescens*

HOW BIRDS LIVE

song of 55 different species in less than one hour. Other imitative species include the warblers, certain Turdidae (thrushes) and certain Sylviidae (woodland birds).

The song is generally a distinctive feature of the various species: birds which are morphologically very alike can be identified through their different song. Songs also vary considerably among populations of the same species, this means that 'dialects' can be distinguished. In certain cases individual variations are used, for example, to identify the other partner of a pair. In species where both sexes have good vocal abilities it is possible to hear duets between male and female, in which, as a rule, the male sings the first notes and the female the last. These duets occur in species such as the African shrikes, the Red-billed Gonolek (*Laniarius erythrogaster*), for example. Voice is, therefore, very important in the life of birds, which is based essentially on visual and audible stimuli. Singing depends on various internal and external factors: the sex hormones control it (particularly

▼ Blue Tit *Parus caeruleus*

Goldfinch
Carduelis carduelis ▶

▼ Rufous Ovenbirds *Furnarius rufus*

HOW BIRDS LIVE

real song) internally, and light (the Nightingale is the best known bird which sings by day and by night), temperature, wind and other environmental factors affect the time and duration of singing. A strange bird, the Guacharo or Oilbird (*Steatornis caripensis*), which lives in the wooded mountains of South America, nests in colonies in caves. In order to move around in these dark caves, where it passes much of its time (it emerges at dusk to feed on fruit), it uses a sonar system similar to that used by bats. In 1953 R. D. Griffin and W. H. Phelps Jr. studied the Oilbird, and carried out various experiments: these showed that by using the syrinx as a transmitting device and the ears as a receiving system, these birds could avoid any obstacles. A similar system is used by certain swiftlets such as *Collocalia brevirostris*, which nests in caves on Sri Lanka.

▼ Hoopoe *Upupa epops*

Other sounds made by birds include the noises produced by the wings in flight, those produced by the Stork when it claps its jaws together, those made by the Common Snipe in flight when it vibrates its wing-quills, and the noise made by woodpeckers when they drum their beaks against wood.

Migration

A feature common virtually throughout the animal kingdom is the mobility of living beings. It is evident that there is a close link between movement, and the quest for better living conditions. Movement, in the animal kingdom, can roughly be divided into two groups: non-periodical movement which occurs when individuals or entire populations cover varying distances and do not return to their point of departure; and periodical movement when, on the contrary, individuals or entire populations cover varying distances and then return whence they came. Dispersion in populations is of three major types: emigration; immigration; and migration or periodic movement. The phenomenon of dispersion plays a part in delineating the structure of populations. Such mobility in varying degrees is found in many areas of the animal kingdom; examples are the periodic movements of certain mammals, such as caribou, bison, elephants, certain cetaceans such as humpback whales (*Megaptera*) which journey each year from the Antarctic to equatorial seas; the migration, often covering huge distances, of numerous species of fishes such as herring, cod and tuna; the periodic migration of other fishes from fresh to salt water and vice versa (salmon and eels); the annual migration of the Monarch butterfly (*Danaus plexippus*) which travels from North America to the shores of the Gulf of Mexico; and the vast periodic movements of locusts, which resemble full-scale invasions. It is among birds, however, that the migratory phenomenon is most widespread.

The origins of the migratory movements of birds have been the object of many theories. Environmental evolution and the extraordinary ability of adaptation shown by birds help explain the altering picture of the distribution of birds across the world, and also show the emergence of migration. In just a century, the nesting area of the Serin (*Serinus serinus*) has extended throughout the continent of Europe and along the shores of the southern Baltic, although, originally, it had a Mediterranean distribution. The Mediterranean populations are non-migratory, whereas the northern populations migrate

Overleaf: flock of migratory birds ▶

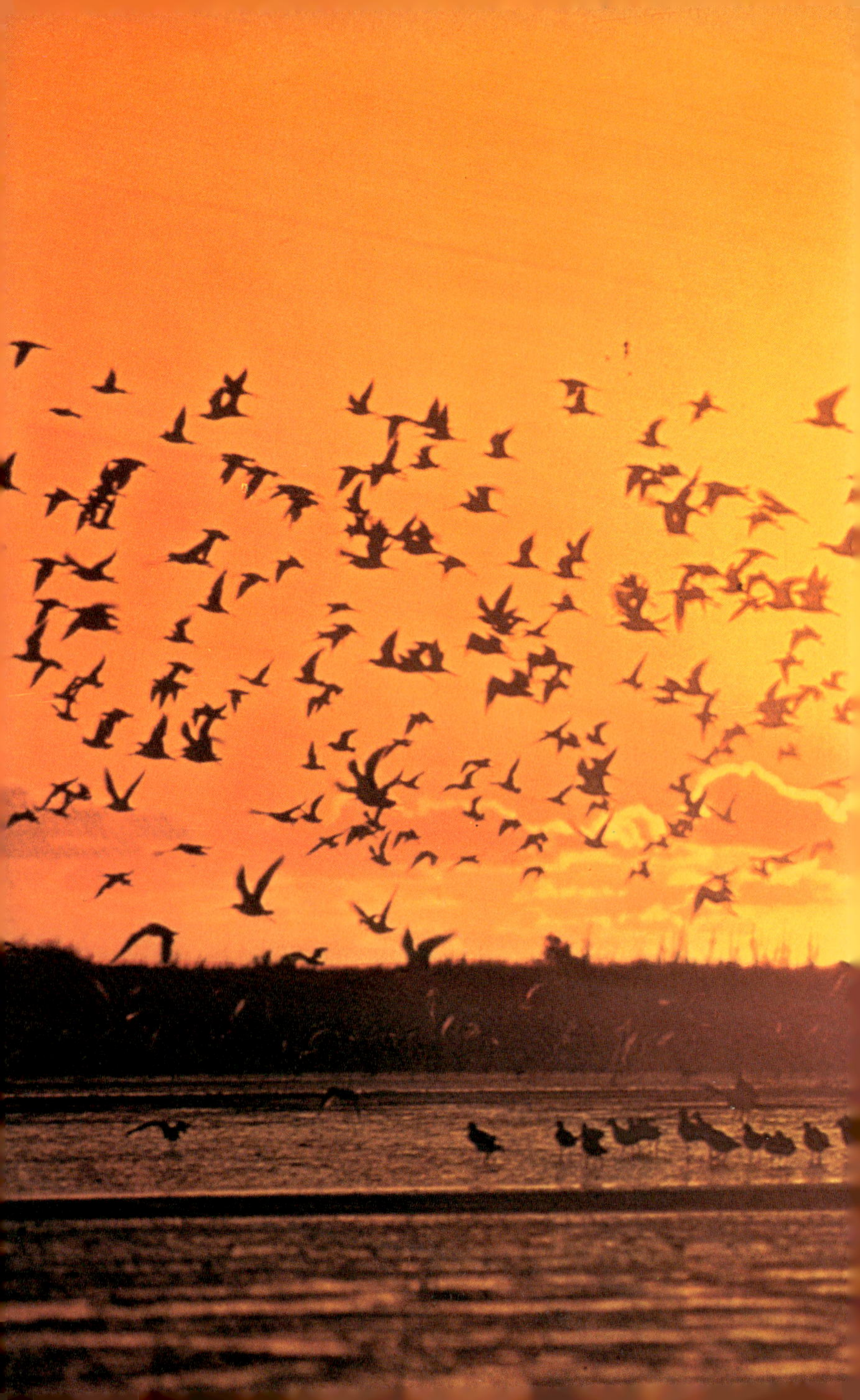

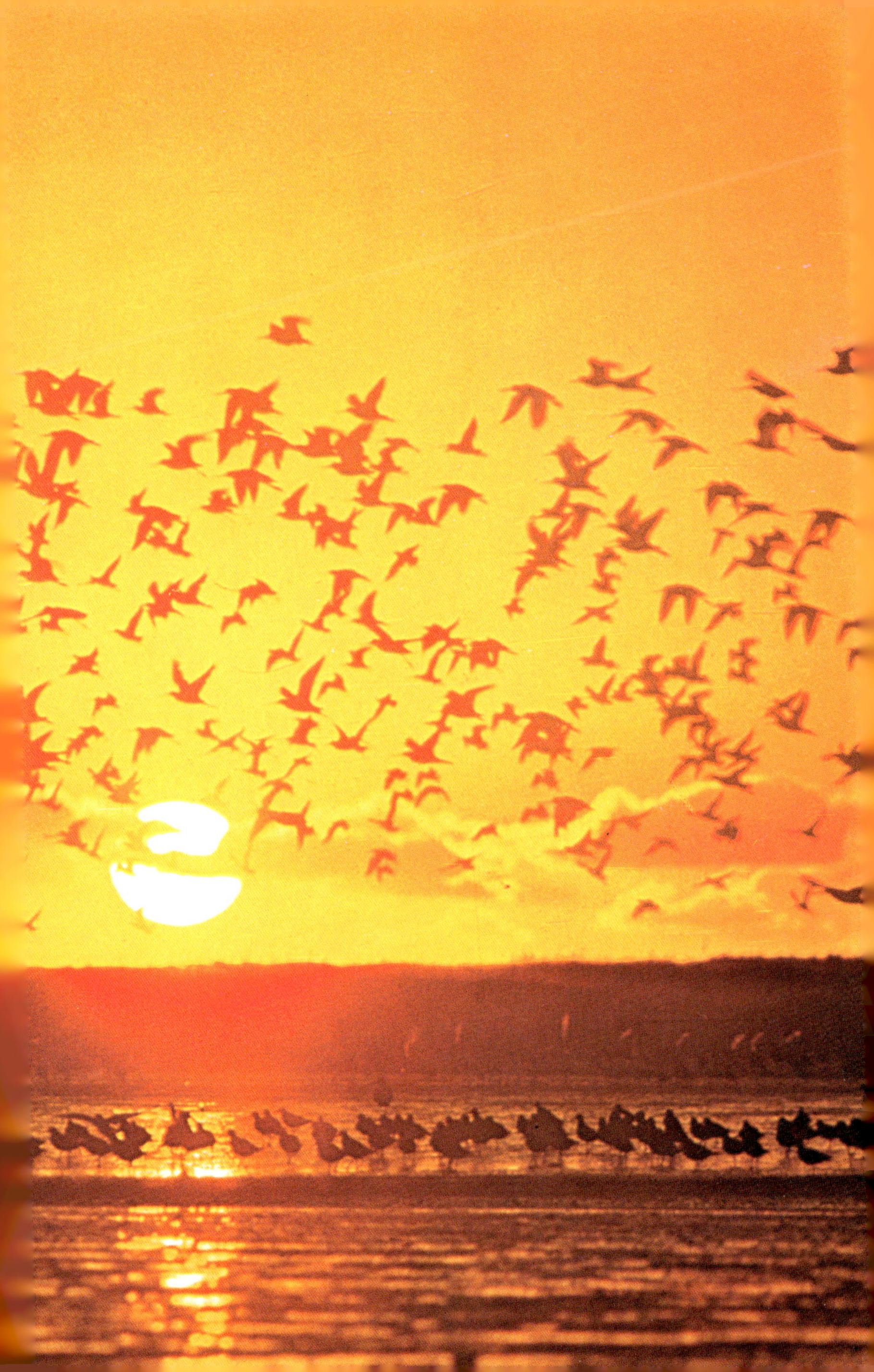

towards the south during the cold season, probably because of the unfavourable climatic conditions existing in the northern breeding areas. Migration dates back to the Tertiary Period, in the course of which the alternation of the seasons probably gave rise to movements similar to those occurring nowadays. This pattern then became more defined during the Quaternary Period in times of glaciation, which were punctuated by periods when milder climatic conditions determined the distribution of various species. During the glacial periods, species with a northerly distribution were forced to move southwards, and in all probability made their way back in the warmer inter-glacial periods. In these periods, populations of tropical species took advantage of the good climatic conditions and moved northwards.

Climate, environment and the inner physiological conditions of various birds form a set of circumstances which give rise to the emergence of migratory movements. The migrations of birds appear to be particularly well-developed in cold and temperate parts of the Northern Hemisphere, where the seasons are very marked, which is why birds tend to move towards zones with more favourable environmental conditions. In the Southern Hemisphere, there are many good examples of migrations although not as impressive as those occurring in the Northern Hemisphere. With the exception of certain sea birds, no birds migrate from the Southern to the Northern Hemisphere. The tropics have their share of migratory species, although they have more constant climatic conditions. In equatorial regions there are few migrations, if any: the environmental and climatic conditions are virtually constant.

It is possible to make a distinction between the various species of birds when discussing migration. In their breeding season birds maintain a specific territory, which they usually leave once the nesting period is over. Some remain fairly close to their territory, moving not more than a mile or two away: these are called non-migratory or sedentary birds. There is a wide range of intermediate stages between the non-migratory and the truly migratory species. Thus there are birds which scatter over wide areas, away from the nesting area (this is referred to as winter dispersion), showing various stages of erratic movement which is not really the same as migration proper. There are situations relating to actual migration, typified by a journey in one direction, known as the postnuptial migration or passage (from the nesting territory to the winter visiting area) and a return journey (from the winter area to the nesting territory) known as the prenuptial migration or return. Other terms indicate specific situations: the species present in a given zone in winter are called winter visitors, and those present in summer, outside the nesting season, summer visitors. Birds present now and then in an area make mass invasions, or major movements, which are generally non-periodical, in as much as in their distribution area there are years when the basic ingredients of their diet are in short

▼ Turnstones *Arenaria interpres*

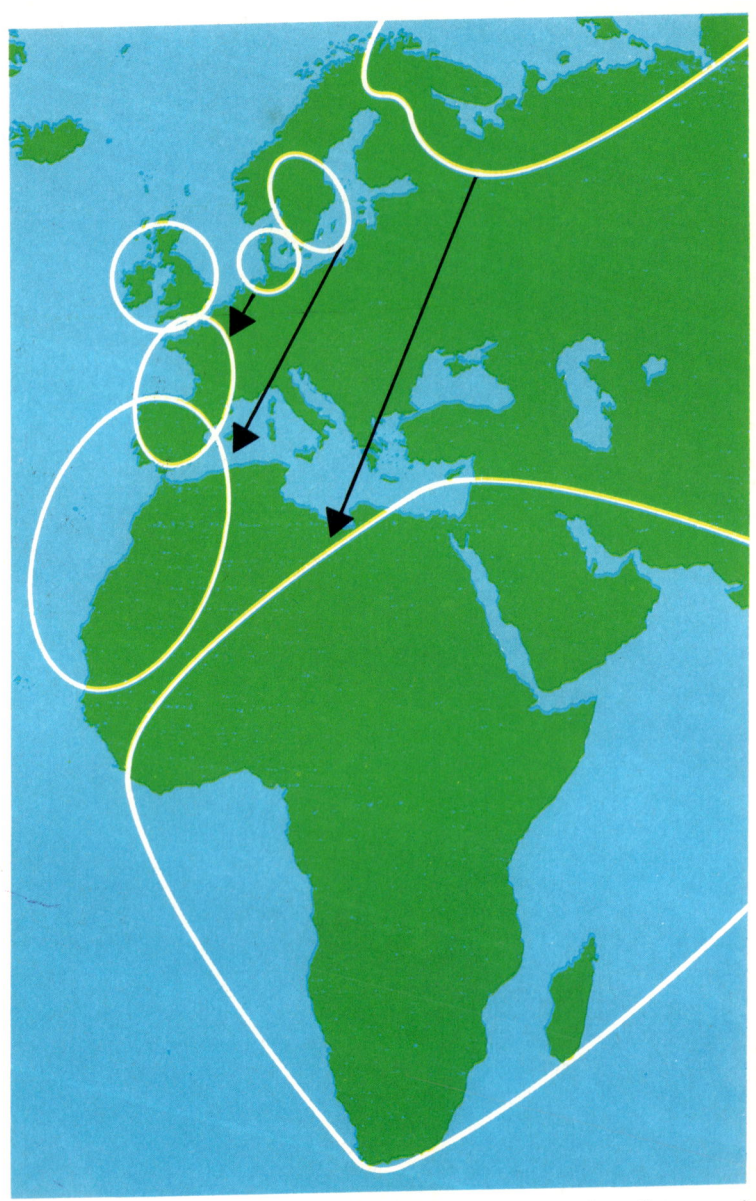

▲ The breeding and hibernation areas of the Ringed Plover *Charadrius hiaticula*

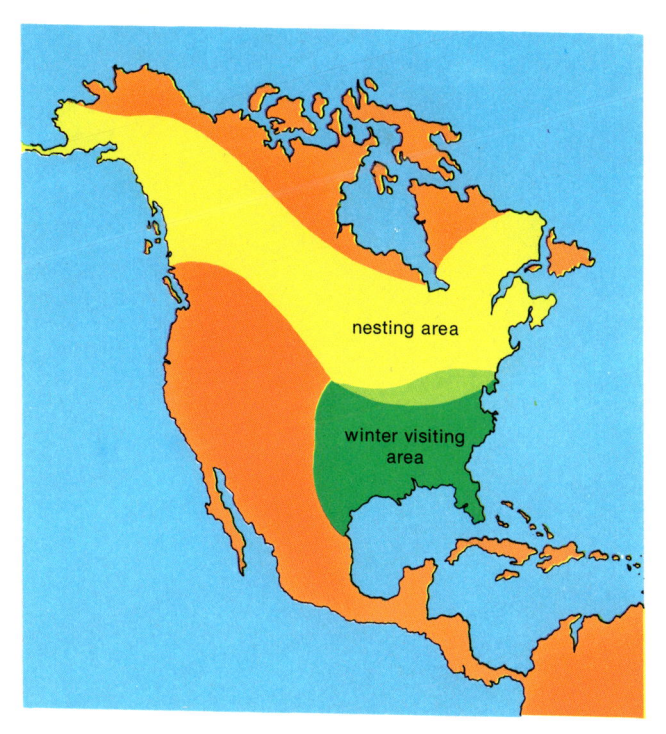

▲ The migration of the American Robin *Turdus migratorius*

supply: examples of this are the Crossbill (*Loxia curvirostra*) and, to a lesser extent, the Two-barred Crossbill (*Loxia leucoptera*) and the Parrot Crossbill (*Loxia pytopsittacus*), the Nutcracker (*Nucifraga caryocatactes*), Pallas's Sandgrouse (*Syrrhaptes paradoxus*), the Waxwing (*Bombycilla garrulus*), the Rose-coloured Pastor (*Sturnus roseus*), certain grouse and the Snowy Owl (*Nyctea scandiaca*). The 'accidental' birds, on the other hand, have gone astray from their normal migratory route for various reasons, and thus touch upon territories which are not part of their own normal distribution area.

Various methods have been used to study migration. Direct observation in the field by experts, noting down the presence of the various species, their direction, the size of the migrating groups, their behaviour, and so on, is undoubtedly the simplest and most widely used method practised today. Ornithologists

G. H. Lowery and R. J. Newman used telescopes aimed at the moon to analyse the number of nocturnal migratory birds passing overhead at high altitude at full moon (although the exact assessment of migrating species is fairly impossible in such conditions). A more effective but still very limited method is based on the use of radar, a method introduced by E. Sutter and used by various ornithologists. For some time people had been observing on radar screens complex sets of signals which no one had been able to interpret; they were called 'angels' then, E. Sutter discovered that they were groups of migrating birds. The ornithologist Donald R. Griffin followed the birds in an aeroplane. The most important method, however, for studying migrations is ringing. Attempts to ring birds were first made some time ago. Jean Dorst (1962) mentions a Peregrine Falcon (*Falco peregrinus*) belonging to Henry IV of France, whose mark it bore, which escaped from Fontainebleau and was recaptured in Malta, more than 2,000 kilometres from its place of origin, having covered the distance in 24 hours. Likewise, the famous ornithologist John James Audubon, in the first half of the nineteenth century, marked birds with a silver wire round one leg. In 1899 the Danish ornithologist H. C. C. Mortensen ringed 164 starlings with zinc rings showing the year and place of ringing. He then ringed many other birds with aluminium rings (the metal usually used for this purpose), and is considered to be the founder of the modern ringing method for studying migrations. In about 1909 in England two ringing centres were set up to study bird migration: one was in the hands of ornithologist Harry Forbes Witherby, and assisted by the scientific journal *British Birds*; the other was in the hands of A. Landsborough Thomson, at the University of Aberdeen.

The rings currently used are metal circles of light, aluminium-based alloy. The outer surface on every ring carries a serial number preceded by a letter and the abbreviated name of the institution – the abbreviation being identifiable internationally – which ringed the bird in question, together with its address. The letter and number refer to special registers where ringing data is recorded; the exact locality, the age of the bird ringed (whether a nestling, young bird or adult), its sex, and all the information that the ringing station has managed to gather about the bird's state of health, size, weight, possible state of moulting and so on. Rings are closed by butting the ends together on the smaller species, and by a slightly more complex device for larger species. Other types of ring and other methods of marking have also been tried. L. Gain, in

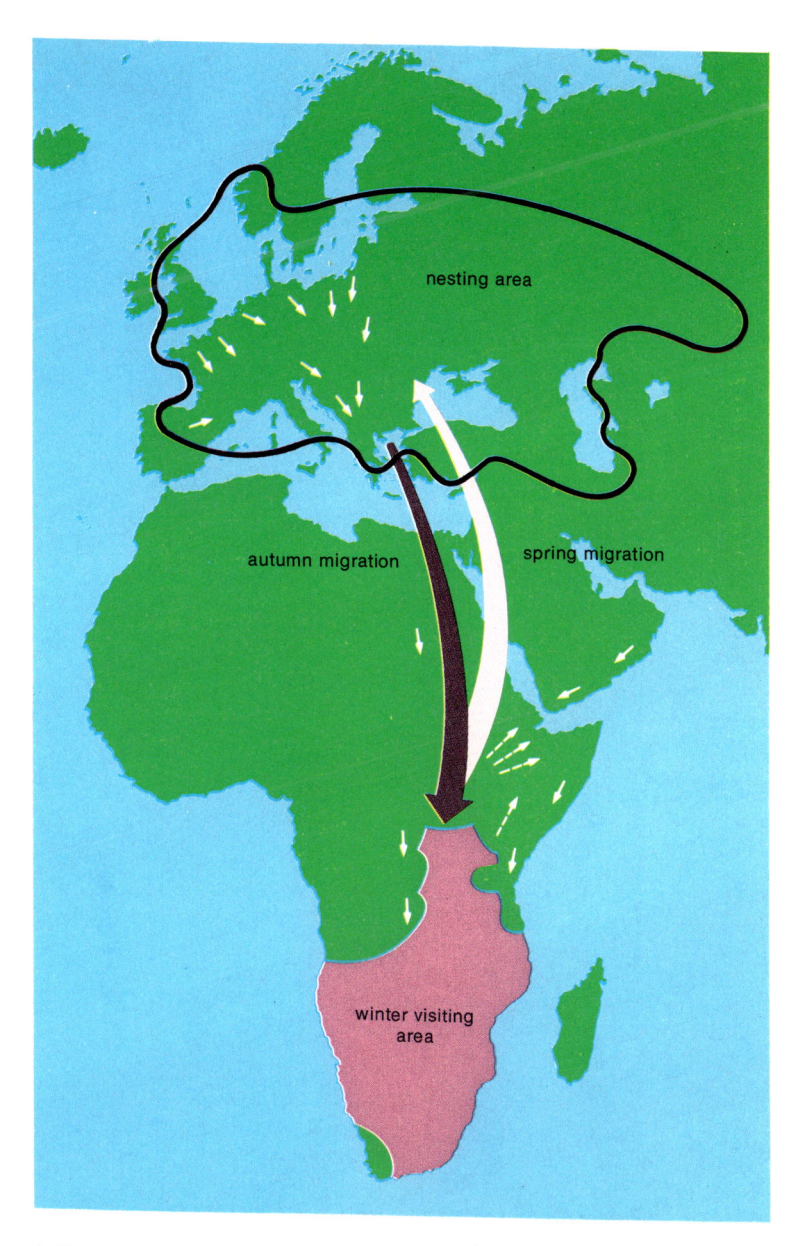

▲ The migration of the Red-backed Shrike *Lanius collurio*

169

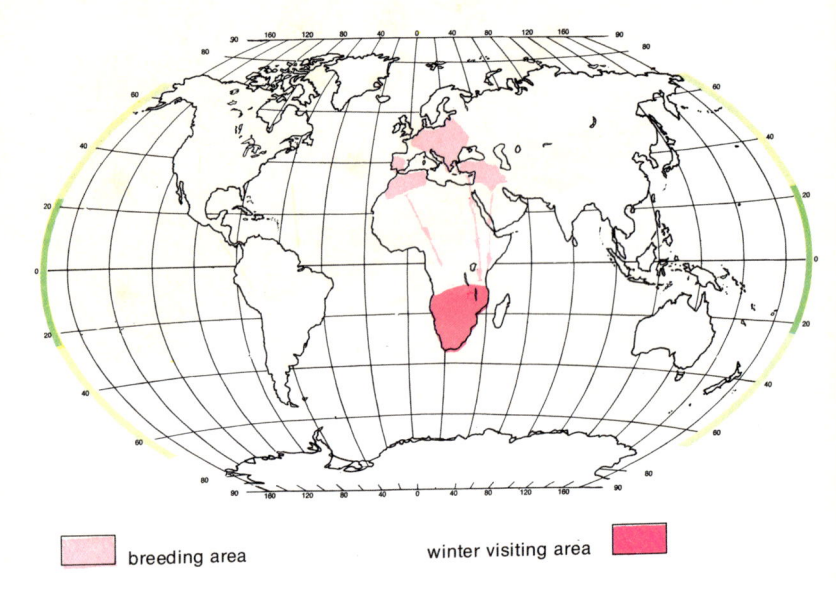

▲ Migration of the Stork

breeding area   winter visiting area

1908, fitted some Gentoo penguins (*Pygoscelis papua*) with strips of green celluloid around their heel-bones. Light metal plaques have been attached to the wings of some ducks and flamingoes and W. J. L. Sladen tried a method using identification bands attached to the tips of the wings of penguins (especially useful because they are identifiable at a distance through binoculars). Ornithologists Cendron, Prevost and Sapin-Jaloustre experimented, on penguins again, with flattened rings fixed with a metal clasp at the base of the wing (a particularly delicate and risky method which, if wrongly applied, may injure the axillary part of the penguin). Other types of ring (large ones, and of different colours) have also been used for identifying birds at a distance with binoculars.

A recent method for the detailed study of animal movements is radiotelemetry, which is used on mammals in particular. Here, the animals in question are fitted with tiny transmitters and once freed the animals can be tracked with a receiver. Radiotelemetric experiments have been carried out with various species: certain Passeriformes, skuas, penguins, pigeons and the Bald Eagle (*Haliaeetus leucocephalus*). As reported by ornithologist Alfred Schifferli, certain migratory thrushes in the state of Illinois (USA), weighing about 30 g, were fitted with tiny transmitters equipped with an antenna (the overall weight being about 2.5 g. One of these thrushes was released in Illinois on May 25, at eight o'clock, pinpointed and then followed with a receiver for an eight-hour flight. It reached Chicago, 225 kilometres away, then crossed Lake Michigan, negotiating fog and storm clouds, and ended up on Washington Island, a further 400 kilometres away.

Ringing in the nest is carried out with extreme caution: it is necessary to wait until the birds due for ringing are fairly advanced, because the ring fixed to the leg must be in proportion with the size of the adult's limb. Care must also be taken not to disturb the brood more than necessary.

Ringing of adults takes place in various ways, all of which try to ensure that no damage will be done, and that no undue stress will be suffered by the birds captured. Nets are used, placed in strategic migratory positions, with sack-like devices in them in which the birds to be ringed remain trapped. For waterfowl, ducks in particular, duck decoys are used, consisting of a series of nets leading from a central marshy area and ending up in actual sacks. Birds in the central area are stimulated to enter the net tunnels by the presence of domestic decoys or other lures; they are then caught and ringed. At the edges of the grazing areas of geese, Sir Peter Scott, founder and head of the *Wildfowl Trust*, arranges rolled-up nets which are released by electrically controlled switches when a sufficient number of geese are in the area. The net is shot into the air, and falls over the grazing geese. To catch other species, Passeriformes in particular, bird watchers and ringing stations use Heligoland traps, consisting of a kind of gigantic funnel of nets: the funnel gradually narrows down to a corridor and ends up in a cage, into which the birds are driven. The birds are then removed through an opening at the side. There are other methods for catching birds but it is important that traps are constantly watched so that birds in them can be removed immediately. All the ringing information is recorded, as mentioned previously.

The re-catching of ringed birds is very important for the study of birds' movements, age, and so on. Ringing should only be carried out by competent and specific organisations. The first ringing station to be set up was done by ornithologist J. Thienemann in 1901, on the shores of the Baltic, and called *Vogelwarte Rossitten*. At the end of World War II the station was moved to the shores of Lake Constance, to Rodolfzell in Schloss Moggingen, and called *Vogelwarte Radolfzell der Max Planck Gesellschaft*. Another important ringing station in

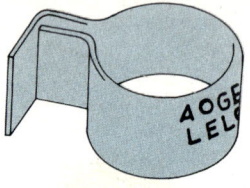

▲ A Mallard's ringed leg

◀ Types of identification rings

Germany was organized by Heinrich Gatke in Heligoland, and officially inaugurated in 1910 under the direction of Hugo Weigold. Britain organized its first ringing centres in 1909; at the present time there are fourteen ornithological observatories and numerous ringing centres co-ordinated by the British Trust for Ornithology, one of the world's major scientific ornithological organizations. Centrally co-ordinated ringing stations and observatories have been organized in almost every country of the world: suffice it to mention the *Centre de Recherches sur les Migrations des Mammifères et des Oiseaux* (CRMMO) and the *Station Biologique de la Tour du Valat* in the Camargue, both in France; the *Station ornithologique Suisse* at Sempach in Switzerland; the numerous stations and centres in Scandinavia; the Ringing Service of the Academy of Sciences in the USSR; and the United States Wildlife Service and the Central Bird Banding Office in the United States. From the start of the ringing programme to the present, several million birds have been ringed and every year several thousand more are ringed. The store of data recorded is truly impressive and requires a great deal of co-operation and collaboration on an international scale, and the use of computers. This international collaboration with standardized methods of gathering data is already well established: in this respect the European Committee for Bird Ringing should be mentioned.

Migratory patterns
The routes taken by migratory birds are extremely varied, but they adhere to precise directions and well-defined destinations. Ornithologist H. Geyr von Schweppenburg observes that there are migrations along narrow routes in which birds follow a thin strip of territory for long distances; this applies to storks which blaze very precise trails as they migrate to and from Europe (using, in particular, the Straits of Gibraltar and the Bosphorus), cranes, and various birds of prey. More frequent are migrations along a variety of routes, in which the birds cover vast expanses of territory. The routes can be narrowed down if local conditions so require, but in general they are very wide over long distances. As they migrate, birds may be scattered along various secondary routes, depending on the environmental climatic conditions prevailing and general weather conditions. As a rule birds make use of straits, passes, watercourses, valleys, stretches of water, all features which are often used to rest in or on. It has been observed that birds manage to alter their direction to take advantage of, for

example, a valley, as has been shown by ornithologist G. Svardson in Sweden for Bramblings and Chaffinches. There is the phenomenon of coasting: assembling in coastal strips of land, and near straits, because most migratory birds, Passeriformes in particular, dislike crossing long stretches of sea. For the species of sea birds proper, matters are quite different, although species such as the Lesser Black-backed Gull (*Larus fuscus*), which starts out from the Baltic Sea, do not hesitate to fly across the entire continent of Europe to spend the winter in the Mediterranean and sometimes even in East Africa, having crossed the desert (Dorst, 1962). Instead of using passes, some migratory birds will fly over mountains at high altitude: a good example of this is given by certain geese which fly over the Himalayas at 9,000 metres. Some species of birds will fly straight across the Sahara although they could use the much less exacting Nile valley. Other species migrate along a circular route, following one half of the circle on the outward journey and the other half on the return. The Lesser Golden Plover (*Pluvialis dominica*) flies from Alaska to the Hawaiian Islands, covering 3,500 kilometres apparently without stopping. Arctic Terns (*Sterna paradisea*) nest along the coast of northern Asia, Europe and Canada, but in winter fly south, and gather in the south Atlantic, the Pacific and the Indian Ocean. Ornithologist Donald R. Griffin mentions (1965) one Arctic Tern found dead off the coast of Natal in the Indian Ocean 116 days after having been ringed in Labrador as a chick. Another Arctic Tern, ringed in western Greenland on July 18 was re-caught in Durban, in Natal, on October 30 of the same year. In just a few weeks these two young terns must have travelled a minimum of 13,680 and 15,300 kilometres respectively. Taking into account the time needed for young terns to grow they could not have left the nest until about a month after they had been ringed: this means that they must have covered an average of some 160 kilometres a day on this, their first autumn migration half way round the world.

In the migratory species the renewal of the plumage must, as a rule, coincide perfectly with the requirements of migratory movement so that all the flight feathers are in prime condition. In most migratory birds moulting takes place before migration commences, so that the birds tackle these journeys with new plumage. The moulting of the contour feathers may continue during migration, but this does not restrict the ability to fly. Various species which undergo one total moult move in such a way so that they are in areas where they can moult in peace and quiet (moulting migrations). Ornithologists Weczetic and

A flight of Bean Geese
Anser fabalis ▶

▲ Bearded Reedlings (also called Bearded Tits) *Panurus biarmicus*

▲ Black-tailed Godwits *Limosa limosa*

Tugarinov report how flocks of ducks (mallards, gadwalls, shovelers, long-tailed ducks, and widgeon), nesting in northern Eurasia, gather in about mid-July at the mouth of the river Volga from where, once moulting has occurred, they start on their migratory routes during the first two weeks in August. Coombes and Goethe report the gathering of Shelduck (*Tadorna tadorna*), large, colourful birds, again in July, in the Bay of Heligoland along the shores of Denmark, France, the British Isles and the Netherlands. Moulting migration also occurs with certain waders. The migration of the Wood Sandpiper (*Tringa glareola*), to the marshland in the Camargue has been closely studied by ornithologist Luc Hoffmann, director of the *Station Biologique de la Tour du*

HOW BIRDS LIVE

Valat. This species, which nests in northern Europe, appears in the Mediterranean between late July and early September; once arrived in the Camargue the birds shed their wing-quills and then continue their migration.

During migrations birds reach considerable altitudes and speeds. Various data have been gathered by ornithologist R. Meinertzhagen: in France migrating cranes have been

▲ Pintail *Anas acuta*

observed at 5,000 metres, Curlew Sandpipers at 3,000 metres and probably Linnets (*Carduelis cannabina*) at 3,300 metres. In Germany sightings have been made of crows at 2,500 metres, and in Iraq, swifts at 2,000 metres. At Dehra Dun in India geese have been observed at about 9,000 metres and curlews and godwits at 6,000 metres. When migrating, flight-speeds increase considerably. A swallow which flies normally at 46–51 kph reaches speeds of 54–60 kph when migrating. Starlings in Baluchistan flew at 69–78 kph, geese in Iraq at 70–80 kph, Dotterels in Britain at 72–80 kph, Whimbrels in Ireland at 64–72 kph, Razorbills in France at 78–86 kph, Yellow Wagtails in Kenya at 46–48 kph, and migratory thrushes in the United States at 27–51 kph.

German ornithologist Erwin Stresemann has calculated that a Red-backed Shrike (*Lanius collurio*) will deploy its time as follows to cover a distance of 1,000 kilometres in five days: two nights for migration, three nights for resting, and five days for feeding, thus covering 500 kilometres in a single night. The meteorological situation is extremely important during migration. Many studies about the influence of the weather on migrations have been made by Kenneth Williamson. It has been discovered that weather conditions determine periods of rest, the directness of the route taken and so on. In many species the pattern and even the routes of migration can vary considerably between the different populations of the species, and between the populations of young and adult individuals: In the case of the Grey Heron, for example, the central European populations move southwards as winter approaches, whereas the young, born that year, move northwards, in a somewhat disorderly fashion.

Birds which migrate at night, include various waterfowl (Anatidae and waders) cuckoos and various Passeriformes (Turdidae, woodland species, flycatchers). Birds which migrate by day include the birds of prey, pelicans, storks, turtle doves, swifts, swallows, various Turdidae, shrikes and certain Fringillidae (finches).

The physiological basis of migration

Migration is determined by a complex set of external (environmental) factors and internal (physiological) factors, associated with the sexual cycle of birds. Migratory birds have a receptive 'phase' which permits the emergence of the migratory impulse. This phase is caused by the annual physiological cycle of the bird and by the external environmental factors. The Germans have defined the inclination to migrate with the word *Zugdisposition*, and the emergence of the migratory impulse with the term *Zugstimmung*. During the annual cycle, in the migratory periods, the bird passes through various specific physiological conditions influenced by the endocrine glands, in particular the hypophysis. The huge amount of energy used in the migratory journey inevitably involves specific physiological adaptations, the most evident of which are fat deposits which do not occur at other times of year. These deposits are used during migration. In the phase prior to migration there is a series of physiological changes designed to facilitate the recovery and renewal of the birds' energy reserves. Thus, a series of concomitant factors determine the migratory impulse. It has been shown, particularly as a result of the experiments made by ornithologist William Rowan, that there is a concomitance between the development of the sex glands, affected by the rhythm of daylight (the photoperiod), and the migratory impulse, even if we cannot be certain that these factors are interdependent, and that one may therefore give rise to the other. Studies have been made of the associations existing between the annual cycle of the thyroid gland the emergence of the migratory phenomenon, and consequently the overall influence wielded by the hypophysis in the physiological determination of migration. Migration is an important phase in the annual cycle of a bird's life, and is closely allied with breeding and moulting and like these latter, therefore, it is regulated and affected by the endocrine system and by external environmental situations.

Orientation

How do birds know the exact direction to be taken when they migrate? How do they stay on course for days on end? How do they acquire a sense of direction during these journeys, which are often fairly lengthy? Migratory birds look for similar areas in which to winter as they do to nest. Numerous studies have been made of this subject. Experiments carried out by Gustav Kramer on starlings have shown that the sun and its movements are undoubtedly important as means of orientation and navigation for diurnal migratory species. Other experiments carried out by Sauer on various Sylviidae (woodland birds) have shown that nocturnal migratory birds are able to use the position of the stars to find their sense of direction. Alfred Schifferli writes (in Frugis *et al.*, 1971–72): 'It would seem that birds also have other means of orientation, apart from the sun and the stars. The constant direction of a wind in a given season, mountain ranges, and river systems can also help them to find and maintain the right direction, even when the sky is overcast. The experience of the older individuals assists young birds when they migrate. Lastly, there is renewed interest in the theory, once considered mistaken, of orientation based on the Earth's magnetic field'. In order to study the patterns and causes of orientation, numerous homing experiments have been carried out. Individuals are removed from the nest and taken to a place some way off: they are then released and their ability to find their way on their possible return to the nest is studied.

Finally, studies by the team working under Floriano Papi have revealed that the sense of smell is of undeniable importance in the orientation of homing pigeons.

Habitats

Due to their ability to fly, birds have colonized many types of habitat. They have adapted themselves, through morphological and physiological modifications, to inhospitable places such as the ice-bound polar regions and the arid sandy wastes of deserts. The many factors which influence and determine the presence of any species in a particular habitat have been studied in detail by ecologists. Ecology is the science which studies the relationships between living organisms and their habitats, including the inorganic world about them. This eclectic and versatile discipline which, perhaps more than any other, embraces a multitude of areas of research, is becoming a basic science for the future of mankind. Man, through ignorance, has indiscriminately destroyed his natural environment. He has plundered and altered it without taking into account the dangerous and often irreversible imbalances in the natural order which result. The outcome of man's overwhelming effect on this order, by which he himself is ruled, has aroused much interest among ecologists who are now attempting to suggest ways of minimizing damage in the future so that man's very survival is not itself endangered. Every living organism on Earth is adapted to the habitat in which it lives. This habitat is formed by the elements which surround creatures, and creatures are bound to these elements in various ways, be they air, water, land, vegetation or other creatures. The perfect interdependence among all the factors which make up an environment – the fruit of millions of years of evolution – shows that there is no single natural entity which exists 'by chance': everything has its value, its importance, its function, its relationships, and its vital niche in the harmony of the natural world. Those people who understand the environment and its overall complexities have increasingly important roles to play in an age when maintaining the balance of nature at all levels has become vital.

The ecologist Odum has drawn up the following list of levels for the organization of life (the last four are of greatest interest to the ecologist): protoplasm, cells, tissues, organs, organisms, populations, communities, ecosystems, and the biosphere. The term population has already been explained on page 11. The term community means a collection of populations of different species living in a given area and forming an organized unit. An ecosystem is a combination of the living community and the inorganic environment in a given area,

HABITATS

with well-defined general characteristics (for some ecologists an ecosystem can be defined as the 'biotope rather than the biocoenosis', biotope meaning the non-living environment and biocoenosis the living community). Lastly, the term biosphere refers to all the Earth's area (surface, underwater and in the air) which is biologically inhabitable – where some form of life is possible.

Life on Earth is made possible by the sun's rays. It is because of solar energy that plants, by means of photosynthetic processes and the use of inorganic compounds (water, mineral salts, carbon dioxide), construct organic substances in which there are large quantities of energy. Animals use the plants they feed on to form their own tissues and to produce the energy necessary for their organism to function. This flow of energy is fundamental to the structure of the various ecosystems and forms a series of food networks. In these food chains, various levels can be defined: the abiotic substances, which are the basic components of the inorganic environment; the productive level, the green plants; the consumer level, animals; and the level of decomposition, in which micro-organisms are formed which direct the food cycle back to abiotic substances. The following is a simple example of a linear food chain: a hare feeds on grass on the ground of a wood, and is subsequently killed by a Bonelli's Eagle; once the eagle is in turn dead, the remains of the hare and the eagle are decomposed into raw material by bacteria, fungi and other micro-organisms; the raw materials resulting from the decomposition are then used by plants which grow and reproduce, and offer food to other hares which, in turn, supply other eagles with meals. Nevertheless, it should be

▼ Flamingoes

remembered that in nature we do not find food chains as simple as this, but complex chains with numerous elements which also act on the same trophic or nutritional levels. To sum up: in nature, every living organism occupies its own vital space and carries out its own function. Odum, in *Fundamentals of Ecology* (1971), differentiates between the habitat of an organism (where it lives) and its ecological niche. The latter term covers not only the physical space which an organism occupies (spatial niche or habitat) but also its function within the natural system (trophic niche) and its environmental position relative, for example, to temperature, humidity, pH and soil (pluridimensional niche or hypervolume). The ecological niche depends, therefore, on what an organism does as well as the place where it lives.

The niche concept is extremely complicated and has led to the formulation of the principle of exclusion or Gause's principle, which states that there cannot be two species occupying the same identical niche (as a result of this, where there are no differences between the niche of one species and the niche of another, there is competition between them). The naturalist Robert MacArthur has compared the niches of four species of American Parulidae (wood warblers) which all breed in the same habitat (a Norway spruce forest), and observed that they build their nests in different parts of trees. The ornithologist David Lack has studied two species of cormorant (the Common or Great Cormorant, *Phalacrocorax carbo*, and the Shag, *P. aristotelis*) on the English coast. These two birds nest on the same rocks, although in different places, and fish in the same waters. The diet, however, is different: *P. carbo* catches fish in deep water on the whole; *P. aristotelis*

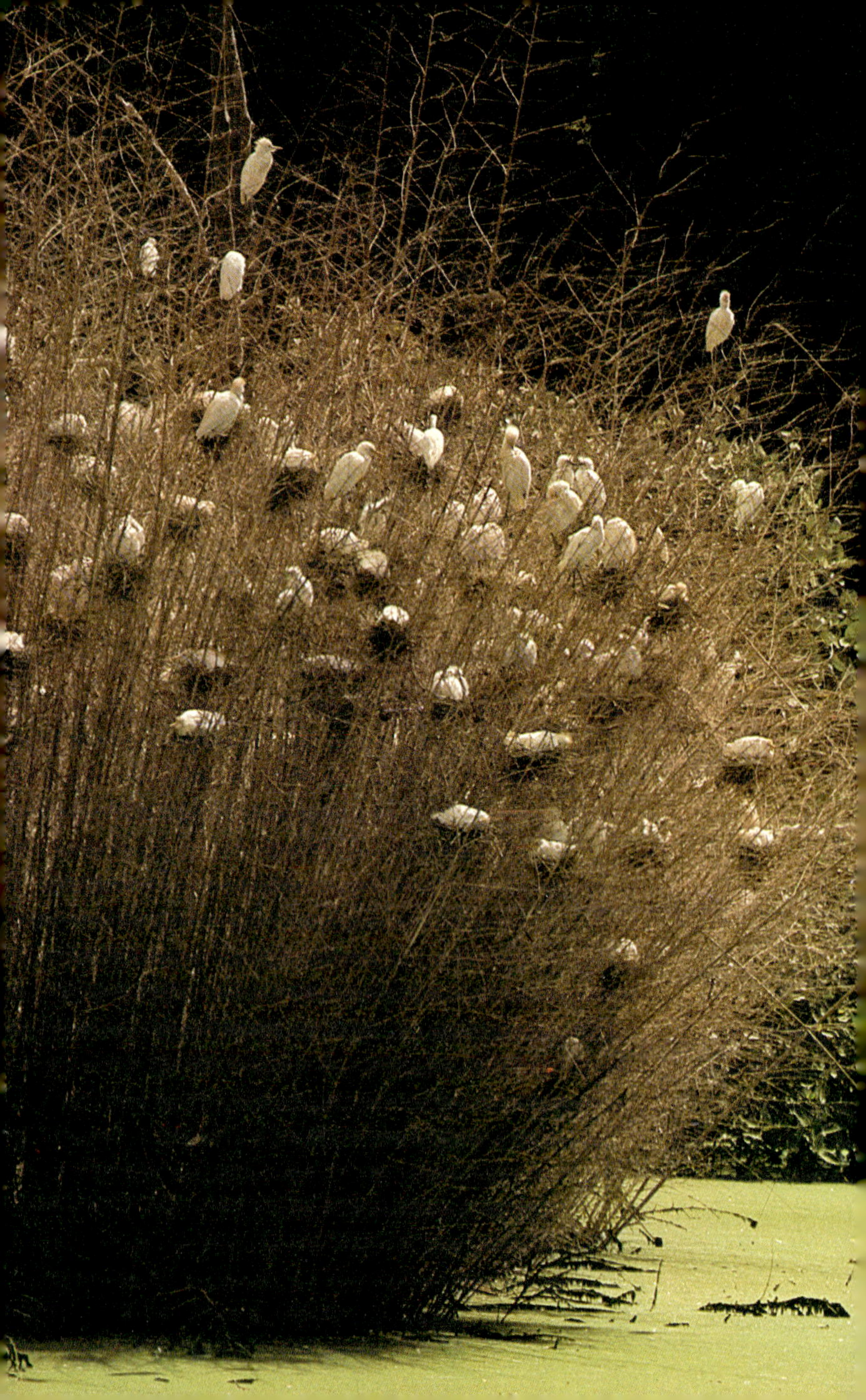

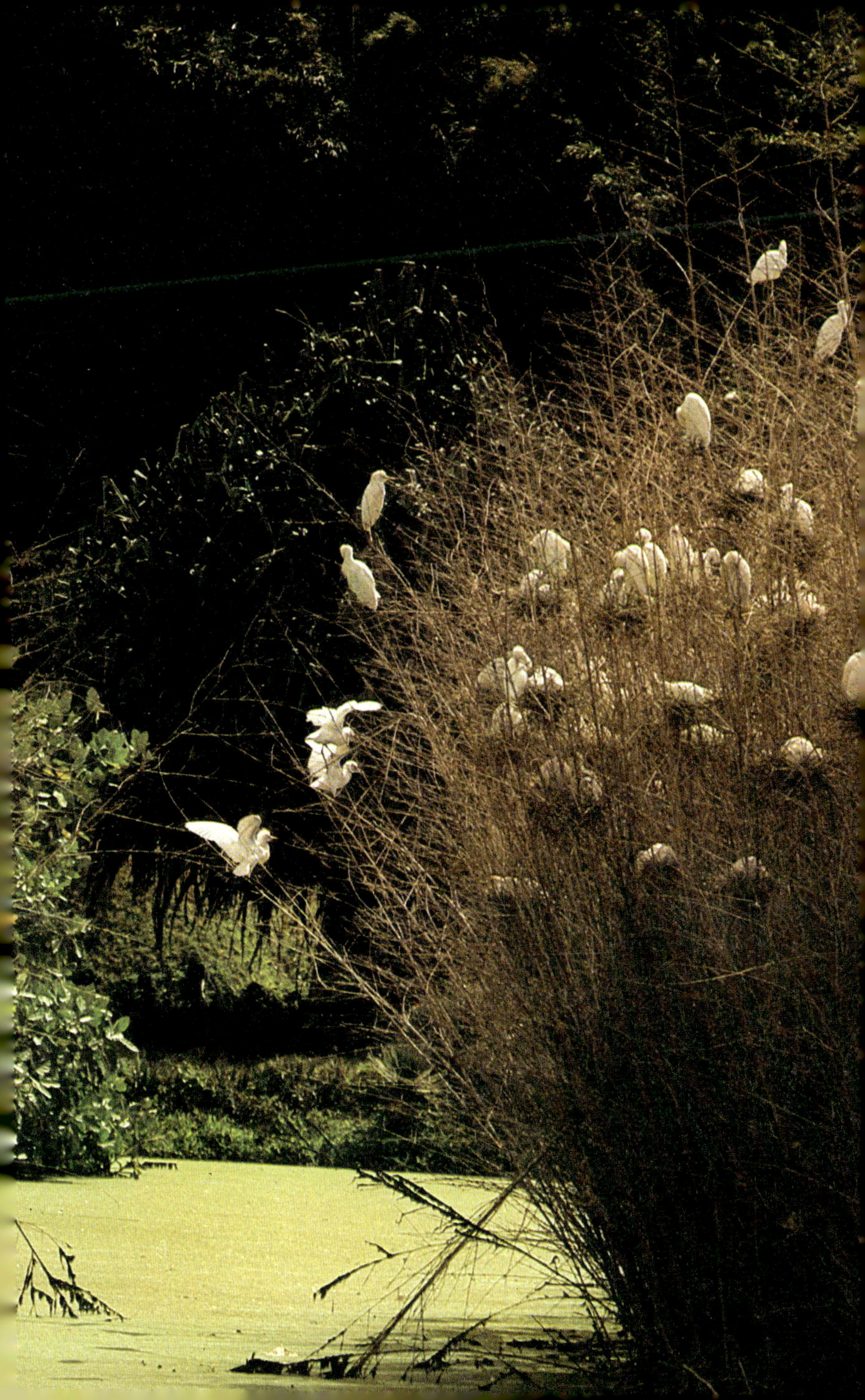

usually catches fish in surface water. Ornithologist Van Valen notes how, in birds, the length and breadth of the beak (which are obviously closely connected with the type of food) also indicate the extent of the niche. In all these cases there is no total similarity between the niches used as there is always some element of difference which makes coexistence possible. In some cases there may also be a sexual separation in the niche as in the case of the Huia, already described when discussing sexual dimorphism, and the case studied by ornithologist J. D. Ligon concerning the sexual differences in the feeding patterns of two species of woodpeckers belonging to the genus *Dendrocopus*, in which the male and the female have beaks of different sizes. Ornithologist Charles Vaurie observes how two species of nuthatches (*Sitta tephronata* and *S. neumayer*) have beaks of a very similar size in populations which are geographically separate (allopatric); in areas where these two species do coexist, on the other hand, the size differs (this evolution is known as character shift).

For an organism to survive and breed in a given environment various conditions must be met. Every organism maintains specific relations with the environment in which it lives. These relations entail different environmental parameters (from temperature and humidity conditions to diet requirements) and have different ranges of tolerance. There are species which have a broad range of tolerance in different environmental conditions, and others, conversely, which are bound to precise environmental conditions without which the survival of the species is seriously at risk. Technically, the more adaptable species are known as euryoecic (these being able to cope with different environmental conditions), and the others as stenoecic or stenecious (these being bound to one or more vital environmental factors). Species which are more versatile, and have no specific and clearly defined requirements are called ubiquitous. The prefixes steno- and eury- are widely used in ecology to indicate a greater or lesser tolerance or value in respect of certain environmental factors. When all the requirements of a species conform, its *optimum* is obtained in its own habitat (as a rule birds breed when the environmental conditions have reached an optimum level). The greater or lesser adaptability of a species to the various environmental factors, which may then limit its presence (which is why they are also known as limiting factors), represents an ecological valency.

◀ Preceding pages: herons in Madagascar

Populations and their dynamics

Populations are the basic unit of evolution (by evolution, a change is meant in the genetic constitution of populations). In nature, bird populations, like those of other animals, are fundamentally characterized by these factors: birth, death, emigration and immigration. As Wilson and Bossert observe, the rate of growth of any population derives from the

▼ A colony of Little Egrets (left) and Cattle Egrets

HABITATS

different rates at which individuals add to the population by birth or immigration, and subtract from it by death or emigration. This type of growth is called exponential: in theory, if natural populations followed it their growth would know no limits. In the natural order there are numerous factors which considerably affect the growth rate of every population, and these can be collectively defined by the term environmental resistance. This 'resistance' entails a series of mortality factors, such as disease, predation, competition for food, food requirements and their availability in the environment and so on, which, in the long term, limit the potential expansion of the population. Expansion thus follows a logistic curve, the population increasing until a limit imposed by the practical capacity of its environment is reached; this is known as the carrying capacity of the environment. Once this limit has been reached, the population becomes stabilized in a state of equilibrium. The dynamics of a population thus depend on two opposing elements: the breeding potential of

▼ Pheasant-tailed Jacana *Hydrophasianus chirurgus*

HABITATS

the species and the resistance of the environment. In the logistic growth of every population, the maximum production tolerable occurs, at a certain juncture – the maximum rate of growth of a population of a given environment. It is at this point that deductions can be made without reducing the number of individuals in a population. Such deductions, where the human activities of hunting and fishing are concerned, must be programmed and planned scientifically, special attention being paid to the demography of the population: close observation must be made of the tables of fertility and survival. The fertility tables record the average number of female offspring produced by a female at every separate age, whereas the survival tables record, for each age, the number of individuals which live, the number which die and the average number of years still to be lived. It is necessary to study the structure of a population and to calculate the net rate of reproduction, or substitution rate (the average number of females that a female produces during its lifetime) in order, eventually, to be able to make carefully planned reductions at the point of maximum tolerable production in such a way that the environmental equilibrium will not be damaged. Unfortunately, fishing and in particular hunting are far from approaching this concept of planned reductions or thinning out of populations. This problem can be discussed from the viewpoint of the breeding value of the individual, particularly a female. The answer largely depends on the age and breeding capacity of the individual.

The factors which give rise to an increase in bird populations concern the number, consistency and variation of broods (see section on nesting, p. 115), the age at which sexual maturity is attained and the longevity of individual animals. The important work carried out by David Lack (1968) revealed interesting information about the age at which sexual maturity is attained. In some Passeriformes, the age of sexual maturity is reached quite fast: in the species *Taeniopygia castanotis*, *Lagonosticta senegala* and *Lonchura striata* some individuals reach sexual maturity at the age of three months (in captivity, *T. castanotis* manages to lay eggs at just six weeks). Some Passeriformes reach sexual maturity within a year, the male House Sparrow acquires its adult plumage in its second year, and other passerines nest for the first time after two years. The Budgerigar (*Melopsittacus undulatus*) nests for the first time as young as two months, and the Little Button Quail (*Turnix sylvatica*) at about five months. Species which nest for the first time between one and two years of age include swifts, bee eaters, various ducks (some ducks nest in their third year and swans as late as the fourth year), and the Grey Heron. Various other species reach sexual maturity at a more advanced age: the male Great Bustard at four to five years, the White Stork at three to five years, the Oystercatcher at three to four years, gulls, terns and skuas at three years, penguins at three years, gannets at five years, the Ostrich at three to five years, various large birds of prey (eagles and vultures) at three to five and even six years, and albatrosses at eight to eleven years. Ornithologist José Antonio Valverde observed that in the period 1954–9 only adult Spanish imperial eagles (*Aquila heliaca adalberti*) nested in the marshes at the mouth of the river Guadalquivir. As the result of being persecuted by man, this eagle is now extremely rare, and various individuals in immature plumage have paired with adults, producing eggs and rearing young. Recent photographs show the nesting of a pair of these eagles, consisting of an adult male and an immature female.

Longevity varies greatly depending on the species and the individuals concerned, and can be calculated by the use of ringing. The bird is ringed as a nestling still nest-bound, and when it is found dead, or is killed, the date on which the ring was attached is compared with the date when the bird is found to obtain the age it has reached. Ornithologist R. Dircksen writes of a record of an Oystercatcher which was caught in 1963 at Mellum (in Germany) wearing a ring 36 years old (the average life of this bird is about ten years). Some species are increasing their distribution area: this is the case with the Cattle Egret (*Bubulcus ibis*) which has invaded the American continent since the establishment of a meagre group in Venezuela; and with the Collared Dove (*Streptopelia decaocto*) which is spreading widely towards the west. Friedrich Goethe writes (in Grzimek, 1972): 'Since 1920 the populations of some species of Laridae, in particular the Herring Gull, in many areas in the Northern Hemisphere have increased at an explosive rate. In 1906 along the German shores of the North Sea there were 3,000 pairs of herring gulls capable of breeding, but after 30 years there were more than 20,000. Today, in this area, there are about 40,000 gulls of this species. There has been a similar increase on the coasts of Holland, the British Isles, Sweden and Finland. Likewise along the Atlantic coast of the United States the population of Herring Gulls has reached huge proportions: in 1920 on the coast of Massachussets there were just a few pairs; 40 years later, there were more than 30,000.'

Maximum life span of certain species
(calculated with the help of ringing methods)

Species	Maximum Age
Pelican	52 years
Cormorant	19 years 7 months
Fulmar	22 years
Gannet	12 years 11 months
Andean Condor	52 years
Bateleur Eagle	55 years
Kestrel	14 years 5 months
Golden Eagle	20 years
Grey Heron	18 years
Coot	19 years
Curlew	31 years
Redshank	14 years 5 months
Knot	13 years
Dunlin	11 years 11 months
Puffin	15 years 9 months
Common Tern	25 years
Herring Gull	16 years 1 month
White Stork	19 years
Mallard	20 years
Wood Pigeon	15 years 11 months
Barn Owl	10 years
Cuckoo	4 years
Swift	21 years
Raven	12 years 5 months
Great Tit	7 years
Wren	4 years 11 months
Blackbird	11 years
Robin	8 years 4 months
Blackcap	6 years 1 month
Starling	13 years
House Sparrow	23 years

Population reduction is caused by predation, physical environmental factors, competition, disease, accidents, the quantity of food available and so on. Although, like the other factors, predation is part of the natural environmental control, it is one of the major factors in population reduction. Despite the numerous devices used for protection against predators (such as camouflaging nests, the mimetism of the eggs, and the nestlings, displays designed to distract attention, alarm calls to warn the group of imminent danger) the effects of predation are always felt by a population. There are cases of cannibalism, especially among birds of prey, where incubation begins once the first egg is laid, which means that the first born is older than the later nestlings and will, in the event of a food shortage, devour its brothers and sisters. The role of predators with regard to populations preyed upon is essential for the equilibrium of the environment. Predators control any potential population expansion, generally catching weak, sick or genetically defective members, thus contributing to the general 'healthiness' of the population subject to predation. The relation between predator and prey is interdependent, since the population of predators is similarly controlled by the availability of food offered by the population preyed upon. The killing of a predator by man – and in the nutritional system predators are at the top of the food chain – tends to break the traditional and essential sequence of events in the food chain. But as zoologists Cockrum and McCauley have rightly pointed out, there is probably no single ecological community which has not been affected by man: nowadays not even deserts, tropical jungles and the depths of the sea are immune from the influence of modern civilization. Other factors which cause population decreases are the physical environmental factors, which occur in the form of waves of extreme cold, storms, heavy rain and gales, and other obviously adverse climatic conditions. Such conditions cause serious losses in migratory groups, as well as in numerous non-migratory or hibernating groups. During the cold winters of 1946–7, 1956–7 and 1962–3, the numbers of many species of birds were drastically reduced.

Similarly, disease and parasites, both internal and external, cause considerable losses. Further competition, involving choice of territory, precise nesting sites and so on, limits the occupation of a given environment by too many birds. We find accidental causes, such as a broken wing or leg, and these also affect the extent of a population's losses. A population can be compared with an individual, and it is possible to analyse its

HABITATS

metabolism, which is linked to that of the ecosystem. Some experiments have shown that if the body of an animal is completely burnt in a calorimetric or heat-measuring bomb in such a way that the energy released can be closely analysed, in general it can be seen that the animal produces between five and seven kilocalories for every net gram of ashes – for every gram of its body-weight the animal can develop, by combustion, enough energy to heat 5–7 litres of water to 1°C. In this respect there are no major differences between the various animal species, whereas plants are more variable and contain less energy. One form of energy supply used by an organism occurs by means of predation or the decomposition of another organism. In an ecosystem, the flow of energy via

▼ A flock of Adelie Penguins *Pygoscelis adeliae*

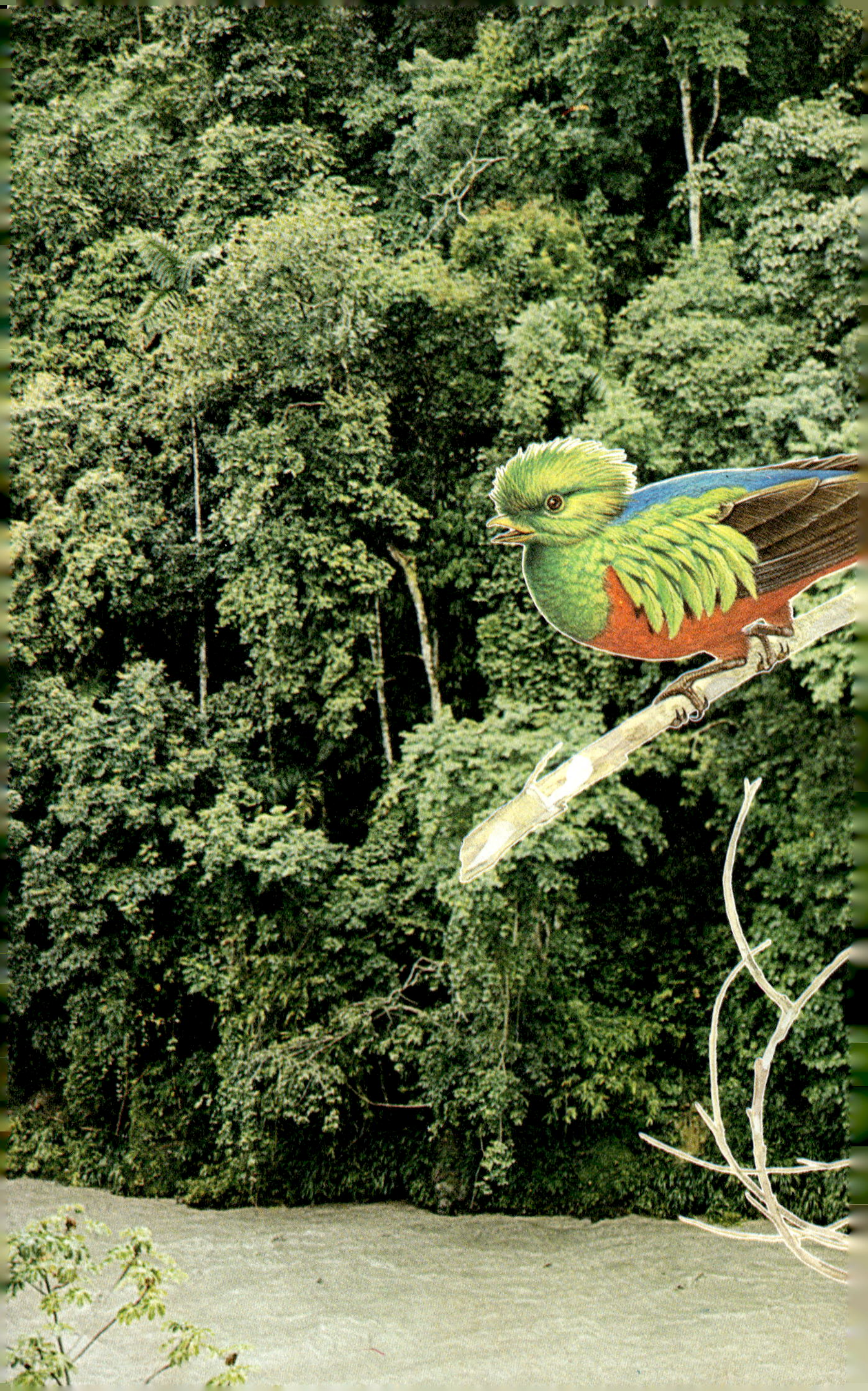

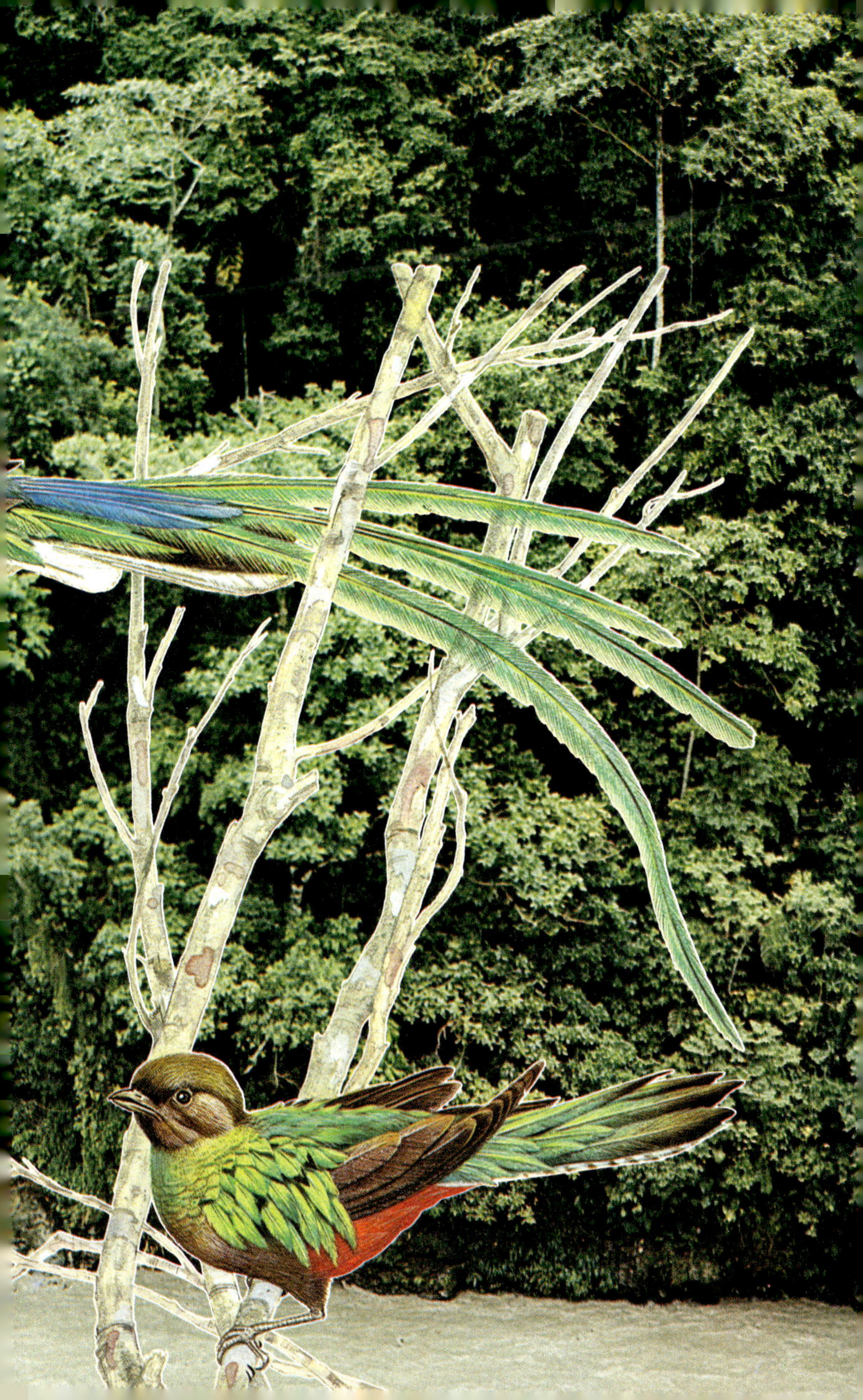

HABITATS

the various food chains is divided into three forms: production (the formation of new tissue, the development process reproduction and accumulation of energy-rich reserves), exportation (the emigration of organisms or the passive conveyance of various organic matter outside the ecosystem by means of natural agents) and respiration (loss by respiration of the ecosystem). Only a small amount of energy is transferred from one trophic level to another. A typical aspect of the dynamics of populations is cyclic fluctuation. This is concerned with species which are particularly dependent on a certain type of diet and food which, when absent, causes considerable fluctuations in the population. These fluctuations are repeated at certain intervals, hence the term cyclic. Such fluctuations occur with the Siberian Nutcracker (*Nucifraga caryocatactes macrorhynchus*), which feeds in particular on the pine-seeds of the Siberian pine (*Pinus cembra sibirica*), the Bohemian Waxwing (*Bombycilla garrulus*), which feeds in particular on the fruit of the rowan (mountain ash – *Sorbus aucuparia*), and the Crossbill (*Loxia curvirostra*), which eats the seeds of conifers, and of the Norway spruce (*Picea excelsa*) more specifically. In periods when their major source of food falls short (because of climatic conditions for example), these species journey considerable distances to other parts in search of food, and these movements can sometimes assume the proportion of full-scale invasions.

The study of population dynamics has led to the analysis and elaboration of research techniques to assess the density and number of birds in various habitats and environments by means, for example, of counts, censuses and regional mapping. It has thus also been possible to analyse density variations of populations in given habitats at different times of year. The importance of these studies lies in the information they yield about habitats and populations and how to manage them, for example, in relation to hunting. Research of this type enables us to know about the structure of populations, calculate the biomass (the overall number of individuals living in a specific environmental area), the energy balance of the habitat, and the movement of energy to the different rungs on the food ladder.

The zoogeographic regions

The distribution of the animal species on Earth is the outcome of a complex series of processes. Changes which have occurred

◄ Preceding pages: Quetzals, male (left) and female

HABITATS

in the climate, in general environmental situations, the arrangement of the land masses (continental drift) and so on have all contributed to the present-day distribution of animal and vegetable species. Over the various geological eras and periods, the Earth's surface has seen major and minor changes. The seas have spread, submerging land, and then shrunk back, and the land has re-emerged. In some periods (the glaciations) the polar ice-caps have advanced and then retreated, causing, among other things, the formation of valleys. The Continental land masses have shifted and merged, and in some mountain ranges have thrust their way upwards while others have been levelled by erosion. Barriers of various types, such as mountains, seas, deserts, and climatic and environmental differences have conditioned the diffusion and distribution of the animal species. By analysing this distribution, naturalists have helped to provide evidence confirming the theory of continental drift formulated by Wegener.

The continents are joined to the rock on the ocean bed, and these in turn rest on the Earth's mantle. The mantle gives rise to new masses which form vast 'plates', and when these shift they drag the continents with them. The contact between two continental masses causes the formation of mountain chains (the Himalayas, for example, from the 'collision' between Asia and India). By analysing the current forms of the continents, it can be seen how they fit together. The original union of the continents in the distant past is confirmed by a great deal of evidence: rocks, for example, of the same type, occur at the

▼ Oystercatchers *Haematopus ostralegus*

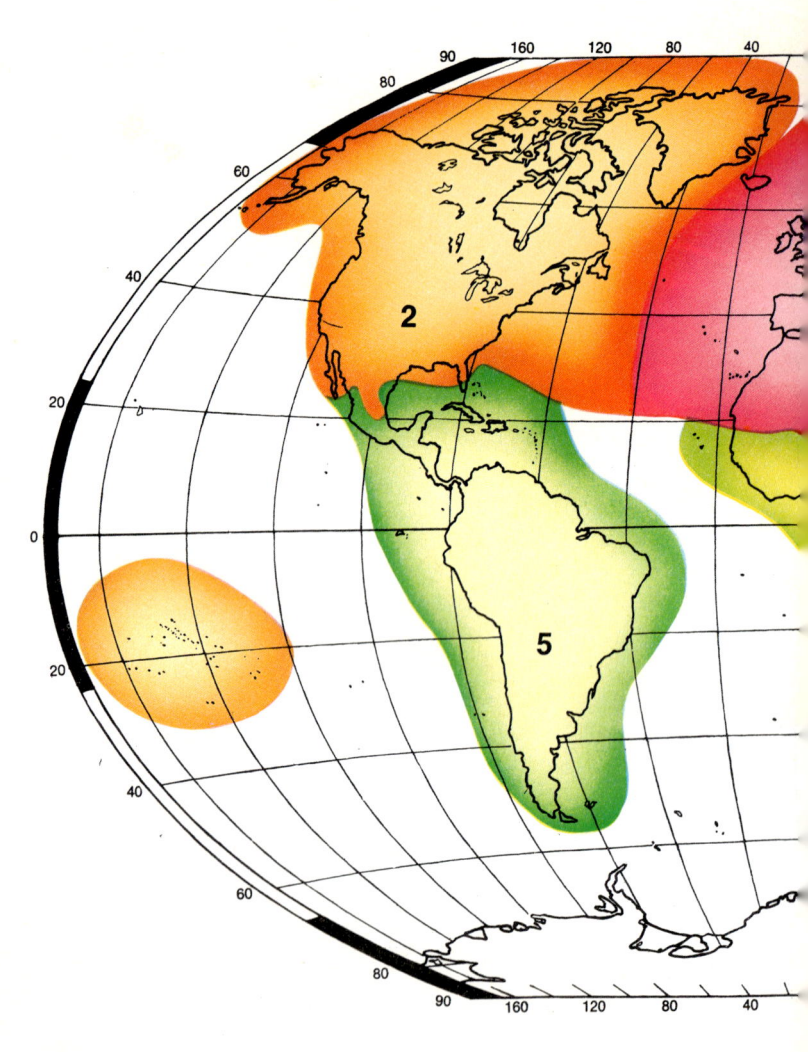

The zoogeographic regions

1. Palaearctic region
2. Nearctic region
3. Oriental region
4. Ethiopian region
5. Neotropical region
6. Australasian region

199

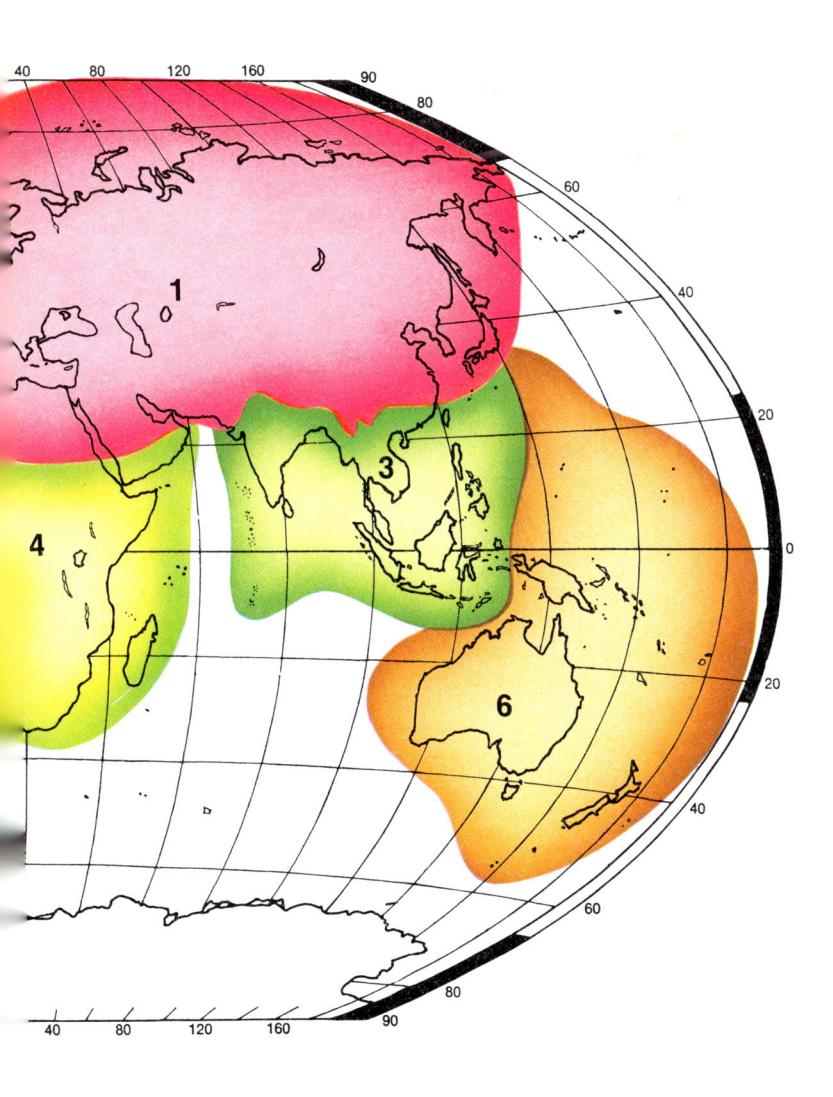

HABITATS

extremities of continents thousands of miles apart. The study of the phenomenon of continental drift has helped considerably to explain the distribution of living beings on Earth, their evolution and their history. The common denominators of the faunas of huge continental areas has made it possible to divide the planet into zoogeographic regions. An initial classification of this type was made by Sclater in 1858, and subsequently improved by the naturalist Alfred Russel Wallace. This division into zoogeographic zones helps to group the very varied distribution of the Earth's fauna. The regions are as follows (see map pp. 198–9):
(1) Palaearctic, covering Europe, North Africa and northern Asia; (2) Nearctic, covering North America (some zoologists group these sub-regions together under the term Holarctic); (3) Oriental, covering tropical Asia and western Indonesia; (4) Ethiopian, covering Africa south of the Sahara (there is a further Malagasy sub-region, covering Madagascar); (5) Neotropical, covering Central and South America (with the Antarctic sub-region, which is often considered as a separate entity); (6) Australasian, covering eastern Indonesia, Australia, Polynesia and New Zealand (the latter often being given its own New Zealand sub-region).

In the Holarctic region, various groups of bird appeared which then spread into other regions: pheasants, cranes, owls, small owls, tawny owls, barn owls, flycatchers, shrikes, finches, tits, tree creepers, nuthatches, crows, waxwings, ouzels, American vultures (and probably gulls, terns, skuas, sandpipers and various waders). Five families occur in this region only: the Gaviidae (divers), Tetraonidae (grouse), Phalaropodidae (phalaropes), Alcidae (puffins, razorbills, guillemots), and Prunellidae (hedge sparrows and accentors). The Ethiopian region hosts many groups, some typical of the region such as the Sagittariidae (secretary birds), Struthionidae (ostriches), Viduidae (widowbirds), Coliidae (mousebirds), Balaenicipitidae (Shoebill), and Scopidae (the Hammerhead). In the Neotropical region we find other typical groups such as the Opisthocomidae (hoatzins), Cariamidae (seriemas), Eurypigidae (the Sunbittern), Steatornithidae (the Oilbird), Rhamphastidae (toucans), Rheidae (rheas) and numerous others. The Australasian region has fewer groups, which include the Dromiceiidae (emus), Casuariidae (cassowaries), Menuridae (lyrebirds), Paradiseidae (birds of paradise) and Ptilonorhynchidae (bowerbirds). In the Oriental region there is one indigenous family, the Irenidae (fairy bluebirds); many others have also spread to adjacent regions.

Habitats

There are various types of habitat on Earth caused essentially by climatic variations. The climate is affected by the action of the sun's rays on the continents, oceans and atmosphere, and changes as a result of the Earth's daily rotation on its own axis, and its annual orbit round the sun. The heating of the Earth by the sun's rays is regulated by the winds, which also affect the ocean currents. Winds and currents are both, obviously, affected by the Earth's rotation, and together with the sun's rays are responsible for the distribution of humidity.

This overall set of factors interacts with specific local conditions such as altitude and type of soil, determining the different climates. However, the action of the sun's rays is fundamental – sunlight supplies plants with the energy

▼ Great Cormorant *Phalacrocorax carbo*

▼ Kingfisher *Alcedo atthis*

HABITATS

necessary for photosynthesis, the process whereby they transform water and carbon dioxide into complex organic substances. Vegetation is extremely important for animal life, and the type of vegetation in a given zone is determined by precise climatic and edaphic (soil) environmental characteristics (the latter are related to the structure of the ground). Environmental factors which determine the type of vegetation in a specific zone include, in particular, light (its intensity, composition, and daily and annual distribution, which vary greatly depending on altitude, latitude, absorption in air or water and so on); temperature; water content of the soil and evaporation conditions; carbon dioxide and oxygen content of the air, soil, and, in the case of aquatic plants, water; and the nutritive substances of the soil. Abiotic mechanical factors (such as storms, snow, and movements of soil and water) are important as are biotic factors such as wind, water and animals involved in the pollination and diffusion of seeds and vegetable and animal parasites.

In order to make an analysis of the environmental sub-divisions a distinction is made between large climatic

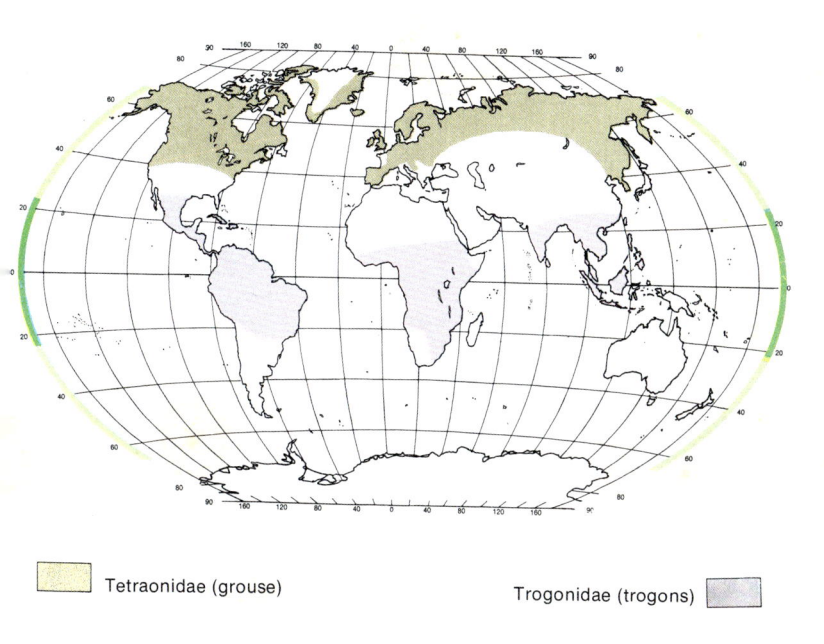

Tetraonidae (grouse)

Trogonidae (trogons)

Honeycreepers (Drepanididae, Hawaii)

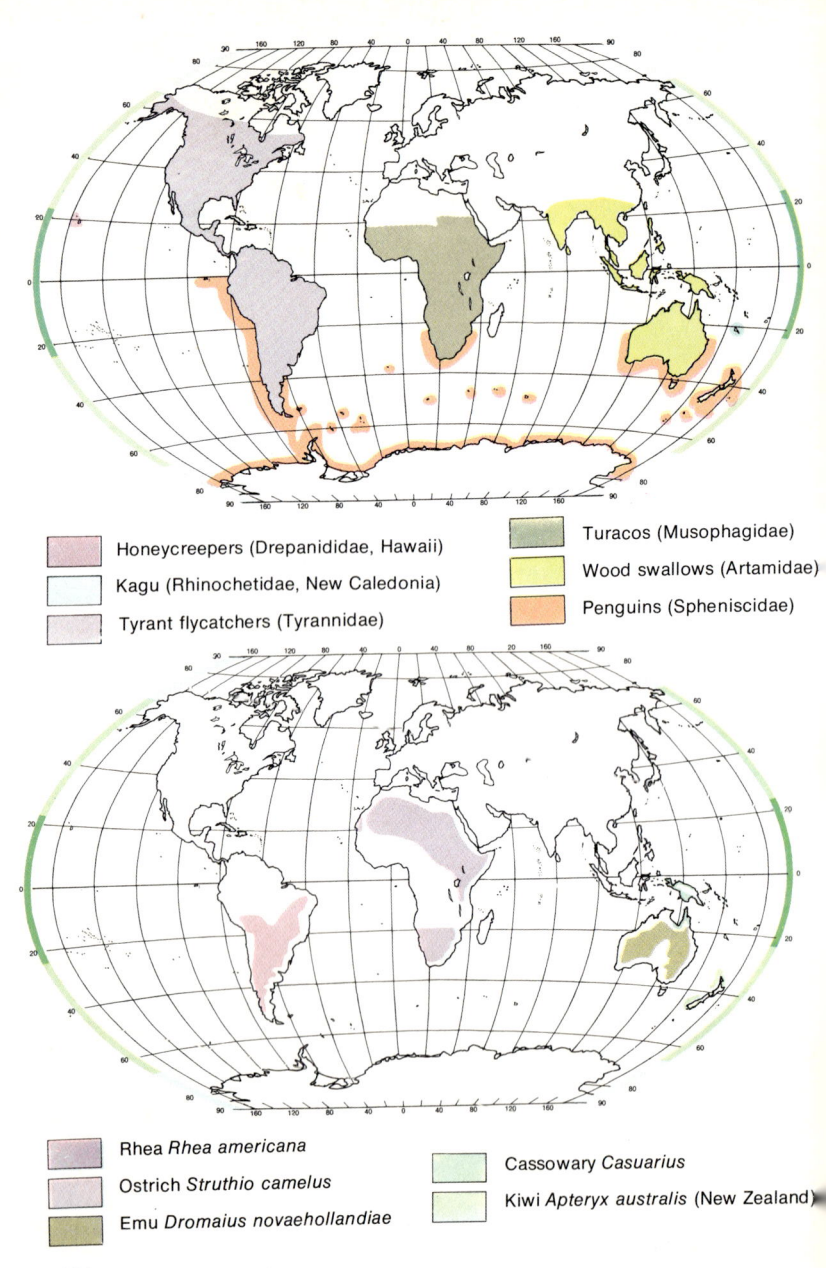

Kagu (Rhinochetidae, New Caledonia)

Tyrant flycatchers (Tyrannidae)

Turacos (Musophagidae)

Wood swallows (Artamidae)

Penguins (Spheniscidae)

Rhea *Rhea americana*

Ostrich *Struthio camelus*

Emu *Dromaius novaehollandiae*

Cassowary *Casuarius*

Kiwi *Apteryx australis* (New Zealand)

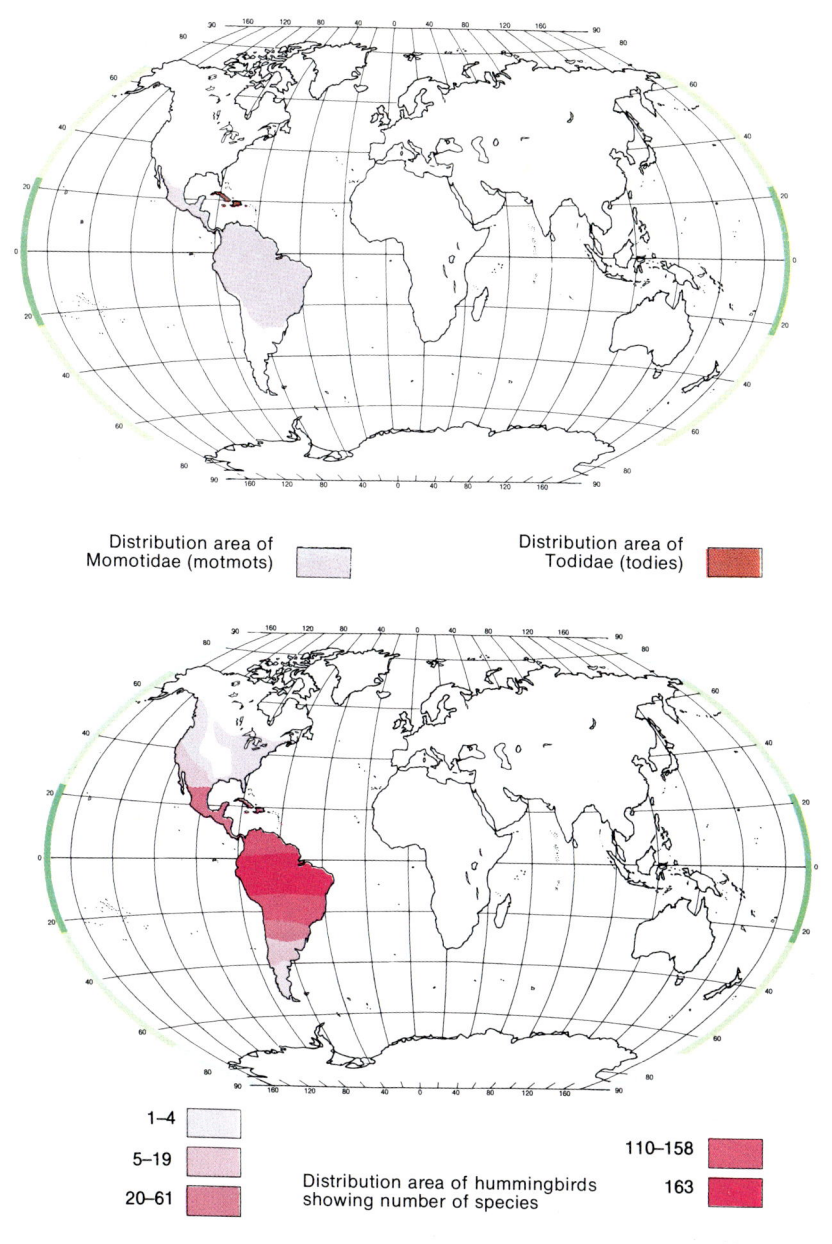

Distribution area of Momotidae (motmots)

Distribution area of Todidae (todies)

1–4
5–19
20–61
110–158
163

Distribution area of hummingbirds showing number of species

205

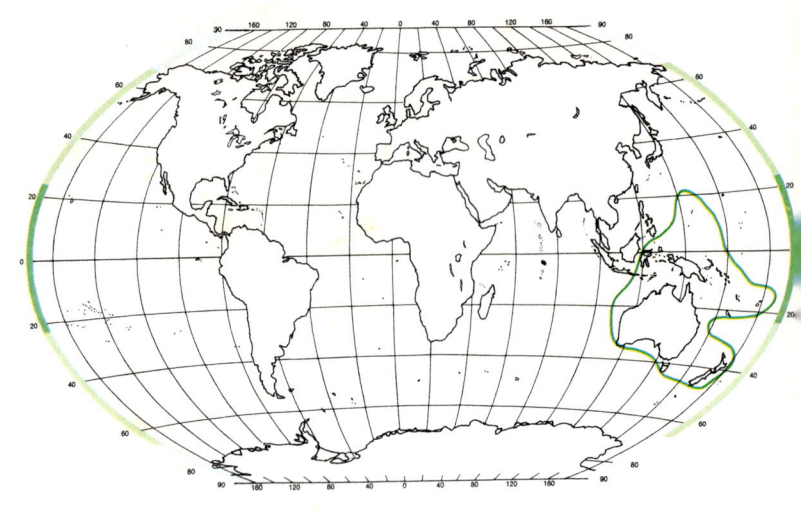

▲ Distribution area of Meliphagidae (honeyeaters)

zones, each one characterized by specific climatic features, and thus by specific vegetation and fauna. There are ten environmental divisions: the polar regions (ice and tundra);

▼ Distribution area of Psittaciformes (parrots)

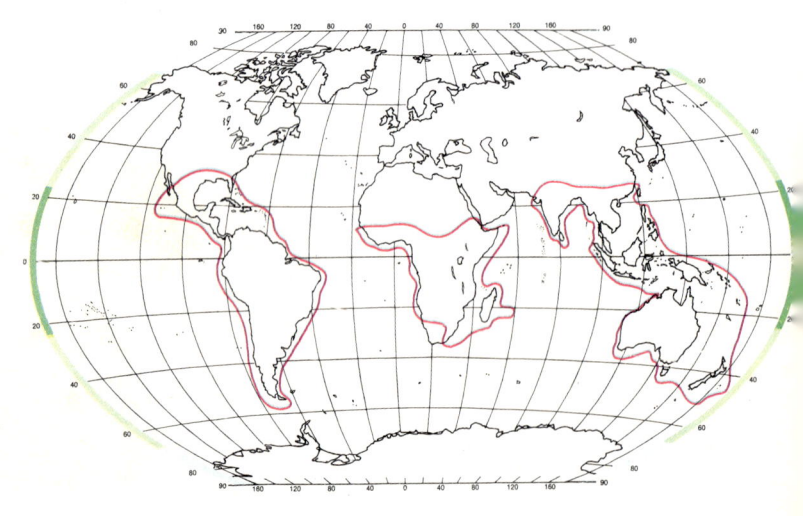

coniferous forest (taiga); temperate forest; grassland (or prairie); deserts; tropical forest; mountains; oceanic islands; continental waters; and seas. In a book about birds and their habitats Jean Dorst analyses the world's avifauna by sub-dividing it into the following environments: sea, polar environment, coastal zones, continental waters, temperate forests, deserts, tropical savannah, humid tropical forests, high mountain zones and islands. Odum lists the following main ecosystems: seas, estuaries and coastal regions, streams and rivers, lakes and ponds, freshwater marshland, deserts, tundra, grassland and forests. Yet another authority, on the other hand, lists the following: the polar regions (tundra), mountains, forests, herbaceous areas (steppe and savannah) and deserts as land-based communities; the sea and its specific sub-divisions as marine communities; and running and stagnant water as freshwater communities. In order to give a brief description of the various habitats and their typical avifauna, the first classification of ten major climatic zones is used here.

The polar regions
The term 'polar regions' embraces both the polar regions proper, where the surface is permanently covered with ice or snow and where the average temperatures, even in summer, are just a few degrees above zero, and the sub-polar regions consisting of rocks and tundra (expanses covered by low vegetation consisting of lichens, mosses, grasses and bushes), bordering on the coniferous forests. The Arctic and Antarctic regions are the central nuclei of this huge climatic zone. As far as temperature is concerned, the limits of both polar regions can be drawn along an imaginary line which links zones where the average temperature in the hottest month is about 10°C. The Arctic has a central nucleus of sea and frozen land of about 14 million square kilometres, including the North Pole, much of Alaska and northern Canada, the coastal regions of Siberia, northern Scandinavia and Greenland. The Antarctic continent, centred around the South Pole, covers all the surrounding sea-enclosed land area. Here lies 95 per cent of the world's permanent ice, which can reach a thickness of up to 3,500 metres. Living conditions in these areas are fairly hard. The sun's rays rarely reach the Poles and a high percentage of them are reflected by the snow and ice. In these areas, day and night both last for six months. The layer of vegetation on the

Overleaf: a colony of gannets ▶

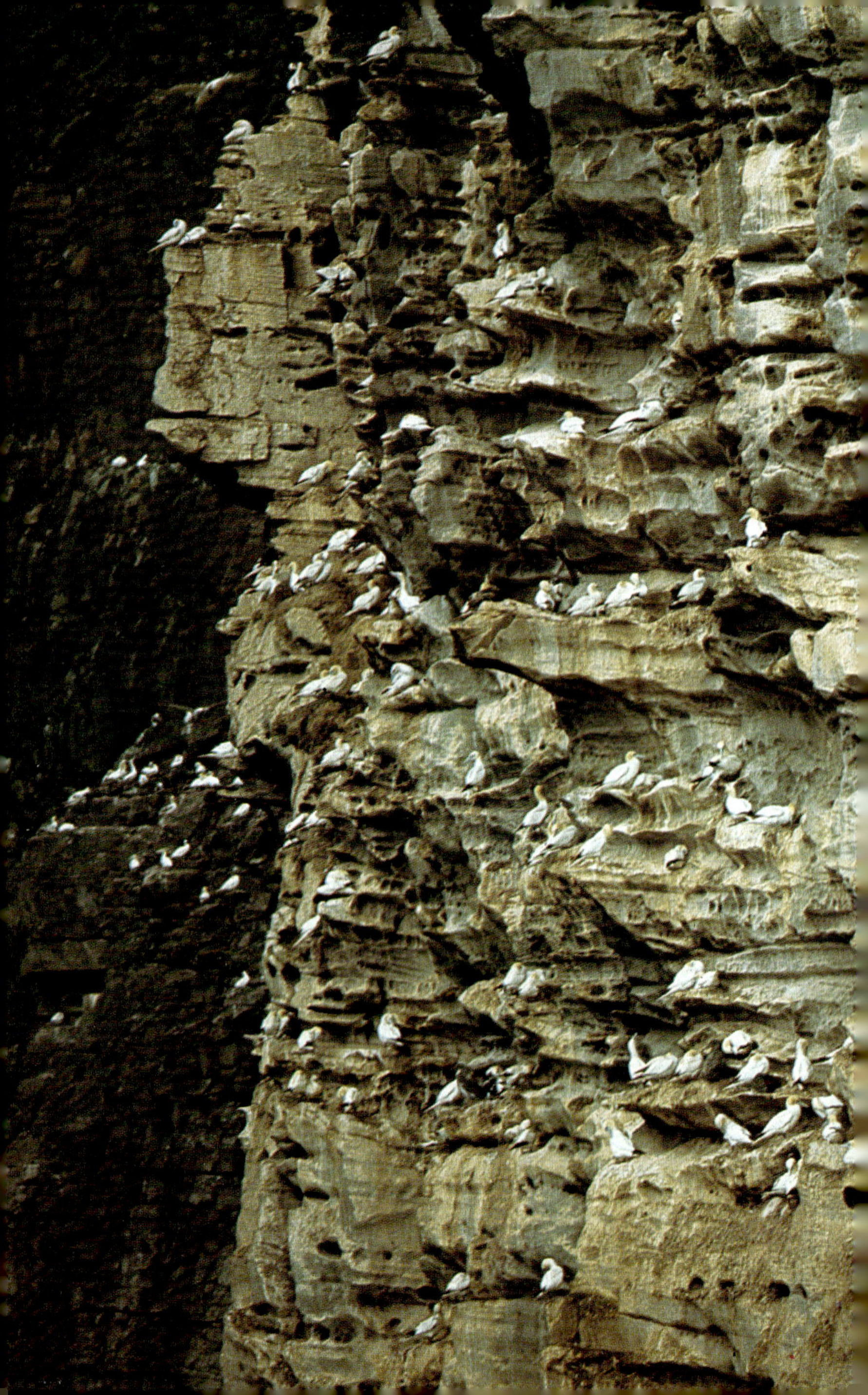

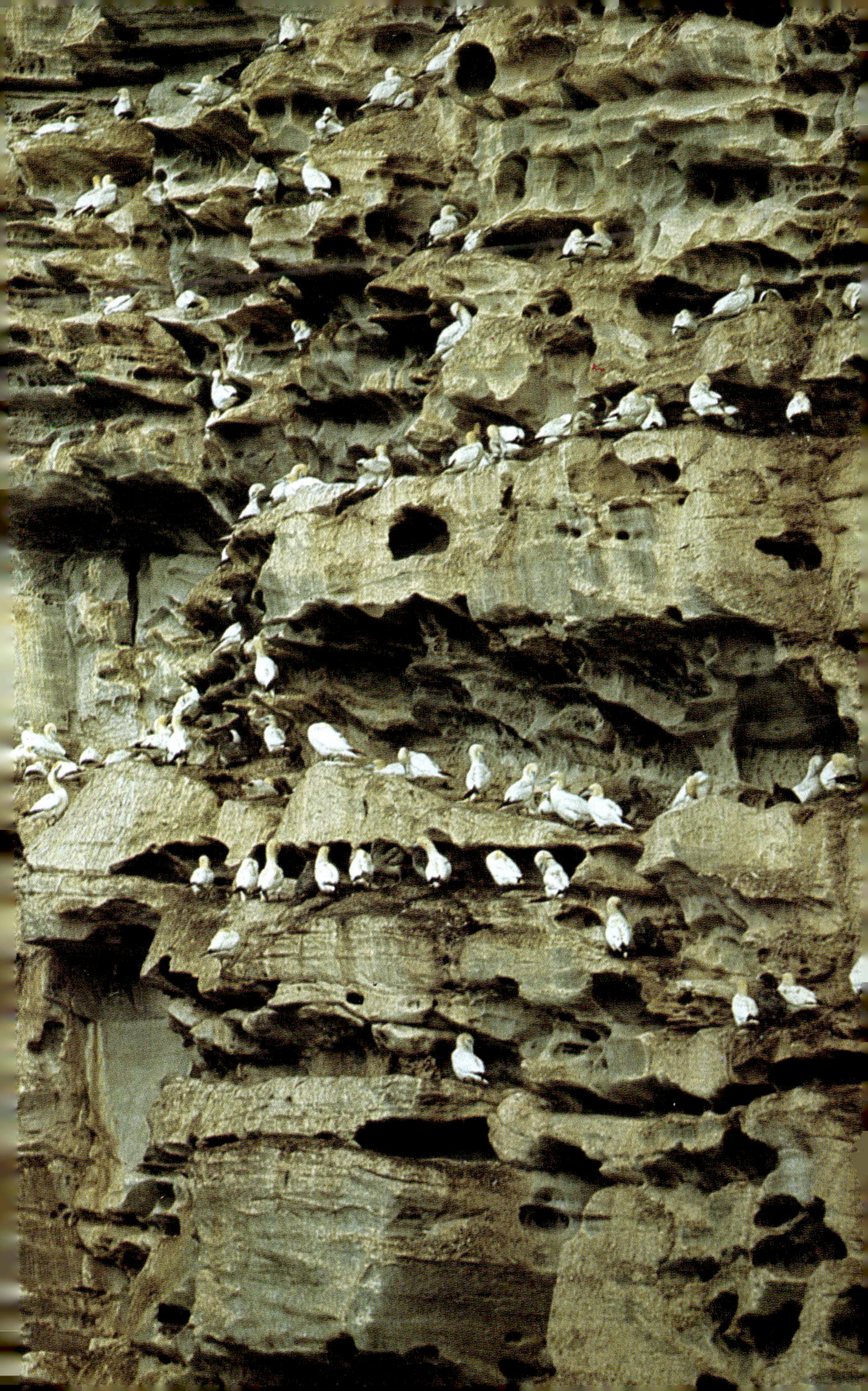

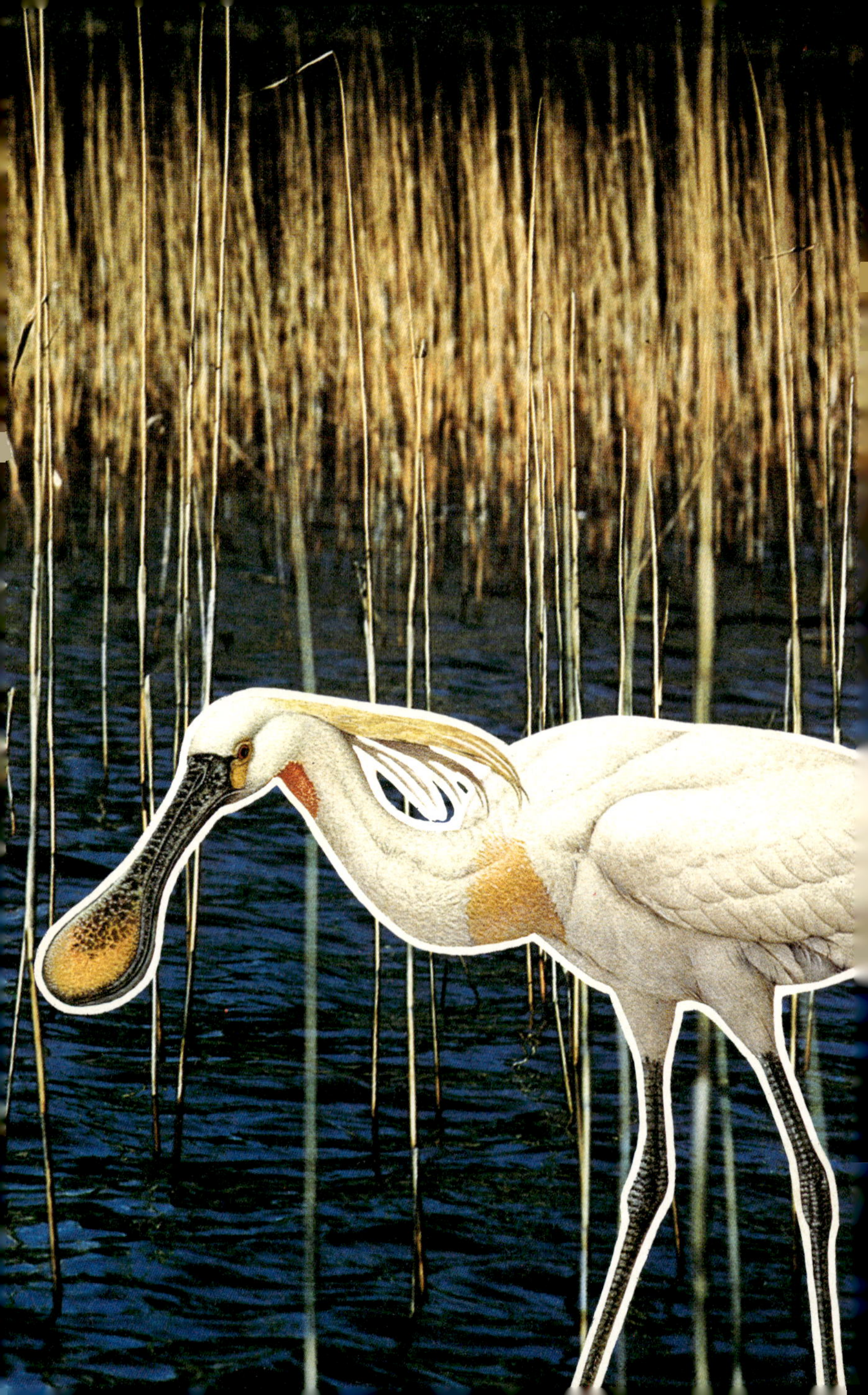

land is buried by snow for long winter periods; the marine phytoplankton and invertebrates (especially crustaceans which form the 'krill') are the main sources of food, along with fishes, for the few animals living here.

In the actual polar regions there are areas which are practically devoid of life. This habitat hosts few birds; most birds are found in the Arctic tundra, and not in the polar regions proper. Many appear only in spring and summer for breeding, and migrate when environmental conditions worsen. Typical birds found in the polar regions are the Antarctic penguins, which are perfectly adapted to this environment. They extend from the ice-floes of Antarctica and the neighbouring islands to the southern coastal zones of South America, Africa and Australia, and one species (*Spheniscus mendiculus*) even occurs in the Galapagos Islands, on the Equator. The species distributed in the coldest areas, in the continent of Antarctica, belong to the genus *Pygoscelis* (*P. adeliae*, *P. papua* and *P. antarctica*), and the Emperor Penguin (*Aptenodytes forsteri*). Various other birds manage to survive in the cold polar habitat too: the Snow Petrel (*Pagodroma nivea*) and the Antarctic Petrel (*Thalassoica antartica*) are perhaps the 'coolest' of all, followed by the Cape Pigeon or Pintado Petrel (*Daption capenses*), the Southern Fulmar or Silver Petrel (*Fulmarus glacialoides*), Wilson's Petrel (*Oceanites oceanicus*), the Giant Petrel (*Macronectes giganteus*) and the skuas. In the Arctic tundra, in summer,

▼ Barred Button Quail *Turnix suscitator*

▼ Plains Wanderer *Pedionomus torquatus*

◀ Spoonbill *Platalea leucorodia*

there is a low layer of vegetation which supplies numerous herbivorous animals with food, such as lemmings, hares and other rodents which are in turn preyed upon by the Snowy Owl, skuas, the Gyrfalcon and so on. In the Arctic region many birds nest in the sub-polar regions, in particular divers, various Anatidae like the Barnacle Goose (*Branta leucopsis*), the Brent Goose (*Branta bernicla*), the King Eider (*Somateria spectabilis*), and various waders. Some even manage to winter here too, such as the Willow Ptarmigan (*Lagopus lagopus*) and Gyrfalcon (*Falco rusticolus*).

The coniferous forest

The climatic belt in which the coniferous forest thrives extends for more than 12,000 kilometres from Norway to the Kamchatka peninsula, and from Alaska to Labrador. The coniferous forest consists mainly of firs, birch and pines, the forest floor being covered with needle-shaped leaves. The soil which supports the forest (called *podzol* from the Russian word for ash) has a low mineral content because of the amount of water which fails to evaporate because of the low temperature. In this region are lakes, marshes, stagnant water and mountain ranges. Conifers are an important food source for birds – seeds, shoots and the summer insects – and provide them with shelter and nesting places. Basic characteristics of this climatic belt include low precipitation (which on average does not exceed 500 mm a year), low temperature (which can often drop to $-40°C$ in winter), and aridity of the soil. Many bird species in this environment are migratory, for example, grouse, crossbills, nutcrackers, certain woodpeckers, certain tits, certain nocturnal birds of prey, and various Passeriformes like the Brambling and the Firecrest.

The temperate forest

Temperate forests extend below the coniferous forests in zones where the climate is temperate and, depending on the specific climatic conditions, the vegetation takes on various forms: maquis and garrigue, typical of the Mediterranean, the chaparral in California and Mexico, and the mallee scrub in Australia.

In the temperate zones there are no sharp climatic differences between the summer and winter and the rainfall averages out at 750–1,000 mm a year.

Many species of birds nest or winter in the temperate zones, and various others pass through when migrating. The range of birds living in this manner is quite extensive.

HABITATS

Grassland
Forest and desert are separated by grassland: it constitutes a climatic belt where dry and humid climates collide. Drought is a permanent threat. In areas where rainfall is too low, grassland or prairie reigns supreme; in areas where it is more plentiful there is a transitional landscape from grassland to forest. Where rain is very rare we find a gradual transition from grassland to shrub-covered steppe and desert. We can make a distinction between temperate grassland (the steppes of Eurasia, the prairies of North America, the pampas of South America, the South African veld and the Australian lowlands) and tropical grassland or savannah. In the latter, temperatures are relatively high all year round, rain falls only in summer and tough grasses thrive, growing to three metres in height, amidst trees and bushes which are particularly drought-resistant (the African, Indian and northern Australian savannah, and the

▼ Osprey *Pandion Haliaetus*

HABITATS

llanos and campos of South America). Typical birds are the ratites (or runners) like the Ostrich and the rheas, certain bustards, guineafowl, certain Bucerotidae (hornbills), prairie fowl, various Passeriformes (weaverbirds, widowbirds, shrikes), Pteroclidae (sandgrouse), Megapodiidae, the Secretary Bird and certain vultures.

Deserts
The climatic belt which embraces the deserts is hallmarked by the absence of water and the sharp temperature fluctuations. In arid areas, there are high daytime temperatures and low

▼ Shoebill *Balaeniceps rex*

▼ Nest of a Spotted Sandgrouse *Pterocles senegallus*

▲ Cream-coloured Courser, *Cursorius cursor*, with an egg.

temperatures at night. In addition rainfall is very scarce, less than 250 mm a year. It is often windy and this feature accentuates the aridity. As a result of these climatic conditions, vegetation is sparse, consisting of tough plants specially adapted to life in these arid areas. There is a distinctive avifauna of species which are specialized for survival in these regions: sand grouse, roadrunners, stone-curlews, burrowing owls, the common poorwill and a few species of woodpecker.

The tropical forest
Tropical forests run along the equatorial belt. They have plenty of rain throughout the year, and very high temperatures and humidity. Near the Equator annual average precipitation may reach four metres, and the average annual temperature is around 25°C. The vegetation is luxuriant, offering good refuge to a large variety of birds. It consists of a grassy stratum, a shrub stratum and a stratum of trees which often reach considerable heights. These forests constitute an extremely important oxygen 'lung' for the rest of the world because of the variety and quantity of plants in them and their constant photosynthetic action. Unfortunately, man is dangerously destroying these tropical forests, creating precarious situations, some of them irreversible, endangering the human race. The World Wildlife Fund declared 1976 a year of fundraising and international propaganda aimed at adequately protecting this priceless legacy. Tropical forests also exist in high mountainous zones, where the height of the trees diminishes with altitude. Numerous species of birds live in these forests: parrots, hummingbirds, birds of paradise, tanagers, cotingas, Dendrocolaptidae (woodcreepers) and Pittidae (pittas).

Mountains
Mountains have a fairly cold climate (as the altitude increases the temperature drops by about one degree every 150 metres) and above 4,500 metres oxygen becomes scarce. Mountains form barriers to wind circulation, and they create vortices which cause local variations in temperature and rainfall. Mountains may offer obstacles to or refuge for the distribution of animal species. The species which live in these zones include, the Alpine Accentor, snow finches, choughs, nuthatches, condors and the Golden Eagle.

Oceanic islands
Oceanic islands form extremely interesting habitats. There are two types: oceanic islands proper and continental islands. The

former originate as the result of submarine volcanic eruptions, which means that they have never previously been linked to a continental landmass and that their living population establishes itself gradually through colonization by species which manage to make their way to them. The latter originate from adjacent continental land masses, with the same geomorphological structure (examples of this are the British Isles, Madagascar, and New Zealand) and were, in remote times, joined to these landmasses. The living population of this second type of island is affected by the whole evolutionary history relating to it down the ages. Islands have specific climates, being exposed to wind and rain in a particular way. Many species have become extinct because of man's interference (deforestation, for example). The avifauna of these islands enables the detailed study of the evolution of certain groups of birds living on them.

Continental waters
This term embraces all habitats constituted by the inland waters of the various continents: lakes, ponds, marshes, rivers, streams and ditches. Such zones are very common throughout the world and extremely valuable when it comes to housing, feeding and offering nesting sites to large numbers of bird species. For the migratory species, and particularly for waterfowl, the presence of water is of prime importance.

Seas
Ornithologist Roger Tory Peterson has commented that oceans account for five-sevenths of the Earth's surface and that for every square mile of land there are 2·5 square miles of salt water. However, true sea birds account for only about three per cent (about 260, grouped in 12 families) of all the species existing in the world. Some of them, like most gulls, terns, cormorants, frigate birds and pelicans, never move too far from the coast, so there are less than 150 species of actual ocean birds.

Dorst (1971) lists in detail the families to which the marine species belong (families in italics are those in which all the members are pelagic): *Spheniscidae* (penguins), *Diomedeidae* (albatrosses), *Procellariidae* (shearwaters and petrels), *Hydrobatidae* (storm petrels), Pelecanidae (pelicans), *Sulidae* (boobies and gannets), Phalacrocoracidae (cormorants and shags), Fregatidae (frigate birds), Stercorariidae (skuas), Laridae (gulls and terns), Rhynchopidae (skimmers and scissorbills) and *Alcidae* (auks, razorbills, guillemots and puffins).

Birds and Man

Birds have always attracted man's keen attention, for a variety of reasons: their extraordinary ability to fly, their plumage, coloration and song, and their food value (meat and eggs). This interest has been expressed in most cultural forms: in art, literature, popular folklore and so on. Man has made extensive use of various species of birds, rearing and developing them. Hunting, once restricted to the procuration of food, is nowadays reduced to a pastime which has sadly spawned far too many hunters (most of whom are uninformed about the natural order of things) in relation to the area available for this pursuit. This is causing serious damage as far as the consistency of bird populations is concerned. Present-day hunting with its advanced weapons (repeating rifles), is yet another extremely worrying factor that has joined the already numerous threats, such as general environmental deterioration and pollution of water, air and soil, which are seriously undermining the avifauna. At present there is only one acceptable type of hunting, based on really scientific principles; due to modern studies of animal populations, this activity plans population control without damaging the fauna which is already so hotly pursued, isolated and hounded by man's progressive and incessant inroads into the natural world.

In this chapter, the study of birds and their protection are discussed.

▲ Mallards *Anas platyrhynchos*

The study of birds
The study of birds is called ornithology (from the Greek words *órnis, órnitos*, bird and *logos*, study, discourse). It falls within the biological and natural sciences and embraces all aspects of the structure, life, habits and characteristics of birds. In order to study birds, it is, of course, necessary first to solve one basic problem: how to identify and recognize birds. The hobby of bird-watching has become very popular in various countries for some years now, particularly in England and America. Although it is usually limited to the simple identification of species observed in the wild and the possible observation of their behaviour, it has often contributed significantly to the advancement of ornithological knowledge. In the numerous countries where there are bird watchers, bird lovers are members of specialized organizations which arrange a wide number of activities including conservation projects.

▲ Mallard taking-off

In order to identify birds it is obviously necessary to use equipment which will bring them closer to the human eye: a good pair of binoculars is vital for every bird watcher and ornithologist. The models advised are 8 × 30, 10 × 40 and 10 × 50, and should be of good quality. In specifying binoculars, the first figure refers to the magnification (how many times nearer the bird observed appears to the observer) the second figure refers to the diameter of the lens in millimetres, and gives a precise indication of the amount of light that can enter the binoculars. Other details refer to the clarity of the image perceived by the human eye and the performance of the binoculars in poor light conditions. When specific detailed studies of certain birds are desired, a telescope is particularly useful, best mounted on a tripod or stand. A telescope with three eyepieces, magnifying 10, 20 and 30 times is best. As well as binoculars and a telescope it is also extremely useful to have a camera to record special situations or important sightings.

When observing birds in the wild it is clearly necessary to learn to identify them: to do this identification guides will be needed (the bibliography suggests a few handbooks for identifying European birds) and it is helpful, especially on the first venture, to have the company of a person who already has a good knowledge. It is also necessary to be mentally prepared for identifying the birds observed by getting used to picking out their most indicative features. Important considerations are

▲ Kokako *Callaeas cinerea*

the size, form, coloration, type of flight, behaviour, and song, together with the habitat in which a bird is seen and the time of year. A swift computation of these factors will enable identification of most subjects to be made.

The dimensions can be easily compared with those of a series of familiar birds such as, in order or size, a tit, a sparrow, a starling, a blackbird, a pigeon, a crow, a pheasant and a swan. When analysing the shape, the form of the body, the wings, the tail, the beak and the legs and feet, should be recorded and any possible similarities with the species listed above noted. As

BIRDS AND MAN

regards the coloration, the most salient features must be noticed: the overall coloration and then any markings or stripes on the body or round the eyes, on the cheeks, chin and so on. A sound knowledge of the terminology used for the parts of a bird's body is obviously essential for recording all data clearly and correctly. An analysis of a bird's behaviour can also be of help in reaching a precise identification: how it moves on the ground, whether it moves its tail, how it climbs up trees, swims, dives, or takes off from water. Its type of flight can also be indicative, undulating or straight for example, as can

▲ Hoatzin *Opisthocomus hoazin*

the sounds it makes and, obviously, the habitat and time of year. Birds can be observed anywhere: in the countryside, in marshes, in mountains and in built-up areas. When setting off to watch birds, it is advisable to wear dull, easily camouflaged clothing, walk unhurriedly without making sudden movements, especially when very near birds and avoid speaking loudly or making any unnecessary noise. It is vital to have a notebook for jotting down observations and making on-the-spot sketches of birds which cannot be identified then and there.

▲ Egyptian Vulture *Neophron percnopterus*

The gathering of data from observations is very important. Observations should be recorded in a consistent and understandable way in appropriate books or card-indexes divided according to both place and species. The use of standard cards for recording data is suggested which might consist of the following information: name and surname of observer; names of any accompanying bird watchers; place where observation took place (where possible include precise map reference, scale: 1:25,000); date of observation (indicate exact times of day and the percentage of the total area covered during the period of observation); data gathered (type of vegetation, environmental features, weather conditions such as cloud cover, wind, temperature, rain and visibility); and a list of species observed. For each species indicate the number of sightings, summing them up perhaps by such terms as 'many', 'very many', or 'several'. Indicate the sighting with the largest number of individuals observed together and, where relevant, the rough total number of individuals present in the area, plus all the various data about behaviour and any other features considered worth recording.

When bird watching, one may well come across some species nesting. It is certainly of use to gather data about nesting, but this must be done as discreetly as possible, because the breeding season is one of the most sensitive in a bird's life, and disturbance may cause a bird to abandon its brood. Every bird watcher and ornithologist should remember that he is out to protect these creatures. Some good advice is given in the original preface to Hoeher's work on nesting habits and eggs (1974) where he strongly recommends avoiding the examination of nests until after the breeding season (until

▼ Kagu *Rhynochetos jubatus*

▲ Harpy Eagle *Harpia harpyja*

September). In the event of wishing to examine a nest and its contents, however, this should be done in a few minutes with the least amount of fuss and without forcing the bird to leave the nest or disturbing the protecting cover. If one wishes to photograph nests and eggs, the greatest care must be taken not to intrude upon the bird in any way. Where a rare species is concerned, photography or disturbance of any kind should be totally avoided as it may upset the whole balance of the breeding birds. Lastly, making a private egg collection should never be attempted.

For some time now, and thanks particularly to the British Trust for Ornithology and the Schloss Moggingen *Vogelwarte Radolfzell*, work has been under way to introduce

▲ White-tailed Eagles *Haliaeetus albicilla*

internationally standardized research methods for data collection. In 1971 a convention was held at the headquarters of the British Trust for Ornithology at Tring in Hertfordshire to discuss the standardization of European ornithology. Thus the methods of collecting data about nesting have been standardized and special index cards have been produced in all the European countries.

Below is a standard card which gives an idea of how to record data about nesting:
1. Name of observer
2. Place of observation (refer to map scale: 1:25,000).
3. Year.
4. Species.

Common Nightjar
Caprimulgus europaeus ▶

Hoopoe *Upupa epops* ▶

5. Position of nest (for example, in a tree, in rocks, on the ground at what height from the ground; in what type of habitat, and so on).
6. Measurements (to be made when nesting is over: length, depth, materials used).
7. Conditions in which found: under construction; with eggs; with young.
8. Visits made. For every visit indicate date, time, number of eggs or young present, and any other features considered worth recording (if there is an adult, if it is sitting on the eggs, feeding the young).

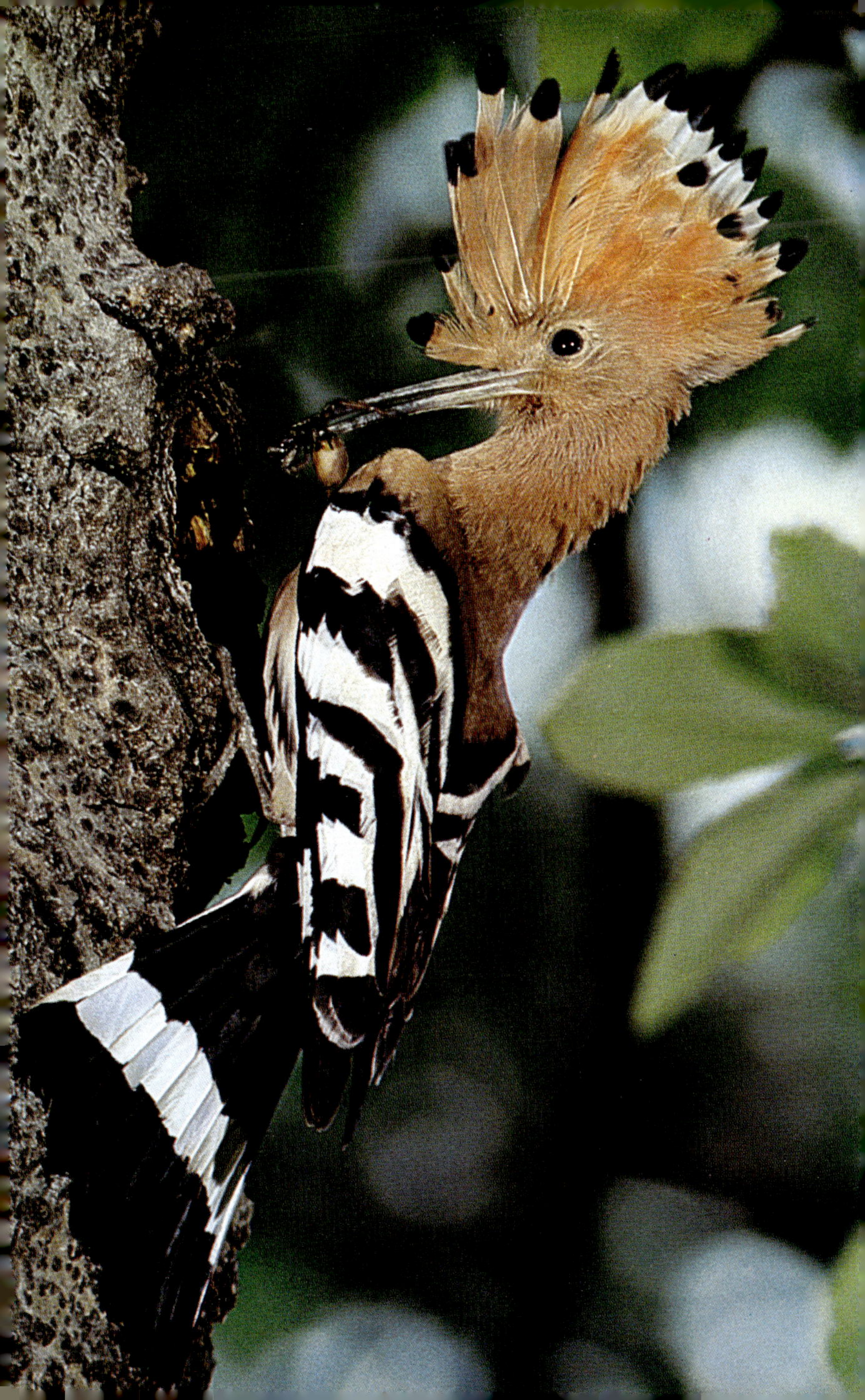

Taking bird-population censuses

Bird population censuses are becoming of ever greater importance today, and tend to provide extremely interesting data, both qualitative and quantitative. Methods of census-taking vary with the situation as it presents itself in the field, but all methods rely on two essential conditions: certain contact (visual, aural or any other sure sign of the bird's presence) with each single individual, and the stability of the population in question in the selected area for a given period of time, sufficient to carry out the visits required for the actual census. A census is, therefore, taken in particularly stable conditions. Flocks of ducks or curlews can be counted with binoculars and powerful telescopes, or by using aerial photographs; colonies of herons, terns, and sea birds can be assessed by the careful counting of the nests, and so on. For some time the International Waterfowl Research Bureau has been carrying out simultaneous winter counts throughout the western Palaearctic zone in places of particular interest, and recording, numerically, all the species of ducks present, as well as the various species of waders (plovers, curlews, redshanks). After several years of research it has been possible to obtain figures indicating the total number of individuals passing the winter in the western Palaearctic region. A census can rarely be complete and refer to all the existing individuals of a given species (this can only occur with species which have a particularly limited distribution and are fairly small in numbers). As a rule a census is partial and based on samples which often reflect complete territorial situations. A census can be absolute when it guarantees a knowledge of the total number of individuals present in a given area, or relative when expressed as a figure proportional to the real density, which remains unknown. Any census taken in closed environments (woods, forests, canebrakes) requires fairly elaborate techniques. Numerous ornithologists have studied, elaborated and applied special methods of census-taking to analyse the avifauna in such areas. Among others can be mentioned Jacques Blondel, David Lack, S. C. Kendeigh, C. Ferry, B. Frochot, A. Enemar and L. R. Dice. The commonest method for taking censuses of birds is mapping. A certain number of visits are made to a clearly defined area which has been previously localized on maps; over a precise route, taken in the same period of time, all contact with individuals present in the area is recorded on detailed maps. While the mapping method makes it possible to obtain an absolute census, the method known as the Kilometric Index of Abundance (KIA) supplies

BIRDS AND MAN

relative censuses. This second method consists of choosing a precise route alongside a certain habitat and then covering the route slowly a certain number of times noting down all contact on one side of it. The data gathered with both these methods are then computed.

Advice to novice bird watchers
Any novice bird watcher will need 1,001 hints if he is to make a successful series of special studies. For example: he can make detailed charts showing the presence of various species in given places at given times of year; analyse the migrations of various species in a given area; study the day-to-day life of a nest discovered during a bird watching sortie, bearing in mind the recommendations already listed; collect the reject pellets of certain species (see p. 58) in order to analyse the contents and

▼ Wild Turkey *Meleagris gallopavo*

Overleaf: domestic turkeys on a turkey farm ▶

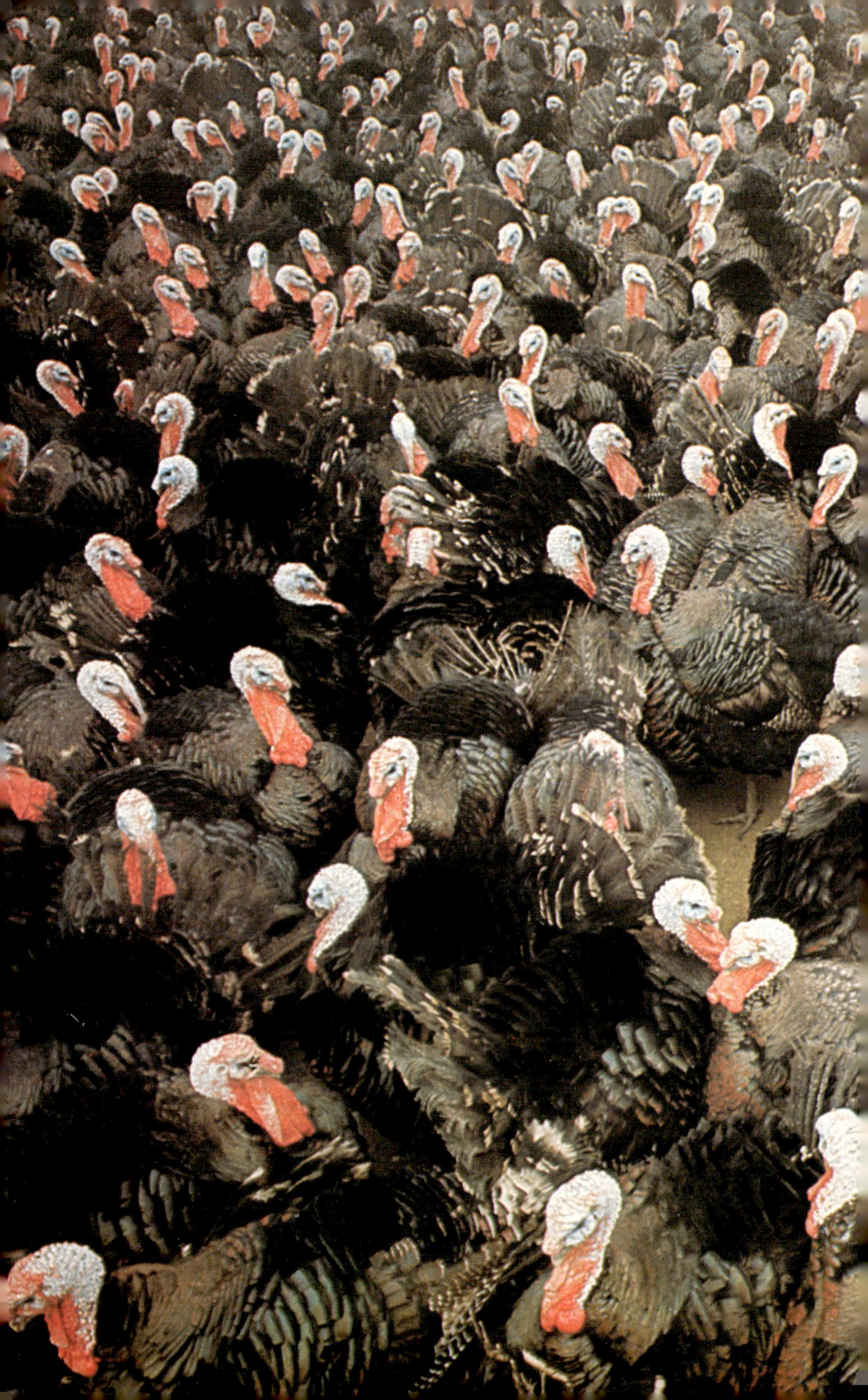

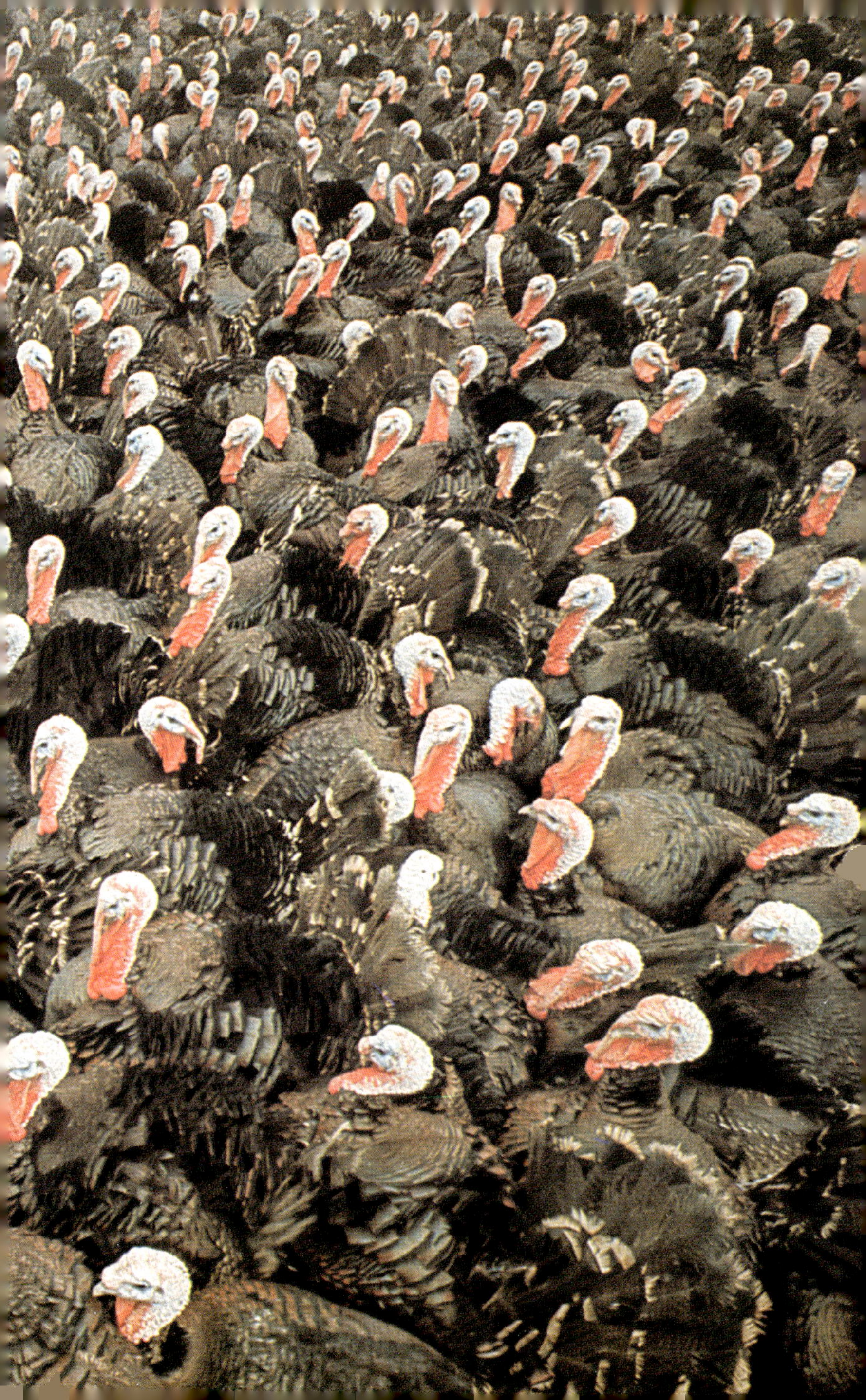

study in detail the quantity and quality of prey; collect and index bones and feathers found during bird watching; or study the behaviour of certain species when feeding, during the breeding season, and in their relations with their own kind or with other species.

Ornithological organizations and journals

It is important for any scholar or mere enthusiast in any field of study not to remain isolated, but to have contact with other enthusiasts and scholars in order to organize activities in common, have discussions and, in other words, form a proper club. It is only by means of continual discussion that large amounts of data can be gathered, ideas and experiences compared, and hints exchanged. In addition, organized groups ensure that research advances and that its quality improves, thus enabling scholars and enthusiasts alike to work together, and supply any data from research via specialized publications. There are ornithological groups and journals in every country in the world. Among the many publications are the following examples: in England, *The Ibis* (published by one of the oldest ornithological associations, the British Ornithologists' Union, founded by Alfred Newton in 1858), *Bird Study* (the journal of the British Trust for Ornithology) and *British Birds*; in The Netherlands, *Ardea* and *Limosa*; in France, *Alauda* and *L'Oiseau et la Revue Française d'Ornithologie*; in Switzerland, *Nos Oiseaux* and *Der Ornitholgische Beobachter*; in Germany, *Journal für Ornithologie, Die Vogelwelt, Ornithologische Mitteilungen*; in the United States, *The Auk, The Condor,* and *Bird Banding*; in Russia, *Ornitologjia*; in Australia, *The Emu*; in Spain, *Ardeola*; and in Italy, *Rivista Italiana di Ornitologia.*

The protection of birds

The current worldwide situation offers little cause for optimism in the immediate future. Man, in our modern civilization, has to a large extent sacrificed the Earth's natural resources, exploited nature, tamed nature, and destroyed nature in every conceivable way.

However, man is part and parcel of nature and inevitably is subject to the natural laws. For this reason he can certainly not delude himself, in this breakneck race towards the cult of the superfluous, that he is constructing his own order which differs from the natural one which originally gave rise to him. Nature conservation and protection are currently popular activities because people have become thoroughly aware that if we continue at this pace man will be the only living being to

Blackcap
Sylvia atricapilla ▶

▼ Young sparrow (*genus Passer*)

BIRDS AND MAN

destroy itself. Today, sadly enough, there is no single natural community where man's interference, be it direct or indirect, has not shown itself. As a result, in many situations, it is now necessary to embark on the task of full-scale environmental reconstitution. The causes of the destruction of our natural heritage are manifold, and range from the progressive devastation of vegetation (a fundamental store of oxygen) to make way for the advance of the concrete jungle, to the indiscriminate pollution of air, water and soil, and further to the direct annihilation of certain animal species by hunting.

Many species of birds have become extinct because of man's activities, one example is the Passenger Pigeon (*Ectopistes migratorius*). There was a time when this species was one of the most abundant in the North American avifauna; 40 cm in length, with a tapering tail, its upper plumage was a delicate shade of slate blue, with purplish-violet highlights at the sides of the neck, and a whitish underside. Passenger Pigeons were so numerous that it was claimed flocks in flight would obscure the sun. Nesting colonies and flocks in flight were the object of merciless hunting, using every means conceivable: guns, sticks and fire. Towards the end of the nineteenth century the Passenger Pigeon became quite rare: attempts to protect it were made in 1910–12, but this was too late. By then the species was doomed to total extinction. In September 1914, in

▼ Woodcock *Scolopax rusticola*

the Cincinnati zoo, the last living specimen of this species died, the last survivor of a small group of these birds which had been reared in captivity.

Other species have become extinct because of a reduction in their area of distribution (especially island species), or because of the specific nature of their ecological requirements. Some species have not been seen or heard of for several years, and there is every likelihood that they too are now extinct. For example the Ivory-billed Woodpecker (*Campephilus principalis*) was studied at length in 1942 by the ornithologist J. T. Tanner (he reported that this species was to be found in the scrublands of Louisiana, Florida and South Carolina). It lived in pairs, and in all probability pairs stayed together for many years with a territory of six to eight square kilometres; it fed on insects and their larvae which it found in old, rotting tree trunks. The numbers of this bird diminished progressively because the large old trees in question were systematically hewn down. The species was last sighted in 1967, in Texas.

The world's rarest bird is most probably the Mauritius Kestrel *Falco punctatus*. This species is kept under permanent supervision by a major protection programme financed by the World Wildlife Fund and operated by the Cornell University Ornithological Laboratory. At the present time there are eight specimens of this species, all on Mauritius. Ornithologist

A young ringed Black Redstart ▶

BIRDS AND MAN

Stanley Temple, in charge of the conservation programme, has managed to catch a pair of this species in the hope that it will breed in captivity; the young will then be released. There are various other endangered species such as the California Condor (*Gymnogyps californianus*) with no more than 40–50 individuals left, and the American Whooping Crane (*Grus americana*) with a world population of about 50 all nesting in certain areas of Canada and migrating to winter in a part of Texas which has now become a nature reserve (Aransas Wildlife Refuge). In the case of the latter species, which lays two eggs but usually only rears one offspring, the practice of removing the unhatched egg from the nest and getting it to hatch in an incubator has begun, thus building up a nucleus of individuals of this species in captivity. The International Union for the Conservation of Nature and its Resources has published (in constantly updated editions) a series of cards for those species of animals and plants throughout the world which are in danger of extinction (the series is called the *IUCN Red Data Book*, red being the colour for danger, hence the red cover on the cards' container).

The picture painted is, sadly, dramatic and depressing, but there may be some or (for the more optimistic) a good chance

▼ A colony of Kittiwakes *Rissa tridactyla*

▲ A Great Skua, *Stercorarius skua,* attacking a photographer

of improving it by decisive action being taken to re-designate areas, provide concrete protection measures and different models of development, because it must be remembered that the extinction of a species is a real gauge for a dramatically changed natural situation across the globe. If the situation is analysed in detail country by country we find grave problems, including the numerical reduction of various species. Nature conservation is the result of conscious efforts, started by making people aware of and then educating them in the environmental problem. The sway of world opinion, which has now been in evidence for several years, in favour of providing effective environmental protection, beginning with a different relationship between man and nature (with a type of social development that encourages collective services and re-evaluates the quality of life), has obtained various results. We must *all*, however, be convinced that to carry on drawing from nature under the impression that nature offers inexhaustible resources and can be despoiled without hitting back is nothing short of madness and will lead to the extinction of man himself. Nature conservation consists not only in educating and informing people, but also of concrete and practical deeds. In this sense, starting in 1961, the World Wildlife Fund now operates throughout the world preparing, organizing and financing conservation operations in every country. As far as the protection of birds is concerned, there are numerous areas in which action can be taken: the establishment and effective administration of protected areas in places of major environmental importance for birds (national parks, protected areas, reserves, wildlife refuges), the reintroduction of species into areas where they once existed but do so no longer because of man; the breeding in captivity of rarer species, and subsequent release of the offspring; measures to assist birds to shelter, feed and nest by means of a whole series of aids (such as artificial nests, planting particularly sought-after plants; legal protection with supervision of hunting, and many more steps. Attempts at reintroduction appear to be particularly delicate, because such attempts have to be based on a series of extremely accurate preliminary studies, and on special release techniques. Reintroductions have been made in various parts of the world: in Europe, the Griffon Vulture has been reintroduced into the Massif Central in France with WWF financing; the White-tailed (or Sea) Eagle into Great Britain; the Bearded Vulture into Haute Savoie, under the auspices of the French Ministry of the Environment; and the Eagle Owl into Germany. These are extremely delicate operations which entail at least four major phases, as described by Colin W. Holloway and Hartmut Jungius: an in-depth investigation of the characteristics and of the ecological and behavioural requirements of the species to be reintroduced; a detailed analysis of the area of reintroduction; a meticulous preparation of the subjects to be released (how many there are, of what subspecies and so on) and the actual release operation, after appropriate studies to find out the best way of carrying out the release; and subsequent supervision of the birds released. Holloway and Jungius observe that past experience in reintroduction programmes shows that it may take from five to twenty years before a programme can be said to have definitely succeeded. Ornithologist E. Herrlinger reports that in Germany (between 1956 and 1972) 222 Eagle Owls were released: more than one-third turned up dead or injured, most

Black-browed Albatross
Diomedea melanophrys ▶

Great Crested Grebe
Podiceps cristatus ▼

BIRDS AND MAN

of them in the months immediately following release. Some were found as far away as 300 kilometres from their point of release.

The use of artificial nests can be beneficial. This procedure has been used for many years – especially in Germany and Great Britain – and is fairly common in Italy too. Artificial nests improve the chances of nesting for various species in habitats where choice of nesting-sites has become restricted. There are many types of artificial nest and their construction and use has been very well explained in a guidebook published by the British Trust for Ornithology (Flegg/Glue, 1972). 'Letter-box' nests are among the most common, and are used for birds which breed in captivity. Their use has encouraged, in numerous places, the breeding of tits, flycatchers, starlings and redstarts. A similar but more rough-and-ready type, using small treetrunks, is the 'treetrunk' nest. Other types of artificial nest include the 'open box' which, depending on the dimensions, can be used by wagtails, robins and by small falcons, like the kestrel, and swifts, swallows, and nocturnal birds of prey.

There are other types of nests used to encourage waterfowl to nest: special wicker baskets for ducks, and special artificial platforms for grebes, geese, ducks, rails and terns, to mention just a few species. The Wildfowlers' Association of Great

▼ Gulls in search of food

Britain and Ireland and the Wildfowl Trust have experimented with this type of platform in the Sevenoaks reserve. Ornithologist Jeffrey Harrison reports that the Grey-lag Goose, Great Crested Grebe, Coot, Moorhen, Mallard and Tufted Duck have all used it for nesting. These platforms are used in various marshy areas. Recently, experiments have started using special platforms to encourage diurnal birds of prey to nest. Bjorn Helander of the Swedish Society for the protection of Nature reports that some of these platforms have been used in Sweden by the majestic White-tailed Eagle and in the United States Roger Tory Peterson reports that they have been successfully used by the Osprey. In Italy in recent years there have been experiments using artificial nests for birds of prey carried out by the *Stazione Romana Osservazione e Protezione Uccelli* (an organization which has concerned itself with promoting the active protection of Italian avifauna since 1946). In 1975 the ornithologist Fabio Perco reported that a pair of Goshawks were nesting in the Eastern Alps on an artificial platform.

There are, therefore, many positive actions being taken to protect avifauna, but because the protection of birds has a wider significance, it is vital that everyone realises the gravity of the environmental problems and becomes actively involved in nature conservation.

Classification

The system currently used by zoologists for naming the various animal species is based on the method used by the Swedish naturalist Carolus Linnaeus in the tenth edition of his *Systema Naturae* published in 1758. In this work, Linnaeus defines every animal and vegetable species described by him with a universal scientific name, in Latin or latinized words. This scientific name has two parts: the first, always written with a capital initial letter, indicates the name of the genus to which the animal belongs, while the second, without a capital initial, indicates the species. This type of system has been progressively improved and modified and is still in use, which is why every living thing is today known by its scientific and universal name. For example, the Osprey is called *Falco pescatore* in Italian, *Balbuzard pêcheur* in French, *Fischadler* in German, *Aguila pescadora* in Spanish, *Visarend* in Dutch, *Fiskgjuse* in

Swedish and so on, but in every language in the world it is known by the scientific name: *Pandion haliaetus*. The binomial system is currently used by zoologists and naturalists throughout the world. In Chapter I, the progress of knowledge which has led to the formulation of a concrete, biological concept of species was described; the genus is a group of species which have a series of close phylogenetic affinities. In his *Systema Naturae* Linnaeus described 4,236 species of animals; since then the progress of zoology has been enormous, and nowadays we know of about one million species of animals, each with a universal scientific name. Continual advances in this field have led scholars to lay down, at an international level, precise rules concerning scientific nomenclature. After the International Zoological Congress of 1898, it was decided to set up a Permanent International Committee for Scientific

CLASSIFICATION

Nomenclature. After many years of hard work, this Committee brought out an International Code for Scientific Nomenclature, for reference in all matters in this field. It is worth noting some of the rules laid down. Firstly, the nomenclature relating to animals is independent of that relating to plants, which means (although best avoided) that there may be animals and plants of the same name. Secondly, the names of families are formed by the suffix *-idae* being added to the root of the genus name, and those of subfamilies by the addition of *-inae*. Thirdly, a special law of Priority lays down that for every animal the generic name and the specific name should be, when they exist, those proposed by Linnaeus in the tenth edition of his *Systema Naturae,* or the names proposed for the first time after that date (1758), and must be accompanied by a precise description of the animal in question. The name of the author of this first description of the species follows the scientific name given to the animal with the year in which the description was made. For example, the scientific name for the Ferruginous Duck is *Aythya nyroca nyroca* (Guldenstadt), 1769. This is a trinomial name as it also refers to the subspecies (the third term does this). The name of the author is in brackets because when he described this species in 1769 Guldenstadt attributed it to a different genus than the one currently accepted. If he had attributed it to the genus currently accepted his name would not be in brackets. Classification procedures thus try to form a precise picture of the kinship existing between living beings by using a hierarchic structure of categories. The main ones are: kingdom, phylum, class, order, suborder, family, subfamily, genus, species, subspecies.

▼ Cape Teals *Anas capensis*

Snowy Egret *Egretta thula* ▶

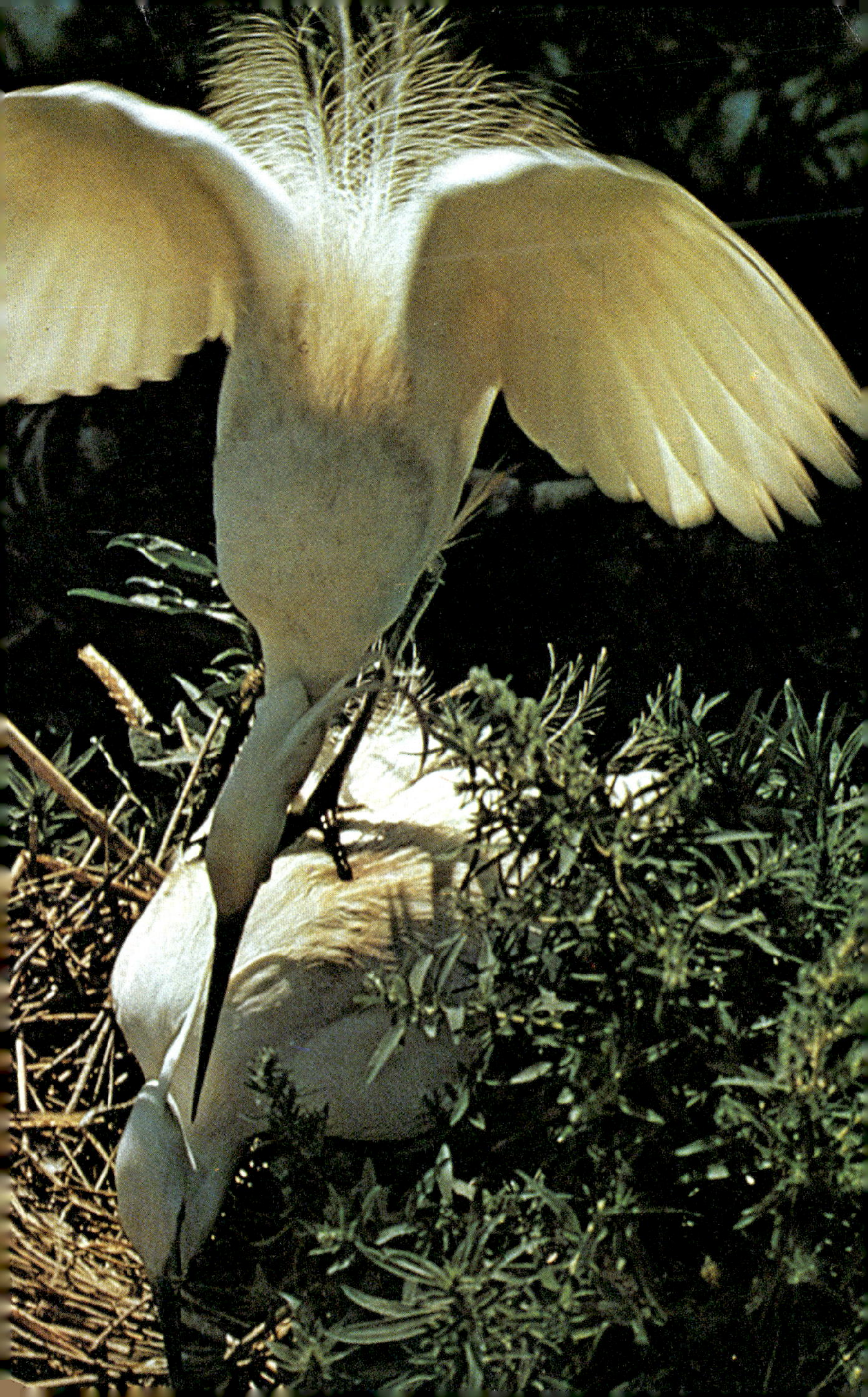

CLASSIFICATION

People are still describing new species of birds today: eleven new species were described between 1971 and 1975. Of these only one has a Palaearctic distribution, the *Locustella amnicola,* a sort of warbler described from specimens from Sakhalin in Siberia. The other ten new species are: a swift, *Cypseloides phelpsi*, from Venezuela and Guyana; a spine-tail *Synallaxis courseni,* from Peru; a woodland bird, *Conirostrum tamaraguensis,* from Chile; a tanager, *Hemispingus parodii,* from Peru; a leaf warbler, *Dendroica angelae* from Puerto Rico; a thrush, *Monticola bensoni,* from Madagascar; two bulbuls, *Phyllastrephus apperti* and *Andropadus hallae,* from Zaire; and two weaverbirds, *Hypochera lorenzi* from Nigeria and *Hypochera incognita* from Angola. In 1975 a new honeycreeper (Drepanididae) was discovered on the Hawaiian island of Maui, the pò-o-uli (*Melamprosops phaeosoma*). Sadly, some of these newly discovered species are already in danger of extinction, particularly those with limited distribution and specific ecological requirements.

Classification inquiry methods

Although systematics may seem to be one of the least interesting areas of zoology, it is important in modern research as it tries to shed light on the evolutionary affinities of the various groups of living beings, Chapter I explained how the biological concept of species reflects this need to draw up, via

▼ Iiwi *Vestiaria coccinea*

Orange-breasted Sunbird *Nectarinia violacea* ▶

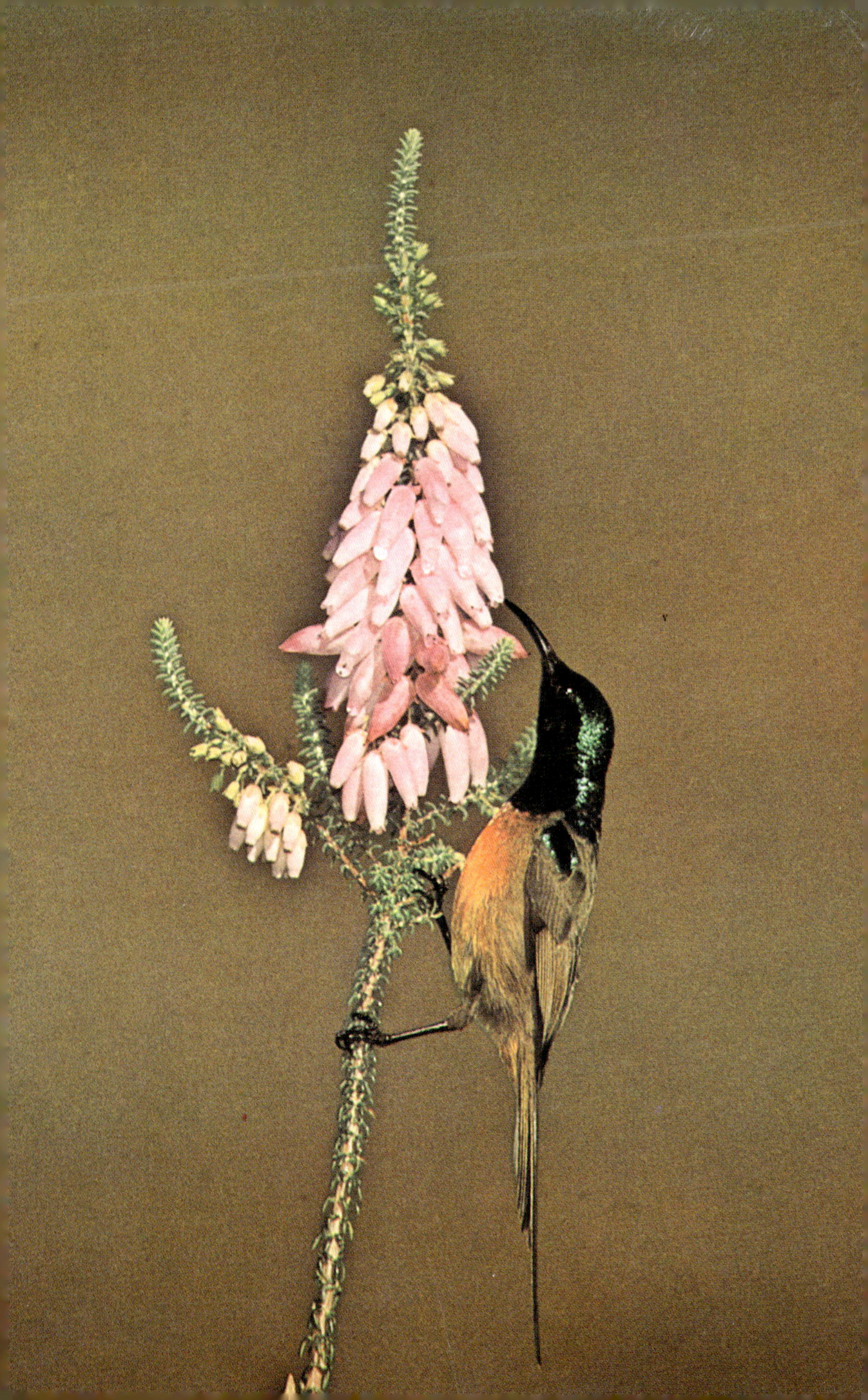

Orders

Struthioniformes	Rheiformes	Casuariiformes	Apterygiformes	Tinamiformes
Sphenisciformes	Gaviiformes	Podicipediformes	Procellariiformes	Pelecaniformes
Ciconiiformes	Phoenicopteriformes	Anseriformes	Falconiformes	Galliformes
Gruiformes	Charadriiformes	Columbiformes	Cuculiformes	Psittaciformes
Strigiformes	Caprimulgiformes	Trogoniformes	Coliiformes	Apodiformes
Coraciiformes	Piciformes	Passeriformes		

systematics, a picture of the evolutionary history and phylogenetic affinities of living beings. The methods of inquiry of systematic research do not therefore stop at the outward morphological appearances or the anatomical differences existing between various species, but use all the fields of modern research to shed light on the real affinities which exist: palaeontology, ecology, ethology, biochemistry, physiology, and so on. In order to outline these affinities, and to give an important significance to systematics as a real and synthetic picture of life on Earth, various fields of inquiry have been used, especially more recently. When discussing birds, the studies of Danilo Mainardi on the immunological properties of the red corpuscles should be remembered. Thanks to these studies it has been possible to detect major affinities between the Phoenicopteriformes and the Ciconiiformes, rather than between the Phoenicopteriformes and the Anseriformes, thus confirming the usefulness, for an exact classification picture (bearing in mind various other differences), of not assimilating the flamingoes in either of the orders which are close to them. Important research has been carried out by G. C. Sibley and J. E. Ahlquist on the electrophoretic properties of albumen. By studying composition of the protein of albumen of various eggs, these men found an affinity between the American vultures (Cathartidae) and the vultures and eagles of the Old World (Accipitridae), rather than between the American vultures and actual falcons (Falconidae). This research confirms the data produced by palaeontology; from these it can in fact be deduced that the Cathartidae originated in the Old World.

The analysis of various fields of research, therefore, contributes greatly in defining the real existence of affinities between living species. The study of behaviour is, in this sense, extremely useful. For example, the Collias man and wife team has classified the various species of weaverbirds according to the degree of complexity achieved in the techniques used in the construction and structure of the nest. Anatomy and morphology are still valuable fields of study for systematics: ornithologist W. Beecher has analysed the muscular system of the head, the form of the beak and tongue, and the plumage, and by taking into account various behavioural features has classified the species of the suborder Oscines (song birds) in the huge order of Passeriformes, by clearly delineating the affinities relating them. Very useful data for producing an exact systematic picture are provided by the close study of the early stages of life, of the eggs and of the breeding patterns.

Bibliography

Armstrong, E. A., *A Study of Bird Song*. Oxford University Press, 1963.
Armstrong, E. A., *Bird Display and Behaviour*. Dover Publications, New York, 1965.
Bannerman, D. A./Lodge, G. E., *The Birds of the British Isles* (12 Vols.). Oliver and Boyd, Edinburgh, 1953–63.
Benson, S. V., *The Observer's Book of British Birds*. Frederick Warne, London, revised edition 1972.
Brown, L./Amadon, D., *Eagles, Hawks and Falcons of the World* (2 Vols.). Country Life Books, London, 1968.
Coward. T. A./Barnes, J. A. G., *The Birds of the British Isles and their Eggs*. Frederick Warne, London, 1969.
Delacour. J., *The Pheasants of the World*. Country Life Books, London, 1951.
Delacour, J., *The Waterfowl of the World* (4 Vols.). Country Life Books, London, 1954–64.
Dorst, J., *Bird Migration*. Heinemann, London, 1962.
Dorst, J., *The Life of Birds*. Weidenfeld & Nicolson, London, 1974.
Fisher, J./Lockley, R. M., *Sea-birds*. Collins, London, 1954
Fisher, J./Simon N./Vincent J., *The Red Book, Wildlife in Danger*. Collins, London, 1969.
Fisher, J./Peterson R. T., *The World of Birds*. MacDonald, New York, 1964.
Fisher, J./Flegg J., *Watching Birds*. Poyser, Berkhampstead, 1974.
Fitter, R. S. R./Richardson R. A., *Collins Pocket Guide to Nests and Eggs*. Collins, London, rev. ed. reprinted 1977.
Flegg, J./Glue D., *Nestboxes – Guide No. 3*. British Trust for Ornithology, Tring, 1972.
Frugis, S. *et.al.*, *Enciclopedia degli uccelli d'Europa* (3 Vols.). Rizzoli, Milan, 1971–72.
Gooders, J., *Where to Watch Birds*. André Deutsch, London, 1967 & Pan Books Ltd., 1974.
Gooders, J., *Where to Watch Birds in Britain and Europe*. André Deutsch, London, 1970.
Goodwin, D., *Instructions to Young Ornithologists, No. 2. Bird Behaviour*. Museum Press, London, 1961.
Greenaway. J. C., *Extinct and Vanishing Birds of the World*. Dover Publications, New York, 1958.
Griffin, D. R., *Bird Migration*. Heinemann Educational, London, 1965.
Grzimek, B., *Animal Life Encyclopedia* (13 Vols.). Van Nostrand Reinhold, Wokingham, 1972–75.
Harrison, C., *A Field Guide to the Nests, Eggs and Nestlings of British and European Birds*. Collins, London, 1975.

Hoeher, S., *Birds' Eggs and Nesting Habits*. Blandford Press, London, 1974.
Hollom, P. A. D., *The Popular Handbook of Rarer British Birds*. H. F. and G. Witherby, London, 1960.
Howard, H. E., *Territory in Bird Life*. John Murray, London, 1920.
Lack, D., *Darwin's Finches*. Cambridge University Press, 1947.
Lack, D., *Ecological Adaptations for Breeding in Birds*. Chapman and Hall, London, 1968.
Lack, D., *Population Studies of Birds*. Oxford University Press, 1966.
Lack, D., *The Natural Regulation of Animal Numbers*. Clarendon Press, Oxford, 1954.
Lorenz, K., *Evolution and Modification of Behaviour*. University of Chicago Press, London, 1965.
Marshall, A. J., *Biology and Comparative Physiology of Birds* (2 Vols.). Academic Press, New York, 1960–61.
Matthews, G. V. T., *Bird Navigation*. Cambridge University Press, 1955.
Mayr, E., *Animal Species and Evolution*. Harvard University Press, 1963.
Mead, C., *Bird Ringing – Guide No. 16*. British Trust for Ornithology, Tring, 1974.
Morse Nice, M., *Studies in the Life History of the Song Sparrow*. Transactions of the Linnean Society of New York, 1938.
Odum, E., *Fundamentals of Ecology*. W. B. Saunders, London, 1971.
Padoa, E., *Manuale di anatomia comparata*. Feltrinelli, Milan, 1969.
Peterson, Roger Tory, *A Field Guide to the Birds of Britain and Europe*. Collins, London, 3rd edition 1974.
Pettingill, O. S. Jr., *Ornithology in Laboratory and Field*. Burgess, Minneapolis, 1970.
Reade, W./Hosking, E., *Nesting Birds*. Blandford Press, 1967.
Singer, A./Bruun, B., *The Hamlyn Guide to Birds of Britain and Europe*. Hamlyn, London, 1970.
Sparks, J., *Bird Behaviour*. Hamlyn, London, 1969.
Stokes, T., *Birds of the Atlantic Ocean*. Country Life Books, London, 1968.
Thomson, A. L., *A New Dictionary of Birds*. Nelson, London, 1964.
Van Tyne, J./Berger A. J., *Fundamentals of Ornithology*. Wiley and Sons, New York, 1965.
Welty, C., *The Life of Birds*. Saunders, Philadelphia, 1962.
Wynne-Edwards, V. C., *Animal Dispersion in Relation to Social Behaviour*. Oliver and Boyd, Edinburgh, 1962.
Yapp, W. B., *The Life and Organization of Birds*. Edward Arnold Ltd., London, 1970.

Index

Acestrura bombus 10
Acrocephalus arundinaceus 156
Alauda arvensis 131
albatrosses 31, 32, 39, 72, 74, 131, 153
  Black-browed *241*
  Black-footed 116
  Laysan 116
  Light-mantled Sooty 116
  Royal 116
  Wandering *9*, 10, 116
Alcedo atthis 202
alula 38
Ammomanes deserti *138*
Anarhynchus frontalis 104
Anas acuta 177
  capensis *246*
  platyrhynchos 220
anatomical structure 6, *53–4*
Anhinga *104*
Anser anser 88
  fabalis 175
Anthus pratensis 131
Aptenodytes forsteri 211
  patagonica *96*
Apteryx australis 68, *204*
Apus apus 83, *83, 94*
Aquila chrysaetos *67*, 123
  heliaca adalberti 190
Ara ararauna 129
  macao 129
Archaeopteryx lithographica *13*, *15, 15*, 16, 17, 18, 33
Archaeornis siemensi 16
Archilochus colubris 97
Ardea cinerea *93*, 130
  purpurea *92, 134, 135*
Arenaria interpres 165
Argusianus argus 131
Artamus superciliosus 95
Atrichornis rufescens 157
Auk, Great 23
Avocet *124*

Balaeniceps rex 104, *214*
bananaquits 110
Baptornis 17, 18
beaks 52, 102, *102*, 104, 108, 112, 114, 161
bee eaters 43, 57
  Common *105*
bills *see* beaks
birds of paradise 32, 120, 200
  Archduke Rudolph's Blue 128
bitterns 30, 69, 130, *136*
blackbirds 108, 123
Blackcap *235*
Boatbill 104
Bombycilla garrulus *167*, 196
boobies 32, 107, 114, 121
  Blue-footed 130
Botaurus stellaris 69
bowerbirds 120, 131
brain 64
Branta bernicla 212
  leucopsis 212

breeding season 57, 61, 63, 116, 119 *et seq*, 128 *et seq*, 153, 164, 179, 225
Bubulcus ibis 190
Budgerigar 189
bustards 27, 38
  Great 190
Buteo buteo 23
  lagopus 115
Buzzard, African 23
  Common 23
  Honey 23
  North American 23
  Rough-legged 115

Callaeas cinerea 222
Calypte annae 86
  costae *8*
Camarhynchus pallidus 112
Camephilus principalis 237
Capercaillie 108, *118*
Caprimulgus europaeus 89, *228*
Carduelis cannabina 177
  carduelis 159
Cariama cristata 50
Cassidix mexicanus 154
cassowaries 17, 27, 28, *204*
  Common *21*
Casuarius casuarius 21
Cathartes aura 73
Centrocercus urophasianus 132
Certhia brachydactyla 86
Chaffinch 25, 123, 156
Charadrius hiaticula 166
Chicken, domestic 91, *114, 145*
Chough, Alpine *127*
Ciconia ciconia 84, 86
Circaetus gallicus *110*
circulatory system 90
classification 248 *et seq*
Cochlearius cochlearius 104
Cockatoo, Greater Sulphur-crested *81*
coloration 49 *et seq*
Columba palumbus *133*
Condor, Andean 46
  Californian *71, 237*
Coot, 123, *147, 149*
cormorants 43, 114
  Common 183
  Great 183, *201*
Corvus cornix 24
  corone 24
  corone cornix 24
  corone corone 24
  frugilegus *127*
cotingas 108, 120
Coturnix coturnix 65
Courser, Cream-coloured *214*
courtship 128 *et seq*
Cowbird, Giant 154
Crake, Spotted 65
cranes 43, 177
  American Whooping 238
  Common 77
  Grey 77
crossbills 104, 108, 167, 196
  Parrot 167
  Two-barred 167
crows 91, 177
  Carrion 24
  Hooded 24

Cuckoo, Common *151*, 153
Cuculus canorus 153
curassows 52, 60
curlews 32, 177
Cursorius cursor 215
Cygnus olor 40

Daption capenses 211
Darter *104*
Dendrocopus major *47*, 65
Diatryma steini *17*, 18
digestion 52 *et seq*
dimorphism 22, 60–1, 186
display 128 *et seq*
Diomedea epomophora 116
  exulans *9*, 116
  melanophrys *241*
distribution 19, 24–5, 161 *et seq*, 183, 186, 187 *et seq*, 196 *et seq*, 230
Diver, Black-throated *48*
doves 42
  Collared 190
  Mourning 150
  Turtle 44
Dromaius novaehollandiae *21*, *204*
ducks *38*, 43, 60, 176
  Black-headed 153

Eagle, Bald *80*, 123, 138, 170
  Bonelli's 182
  Golden *67*, 123
  Harpy *226*
  Indian Black 106
  Martial *72*
  Sea 240
  Short-tailed *110*
  Spanish Imperial 190
  White-tailed *227*, 240, *243*
Eclectus roratus 22
Ectopistes migratorius 236
eggs 63 *et seq*, 148–9, 215
egg laying 146 *et seq*
Egret, Cattle *103*, *187*, 190
  Little *187*
  Snowy *247*
Egretta alba 20
  thula *247*
Eider *148, 212*
Elephant Bird 11
Emu 17, *21*, 28, *204*
Ensifera ensifera 104
Eremophila alpestris 32
Erithacus rubecula *79*, 123
evolution 11 *et seq*, 19 *et seq*
excretion 58 *et seq*

falcons 43
  Peregrine 20, 44, 168
Falco peregrinus 20, 168
  punctatus 237
feathers *see* plumage
feeding 102 *et seq*
feet *35*, *46*
Finch, Galapagos 112
  Sharp-beaked Ground 106
  Woodpecker 112
flamingoes *53*, 57, 170, *182*
flight 6 *et seq*, 37 *et seq*
flycatchers, tyrant 76, *204*
Fratercula arctica 101
Fregata minor 122
Frigate Bird, Great *122*
Fringilla coelebs 25, 123

INDEX

Fringilla coelebs tintillon 25
 teydea 25
Frogmouth, Tawny *90*
Fulica atra 123
Fulmar 23, *42*
 Southern 211
Fulmarus glacialis 23, *42*
 glacialoides 211
Furnarius rufus 159

gannets 114, 150, *208–9*
Gavia arctica 48
geese 43
Geococcyx californianus 85
Geospiza difficilis 107
Glareola nordmanni 18
 pratincola 18
gliding 38
gnat eaters 76
Godwit, Black-tailed *176*
Goldfinch *149*
Gonolek, Red-billed 158
Goose, Barnacle 212
 Bean *175*
 Brent 212
 Grey-lag *86*
Grackle, Great-tailed *154*
grebes 49
 Great Crested 130, *241*
Grouse, Black 108, 132
 Sage 132
Grus americana 238
 grus 77
Guacharo 160
Gull, Black-headed 123
 Herring 190
 Lesser Black-backed 174
Gymnogyps californianus 71, 238
Gyps fulvus 25
Gyrfalcon 212

habitats 201 *et seq*
Haematopus ostralegus 112, *120*, *197*
Haliaeetus leucocephalus 80, 123, 138, 170
 albicilla 227
Hammerhead, African 145
Harpia harpyja 226
Hawfinch 108
hearing 70
herons 30, 114, *184–5*
 Great White *20*
 Grey *93*, 130, 178, 190
 Night 130
 Purple *92*, *134*, *135*
Hesperornis 16, 17, 18
Heteralocha acutirostris 20
Heteronetta atricapilla 153
Himantopus himantopus mexicanus 146
Hirundo rustica 112, *139*
Hoatzin 57, 108, *223*
homoiothermy 78 *et seq*
honeyeaters 104, 110, *206*
honeycreepers, Hawaiian 110, *204*, 248
Hornbill, Yellow-billed *9*
Hoopoe *160*, *229*
Huia 20
hummingbirds 9, 11, *36*, 43, 46, 52, 78, *82*, 86, 104, 110
 Bee 10
 Costa's *8*
 Ruby-throated *97*
 Streamer-tailed *97*
Hydrobates pelagicus 71
Hydrophasianus chirurgus 188
hypothermia 80
hyperthermia 80

Ichthyornis 16, 18
Ictinaetus malayensis 106
Iwii *248*
Ixobrychus minutus 136

Jacana, Pheasant-tailed *188*

Kagu *204*, *225*
Kakatoe galerita 81
Kestrel, Mauritius 237
kingfishers 42, 58, *202*
Kittiwakes *238*
Kiwi 17, 72, *204*
 Brown *68*

Lagonosticta senegala 189
Laniarius erythrogaster 158
Lanius collurio 169, 178
Lark, Desert *138*
 Shore 32
Larus fuscus 174
 ridibundus 123
Leptoptilos crumeniferus 86
Limosa limosa 176
Linnet *149*, 177
Lonchura striata 189
lorikeets 110
 Rainbow *45*, 110
Loxia curvirostra 167, 196
 leucoptera 167
 pytopsittacus 167
Lyrurus tetrix 132

macaws, *129*
Macronectes giganteus 211
Macronyx crocea 23
Mallard *149*, *220*
manakins 76
mating *see* breeding season, courtship
Megapodius freycinet 137
Meleagris gallopavo 231
Melopsittacus undulatus 189
Merops apiaster 105
 nubicus 51
metabolism 78
Micrathene whitneyi 87
migration 153, 161 *et seq*, 173 *et seq*, 178 *et seq*
Mimus polyglottus 157
moas 10, 18
Mockingbird, Northern 157
morphological structure 6
Morus bassana 130
Motacilla alba 91
moulting 28, 32, 51
Mound Bird *123*
muscular apparatus 36 *et seq*
Mycteria americana 86

Nectarinia violacea 249
Neophron percnopterus 106, *224*
nervous system 64
nests 135 *et seq*
Nightingale *148*
Nightjar, European 89
Nucifraga caryocatactes 167

Nucifraga caryocatactes macrorhynchus 196
nutcrackers 105, 167
 Siberian 196
nuthatches 186
 Canadian 24
 Corsican 24
Nyctea scandiaca 87, 115, 167
Nycticorax nycticorax 130

Oceanites oceanicus 211
Oenanthe deserti 119
 hispanica 119
 leucura 119
 oenanthe 119
Oilbird *73*, 160, 200
Opisthocomus hoazin 57, *223*
Oreotrochilus estella 88
Oriole, Black-naped *89*
Oriolus chinensis 89
Osprey 114, *213*
Ostrich 6, *10*, 11, 17, 18, 27, 28, 52, 58, 190, *204*
Otus scops 65
ovenbirds 76
 Rufous *159*
oviparity 8
Owl, Barn 68, *109*, 114
 Elf *87*
 Hawk 116
 Scops 65
 Snowy *87*, 115, 167
 Tawny 114
Oystercatcher 112, *120*, 190, *197*

Pagodroma nivea 211
Pandion haliaetus 114, *213*, 245
Panurus biarmicus 175
Paradisea rudolphi 128
parrots 27, 52, 57, 58, 65, 108
 distribution *206*
 Eclectus 22
Parus caeruleus 158
Pastor, Rose-coloured 167
Pavo cristatus 117
Peacock *117*, 128
Pedionomus torquatus 211
Pelecanus onocrotalus 22, *100*
pelicans 32, 43, 121
 European White *100*
 White *22*
penguins 6, 49, 57, 121, *204*
 Adelie *44*, *193*
 Emperor 57, 137, 211
 Gentoo 170
 King *96*
Pernis apivorus 23
Petrel, Antarctic 211
 Giant 211
 Pintado 211
 Silver 211
 Snow 211
 Storm 211
 Wilson's 211
Phalacrocorax aristotelis 183, 186
 carbo 183, *201*
Phalaenoptilus nuttallii 88
Pheasant, Great Argus 131
Philetairus socius 141, *141*
Philomachus pugnax 132, *132*
Phoenicopterus roseus 53
Phoenix 9
pigeons 42, 52, 57, 66, 68, *86*, 91, 108

255

INDEX

Pigeon, Cape 211
  Passenger 236
  Wood *133*
Pintail *177*
Pipit, Meadow 131
Plains Wanderer *211*
Plantain Eater 49
Platalea leucorodia 210
plovers 32
  Golden 24
  Lesser Golden 24, 174
  Little Ringed *148*
  Ringed *166*
plumage 26 *et seq*
Pluvialis apricaria 24
  domestica 24
  dominica 174
Podargus strigoides 90
Podiceps cristatus 130, *241*
poikilothermia 86 *et seq*
Polemaetus bellicosus 72
polymorphism 22
Poorwills 88, 89
populations 11 *et seq*, 24 *et seq*, 161, 187 *et seq*
Porzana porzana 65
Pratincole, Collared 19
  Black-winged 19
preening 26–7, 49
protection 234 *et seq*
Ptarmigan, Willow 212
Pterocles senegallus 215
Ptilonorhynchus violaceus 131
puffins *101*
Puffinus puffinus 42, *150*
Pygoscelis adeliae 44, *193*, 211
  antarctica 211
  papua 170, 211
Pyrrhocorax graculus 127

Quail, Barred Button *211*
  Little Button 189

Razorbill 114
Recurvirostra avosetta 124
Reedlings, Bearded *175*
Remix pendulinus 138, *140*
reproduction 60 *et seq*
respiratory apparatus 94
Rhea *21*, *204*
Rhea americana 21, *204*
Rhynochetos jubatus 225
Rhynchops nigra 112
ringing 168 *et seq*
Rissa tridactyla 238
Roadrunner *85*, 216
Robin *79*, 123, 125, 126
rooks *127*
Ruff 120, 132, *132*, 134, 179

Sagittarius serpentarius 113
Sandpiper, Curlew 177
  Wood 176
Sandgrouse, Pallas's 167
  Spotted *215*
Sarcorhamphus papa 73
Scaphidura oryzivora 154
Scolopax rusticola 67, *236*
Scopus umbretta 145
Scrub Bird, Rufous *157*
Secretary Bird *113*, 200
Selasphorus sasin 86
Seleucidis melanoleucos 32
senses 64 *et seq*

Seriema, Crested *50*
Serin 161
Serinus serinus 161
sex organs *54*, 60 *et seq*, *62*
shearwaters 39, 72, 74
  Manx *42*, 150
Shoebill *214*, 105
shrikes 42, 105, 121
  African 158
  Red-backed *169*, 178
sight *65*, *66*, 66 *et seq*
Sitta canadensis 24
  neumayer 186
  tephronata 186
  whiteheadi 24
skeleton 33 *et seq*
Skimmer, Black 104, 112
skuas 52, 170
  Great *239*
  Pomarine 123
smell, sense of 70 *et seq*
Snakebird *104*
soaring 38
Somateria spectabilis 212
sparrows *148*, *235*
speciation 19 *et seq*
Spheniscus mendiculus 211
Spoonbill *210*
Starling, Common 65
Steatornis caripensis 72, 160
Stercorarius pomarinus 123
  skua *239*
Sterna fuscata 116
  paradisea 174
Stilt, Mexican *146*
storks *38*, *170*
  American Wood 86
  White *84*, 86, 190
Streptopelia decaocto 190
Struthio camelus 10, *204*
Sturnella magna 23
Sturnus roseus 167
  vulgaris 65
Sula dactylatra 107
  nebouxi 130
  sula 107
Sunbird, Orange-breasted *249*
Surnia ulula 116
swallows 42, 46, *112*, 177, *139*
  White-browed Wood *95*
  Wood, *204*
swans 33, 120
  Mute *40*
swifts 43, 44, 46, 52, *83*, *94*, 190
  Common 43, 78, 83
Sylvia atricapilla 235
Syrrhaptes paradoxus 167

Tadorna tadorna 176
Taeniopygia castanotis 189
tailorbirds 138
tanagers 108
Teal, Cape *246*
terns 42
  Arctic 43, 174
  Black *148*
  Common *148*
  Sooty 116
territory 119 *et seq*, *125*
Tetrao urogallus 118
Thalassoica antarctica 211
thermoregulation 80 *et seq*, 152
Thrush, Song 123
Tichodroma muraria 41

Tit, Bearded *175*
  Blue 43, *158*
  Great 153
Titmouse, Penduline 138, *140*
Tockus flavirostris 59
toucans 108
  Keel-billed *111*
Tree Creeper, Short-toed 86
Trichoglossus haematodus 45
Tringa glareola 176
Trochilius polytmus 97
Troglodytes aedon 123
  troglodytes 157
turacos 49, 50, 108, *204*
Turdus merula 123
  migratorius 167
  philomelos 123
Turkey, Wild *231*
Turnix suscitator 211
  sylvatica 189
turnstones *165*
Tympanachus cupido 132
Tyto alba 109

Upupa epops 160, *229*

Vestiaria coccinea 248
vocal organs 76 *et seq*
voice 155 *et seq*
vultures 38, 43, 72, *106*
  African 106
  American 73
  Bearded 46, 51, 240
  Egyptian 106, *224*
  Griffon *25*, 240
  King 73
  Nevada 10
  Rüppell's 46
  Turkey 73

waders 32, *35*, 42, 43, 52, 141, 236
Wagtail, Yellow 69, 177
  White *91*
Wall Creeper *41*
Warbler, Great Reed 156
  Reed *151*
  Savi's *149*
  Wood 183
waterfowl 32, 43, 76, 112, 171, 178
wattle birds, New Zealand 22
waxbills 155
Waxwing, Bohemian 167, 196
weaverbirds 153, 248
  Sociable 141, *141*
Wheatear 119, 128
  Black 119
  Black-eared 119
  Desert 119
widowbirds 155, 200
Woodcock 67, *236*
wood creepers 76
woodpeckers 42, *46*, 49, 56, 65, 108, 112, 137, 153, 186, 216
  Great Spotted *47*, 65
  Ivory-billed 237
Wren *157*
  American House 123
Wrybill 104

Yokohama Cock 9

Zarhynchus wagleri 154
Zenaida macroura 150
zoogeographic regions 196 *et seq*